HISTORICAL THEOLOGY
CONTINUITY AND CHANGE
IN CHRISTIAN DOCTRINE

THEOLOGICAL RESOURCES is a series of books taking its impulse from the striking renewal of interest in theology to-day. That renewal is unique in theological history, because its impetus derives from all the churches and because evidence for it abounds in all countries. The contributors to the series have been chosen, therefore, for their suitability to particular subjects rather than for denominational uniformity. There are two General Editors, John P. Whalen, formerly acting head of the Catholic University of America, and Jaroslav Pelikan, a prominent Lutheran Pastor, at present the Titus Street Professor of Ecclesiastical History at Yale University.

In commenting on the current theological revival, the General Editors write—'this interest, vital though it is, stands in danger of being lost in superficiality and trivialized into a fad. The answer to this danger is greater depth. *THEOLOGICAL RESOURCES* is intended to supply that depth.'

JAROSLAV PELIKAN

HISTORICAL THEOLOGY

CONTINUITY AND CHANGE IN CHRISTIAN DOCTRINE

WIPF & STOCK · Eugene, Oregon

Wipf and Stock Publishers
199 W 8th Ave, Suite 3
Eugene, OR 97401

Historical Theology
Continuity and Change in Christian Doctrine
By Pelikan, Jaroslav
Copyright©1971 by Pelikan, Jaroslav
ISBN 13: 978-1-62564-647-7
Publication date 1/20/2014
Previously published by Corpus Instrumentorum, 1971

TO MY PROFESSORS AND FELLOW STUDENTS (1944–1946)
TO MY STUDENTS AND FELLOW PROFESSORS (1953–1962)
THE DIVINITY SCHOOL OF THE UNIVERSITY OF CHICAGO

Crescat scientia, vita excolatur

Foreword to the Jaroslav Pelikan 2014 Reprint Series

WHILE COMPILING A COMPREHENSIVE bibliography of the works of Jaroslav Pelikan for a Festschrift celebrating his 80th birthday in 2003, I occasionally brought to light an article or lecture that Jary himself had all but forgotten.[1] This is not surprising, given his prolific, fifty-eight-year publishing history. Called "the premier historical theologian of our time," Pelikan took on the history of Christianity and Christian doctrine in its entirety--from East to West and from the apostolic age to contemporary issues. Indeed, to say he is the "premier" or "foremost" scholar in this field is an understatement, for he is the only scholar recognized as the authority for the immense field of all of Christian history.

This Wipf and Stock series aims to reprint a selection of Pelikan's writings that are no longer in print, such as *Historical Theology*, an erudite survey of the history of theology as both bound by tradition and ever-changing, or *The Melody of Theology*, a collection of brief reflections on important theological topics which one reviewer called "the ultimate bedside book." The versatility of Pelikan's thinking is apparent in another work reprinted in this series, *The Excellent Empire*, which juxtaposes Gibbons *Decline and Fall of the Roman Empire* with the "rise and triumph" of the Christian Church. Pelikan's facile mind comprehended big, expansive ideas and as an author he could synthesize, analyze, compare, and interpret large periods of history. His sweeping views of theological history, as in *From Luther to Kierkegaard*, are invaluable for understanding the field, but he could also zero in on a particular author or topic, as in his elegant study of *Faust the Theologian*, or his last publication, a commentary on The Acts of the Apostles. From great editorial projects such as Luther's *Works* (55 volumes) to succinct and cogent essays such as *Whose Bible Is It?*, Jaroslav Pelikan considered himself "a chronicler of one of the most overwhelming explosions in the history of the human mind and spirit," that is, Christianity and its impact on theology, philosophy, culture, and world history.

The reprinting of Pelikan's writings is a worthy undertaking not only because they were so influential in the twentieth century, but also because they will stand the test of time and continue to influence students, scholars, ministers, and laypeople. Though scholarly in nature and dealing with complex themes, Pelikan's work is nonetheless accessible and his topics are compelling. *Jesus Through the Centuries* (1985) and *Mary Through the Centuries* (1996) were popular best-sellers. Other examples include his *Bach Among the Theologians* (1989), which is required reading for musicians. And several of his books began as public lecture series, including *Imago Dei* (1990), *What Has Athens to Do with Jerusalem?* (1997) and *Interpreting the Constitution* (2004), in addition to the *Jesus* and *Mary* works. Pelikan's writings show us the interrelation of Christian tradition and intellectual history within broad cultural frames of reference drawn from philosophy, music, the visual arts, literature, rhetoric, political and legal theory, and the natural sciences. Crossing boundaries and making connections was Pelikan's strength. He knew the primary literature and the languages in which they were written. He saw the larger picture and he painted it with breathtaking majesty and mastery.

Jaroslav Pelikan was a man of many achievements. In addition to his prodigious publishing career, he also served in positions of distinction from Dean of the Graduate School at Yale to president of the American Academy of Arts and Sciences. He received prestigious awards such as the Jefferson Award of the National Endowment for the Humanities and the John W. Kluge Prize for Lifetime Achievement in the Human Sciences (bestowed by the Library of Congress which in 2000 named him a "Living Legend"), and accepted some forty-six honorary degrees. Now through this reprint series, the legend continues and the man lives on through his writings.

Valerie Hotchkiss
Andrew S. G. Turyn Endowed Professor and
Director of the Rare Book & Manuscript Library
University of Illinois at Urbana-Champaign
June 2013

1. *Orthodoxy and Western Culture: A Collection of Essays Honoring Jaroslav Pelikan on this Eightieth Birthday*, edited by Valerie Hotchkiss and Patrick Henry (Crestwood, NY: St. Vladimir's Press, 2005), 185-228.

Contents

PREFACE	ix
EDITOR'S FOREWORD	xi
INTRODUCTION	xiii

CHAPTER ONE
THE PROBLEM OF DOCTRINAL CHANGE — 1
Christian Doctrine as Unchangeable	4
The Dogmatic Solution	21
The Dialectical Interpretation of Change	26
The Method of St. Thomas	28

CHAPTER TWO
THE EVOLUTION OF THE HISTORICAL — 33
Renaissance and Reformation	33
The Enlightenment	43
The 19th Century	51
The Work of Adolf von Harnack	58

CHAPTER THREE
THE PRESENT TASK OF THE HISTORY OF DOGMA — 68
The New Situation of Theological Scholarship	68
Scope and Subject Matter	83
Toward a Redefinition	93

CHAPTER FOUR
The Historiography of Doctrine — 99
- Historical and Theological Methods — 99
- The Contexts of Theological History — 110
- Periodization in Historical Theology — 120

CHAPTER FIVE
Historical Theology as a Theological Discipline — 128
- Historical Research and Biblical Study — 132
- History—Doctrinal and Ecclesiastical — 141
- Dogmatics and History of Dogma — 149

Conclusion — 156

Abbreviations Used in the Notes — 163

Notes — 165

Bibliography — 219

Index — 225

Preface

This study of historical theology is intended to serve several purposes simultaneously.

As part of the current theological discussion, it is aimed at justifying the historical method of 'doing theology'—a method that is employed, though often without explicit justification, in many other theological works today. It is meant to state some of the principal reasons for the intimate connection between the discipline of history and the study of theology. In relation to my history of the development of Christian doctrine, entitled *The Christian Tradition*, it seeks to spell out the theological and methodological assumptions that have guided me in my historical-theological scholarship.

Such a monograph necessarily ranges rather far, and therefore I have documented my discussion more fully than I might have otherwise, on the assumption that a specialist in one of the involved fields might benefit from such documentation in other fields, if not in his own. As a result, the bibliography does not include every conceivable book in or near the field of historical theology but largely is confined to standard manuals of the history of Christian doctrine; these I have listed only in their first editions and English translations.

I want to thank all those who have helped me as I have developed this monograph: my colleagues of Corpus Instrumentorum, who invited me to undertake this assignment; my students and audiences (including the hearers of the Thirteenth Annual Robert Cardinal Bellarmine Lecture at Saint Louis University), whose reactions and criticisms have helped me to strengthen the book; and my secretary and editorial assistant, Mrs. Margaret Schulze, who typed the manuscript through several revisions and verified footnotes, bibliography, etc.

Yale University

JAROSLAV PELIKAN

Editors' Foreword

The catalogue of topics discussed in a series of monographs entitled 'Theological Resources' (or its Latin equivalent) a thousand years ago would in many ways have been similar to the list of subjects projected for this series. Whether there is such a thing as a *philosophia perennis* or not, there are persistent issues to which Christian theology in every generation has been obliged to address itself. What would have been remarkably different in such a series a thousand years ago, or for that matter two hundred years ago, is the method of addressing these issues. For in the final third of the twentieth century almost every theological scholar, regardless of his official confession or personal position, looks at the topics of Christian thought from a historical perspective. Every monograph in this series will be different from its counterpart in earlier times because that perspective will be present and will, to a greater or lesser degree, determine the procedure, if not indeed also the results, of the theological investigation set forth in it.

It is by no means self-evident that this should be so. History as a theological method requires explanation, perhaps even justification, and what better justification than a history of the history of Christian doctrine? This monograph on *Historical Theology* includes such a history, concentrating on the eighteenth and nineteenth centuries. But it would be an argument in a circle if this account of the historical method in theology did not attempt in some way to come to terms with other and older methods. The central point at which older and newer methods collide is the question of doctrinal change and the resultant quest for doctrinal continuity. Therefore this analysis of historical theology is put into the context of continuity and change as an unavoidable challenge to theological reflection. The historical method did not invent this challenge; for the phenomenon of doctrinal change has never been absent from the theological horizon. But as the historical method was introduced to cope with this phenomenon, it also came to accentuate and sometimes exaggerate, change at the expense of continuity. In *Historical Theology* the attempt is made to redress the balance and to take change seriously without ignoring continuity.

The history of Christian doctrine is, in one sense, a theological problem, one with which classical Christian theology, be it Eastern Orthodox or Roman Catholic or Protestant, has not dealt very successfully. But in another and deeper sense, historical theology is a 'theological resource,' for it makes possible a more comprehensive and more honest treatment of classical theological themes. This monograph is itself an attempt to vindicate the historical method, but the real vindication comes in the concrete application of the method to the tracts of Christian dogmatics. Thus it serves as an introduction to the monographs that will follow it, and they in turn will provide documentation of its principles. At the same time, the student of the history of ideas can find here an assessment of the place of the history of Christian thought in Western intellectual development.

J.P.W.
J.P.

Introduction

Historical theology is the genetic study of Christian faith and doctrine. Nevertheless, it may seem, by definition, to be a contradiction in terms to combine the noun 'theology' with the adjective 'historical.' For on the one hand, theology lays claim to the title of 'sacred science' chiefly on the grounds that it 'derives its principles, not from any human knowledge, but from the divine knowledge, by which, as by the highest wisdom, all our knowledge is ordered.'[1] To be historical, on the other hand, is to be relative, to be involved in flux. History speaks of becoming; theology deals with being.

Theologians of various denominational traditions have called attention to the apparent anomaly of linking the two. In the 19th century a seminal Roman Catholic thinker, Johann Adam Möhler, asked:

> How is it possible for the truth given by Christ to have a history? We cannot conceive of a history in any other way than that some object passes through a series of changes. But it has been said that the truth revealed and imparted by Christ is to remain as it was originally given. Here, therefore, there does not seem to be any object of history present. For that which abides transcends all change; it is a continuous being, not a becoming.[2]

A century later the eminent Lutheran theologian Werner Elert formulated the same contrast in even more striking terms:

> The term 'history of dogma' combines two concepts that belong to different dimensions. Ecclesiastical dogmas are doctrinal propositions that lay claim to validity on the basis of their assertion that they are declaring the truth or rejecting error. They champion a reality that is, or professes to be, independent of and separable from their historical genesis. . . . History, by contrast, means a reality that is caught in coming and going and that, since it arises with time, also passes away with time. If we assert that dogmas, too, have a history, this seems to be permitted only on the assumption that they also pass away with time just as they arose with time.[3]

The purpose of this study of historical theology is to attempt an answer to the question asked by both these historical theologians.

The genetic study of Christian faith and doctrine has been designated in various ways, the most important of which are 'historical theology,' 'history of dogma,' 'history of theology,' 'history of Christian thought,' and 'history of doctrine.' As Adolf von Harnack pointed out,[4] these terms have themselves been the subject of some confusion and even of occasional controversy. Except where the distinction between them has become an issue on its own, however, they have not in fact been distinguished with either clarity or consistency. Distinctions between the specific emphases suggested by these several terms are not trivial, as will be pointed out repeatedly here, but it is difficult to attach those distinctions to the various terms themselves with any uniformity. In the present exposition of the task of historical study, several of them will be used almost interchangeably. Before using the terms, however, it is appropriate to analyze each of them; and in a work concerned with history it is also appropriate that such an analysis proceed partly by means of a historical examination.

Of all five terms, *historical theology* is, in the history of its usage, the most equivocal; for it has been used to designate not only the genetic study of Christian faith and doctrine but the entire study of the history of the Church and even, occasionally, all those theological and paratheological disciplines whose methodology is historical. As a propaedeutic to the formal study of theology, especially in the Protestant theological faculties of Germany, there developed a course of lectures entitled 'theological encyclopedia,' and a body of theological literature to match this.[5] Theological encyclopedia was an attempt to arrange all the subject matter of theological study in a systematic whole, with the distinctions between the several fields delineated as precisely as possible. With the growth of historical studies in the theological curriculum (aspects of which will be summarized below), historical theology became a major genus in theological taxonomy. Karl Rudolf Hagenbach was the author of a widely accepted textbook of theological encyclopedia, which originally appeared in 1833 and which had gone through 12 editions by the end of the 19th century.[6] He also wrote not only the article on 'Theological Encyclopedia'[7] but also the article on 'Church History'[8] in the first edition of the standard reference work of Protestant theology. In the latter article, as in his handbook, Hagenbach tried to set historical studies into a total architectonic framework. Therefore he insisted that church history was less inclusive than historical theology, even if the latter were to be defined 'more narrowly' by the exclusion of dogmatics and exegesis; for such subjects as biblical history and archeology presupposed church history and yet were part of historical theology within what Hagenbach called 'the organism of the theological sciences.'[9]

More often, historical theology was used as a loose synonym for church history. Theological studies were divided into four basic categories: biblical theology, systematic theology, historical theology, and practical theology.[10] Within this structure, historical theology was the term for the history of Christianity, which usually was equivalent to church history,[11] with such areas of special interest as history of doctrine or history of missions included in the broader field. The 'theology' in these titles comprehended all the subjects on which members of the theological faculty lectured, and historical theology was theological not in the sense of dealing with doctrine and theology as its content but through its participation in the overall discipline of theological study. As the term has developed, however, it has been narrowed even more. In the catalogues of theological faculties, professors and courses with 'historical theology' in their titles are distinguished from those with the title 'church history' by their concentration on what we are here calling the genetic history of Christian faith and doctrine.[12] The term is used this way in recent theological literature, and will be used this way in the present study.

History of dogma is the time-honored term for this field. Both its history and its appropriateness will engage our attention at some length in the main body of our discussion. It was as history of dogma that the historical study of doctrine became a field of theological inquiry. Dogma is a term ordinarily used to designate the orthodox doctrinal affirmations of the Christian Church.[13] Although the Greek word *dogma* appears five (perhaps six) times in the New Testament,[14] the only passage in which it has this connotation is Acts 16.4, and even there it would seem to be primarily ethical and ceremonial decisions, rather than doctrinal ones, that the writer has in mind. In St. Ignatius' *Epistle to the Magnesians* the word begins to acquire its later meaning,[15] which is also evident in Origen[16] and other Fathers.[17] But only when the councils of the Church actually began to formulate doctrine could the term begin to be used in the official, quasi-legal sense it has in the history of dogma. In the strictest sense, nothing less than the whole of the Church is qualified to define dogmas. Therefore it could be argued that the only dogmas in the precise sense of the word are the dogmas of the Trinity and of the person of Christ, as these were defined in the first four (or seven) ecumenical councils. Harnack's account of history of dogma concentrates on these two doctrines;[18] but in most of the Church Fathers and in most of the histories the term is used in a somewhat looser sense, yet still with the connotation of dogma as the public doctrine of the Church.[19] The discussion here proceeds on the assumption that such decisions are inseparable, both historically and theologically, from the whole of what a particular church has believed, taught, and confessed, and that therefore history of dogma must include, for example, the doctrine of the work of Christ (not defined in formal dogmatic decisions)[20] no less than the doctrine of the person of Christ. While the term dogma also in the usage here still carries some overtones of the strict construction given to it by Harnack, 'history of dogma' will be used to include also the history of doctrines that do not qualify as dogmas by his criteria.

Although even history of dogma has incorporated materials that go beyond these criteria, *history of theology* is sometimes distinguished from history of dogma as the proper heading for the consideration of such matters.[21] Much of the development of Scholasticism, although more or less based on the dogmatic con-

Introduction   xvii

sensus of earlier centuries,²² does not really fit into history of dogma. Early medieval discussions of the Real Presence might qualify,²³ on the grounds that the doctrine of transubstantiation as eventually adopted at the Fourth Lateran Council²⁴ and the Council of Trent²⁵ was derived from them, but many of the theological disputes among the Scholastics have never been resolved by a dogmatic definition. Similarly, a strict application of the thesis that dogma is appropriate only for the doctrinal formulations of an undivided Christendom relegated the doctrinal movements within Protestantism to history of theology.²⁶ But theology in this designation has usually meant the learned theology of the professionals, rather than the doctrine contained in the preaching, teaching, and worship of the Church. In fact, not even all of learned theology was included: the theological systems overshadowed the theology expressed in biblical commentaries or in expositions of the liturgy, even though the latter were fully as scientific as the former. The history of theological systems thus forms a parallel to the history of philosophical systems. As such a parallel, it is a legitimate object of historical study and an important part of the history of ideas. A volume of historical theology in this sense would correspond to a reference work such as J. E. Sandys' *A History of Classical Scholarship*.²⁷ Important and interesting though such study is, its concentration on academic theology makes it too narrow for the purposes of this study; 'history of theology' will usually be referring to the broader history of doctrine rather than merely to the history of books of dogmatics.

Sometimes employed as a synonym for history of theology,²⁸ the *history of Christian thought* should probably be defined in broader terms, to include not only dogmas or doctrines but ethics and the Christian reflection upon other problems both of thought and of society. The series of volumes entitled 'A Library of Protestant Thought,' for example, incorporates many works of dogmatic theology, but it also reprints treatises that deal with piety, ethics, and politics.²⁹ Unless Christian thought simply means the thought of Christians, however, even this term involves a judgment about the specifically Christian presuppositions and contents of such thought—and this finally means doctrine. Yet it may be argued with some cogency that the history of dogma has long made the history of Christian thought about

A*

philosophical issues an object of its research, and that Christian thought about society is no less important. Why should the medieval debate about universals claim as much space as it does in some histories of doctrine[30] while Puritan controversies about the nature of the holy commonwealth have only rarely merited inclusion?[31] With recognition of the validity of this criticism and therefore of the need for studying the history of Christian thought, the present discussion will nevertheless concentrate on doctrine and will generally avoid use of this more inclusive term.

Probably the most fitting name for the subject here treated would be the *history of Christian doctrine*, which was used by such scholars as George Park Fisher.[32] This name clearly distinguishes the field from general church history, as well as from other branches of church history, such as the history of liturgy or the history of canon law. Even though 'history of doctrines' is used in the English translation of the title of Reinhold Seeberg's book on the history of dogma,[33] the term should not be confined to those doctrines that have been codified in creeds or confessions. Fisher's *History of Christian Doctrine*, by contrast, sought 'to trace the history of theology, not only so far as theological inquiry and discussion have issued in articles of faith, but likewise so far as movements of religious thought are of signal interest, and are often not unlikely to influence sooner or later the molding of the Christian creed.'[34] Yet the molding of the Christian creed is the result not only of the thought of theologians but also of the life and worship of the entire Christian community. Therefore history of Christian doctrine, while certainly more inclusive than history of dogma, is also more comprehensive than history of theology. In the New Testament and in other early Christian literature, to be sure, 'doctrine' was often used for ethical instruction.[35] But ecclesiastical usage—exemplified by authors as diverse as St. Gregory of Nyssa,[36] Theodore of Mopsuestia,[37] and St. Cyril of Jerusalem[38]—eventually came to distinguish between that form of Christian instruction dealing with behavior and that dealing with what was to be believed; this latter was what dogma often meant, and it is what doctrine means when the term is used here.

An introduction to the genetic study of Christian faith and doctrine could conceivably take any of several forms. It could attempt to outline the history of doctrine, condensing into the format of a monograph the principal points of a multivolume work. This was done by historians of dogma such as Nathanael Bonwetsch, Reinhold Seeberg, and Adolf von Harnack, each of whom issued a single compact volume on the history of dogma in addition to his full-length history.[39] Another approach to the subject would be by way of the history of historical theology since its beginnings in the 17th and 18th centuries. As the histories of historical writing by Eduard Fueter, James Westfall Thompson, and others show,[40] such a narrative can illumine many aspects of the problem of writing and interpreting history. Apart from encyclopedia articles and brief résumés at the beginning of the standard manuals of history of dogma,[41] there is no such treatment of the development of historical theology, but a careful and scholarly volume on the subject would be a significant contribution to both theological and historiographical literature. It would also be possible to analyze the task of historical theology chiefly on the basis of the theological and philosophical issues that it raises. No historian, regardless of his specialty, can ignore *The Idea of History* by R. G. Collingwood, which, by a judicious concentration on certain historians, opens up these issues in a probing and provocative way.[42] Partly in reliance upon Collingwood, several theologians have taken up the problem of history, but at their hands it has become so predominantly a theological question that their discussions seem less and less pertinent to the task of the working historian.[43]

The present monograph, somewhat eclectically, combines some of the features of each of these methods and adds features of its own. This it does by relating most of its discussion, directly or indirectly, to the work of the most influential of historical theologians, Adolf von Harnack. Agreement or disagreement with Harnack thus becomes a way of considering various proposals and possibilities in the writing of historical theology. The unrivaled breadth and depth of Harnack's scholarship enable such a presentation of the task of the history of doctrine to cover most of the crucial questions. As Harnack's magisterial *History of Dogma* was once criticized by one of his pupils as essentially a monograph on the 4th century,[44] so this volume could be called a long essay on Harnack. This approach has certain drawbacks, especially in its handling of methodological problems, which he tended to dismiss in rather cavalier fashion.[45] But it is perhaps the most appropriate way for a historian of doctrine to analyze his own craft. The philosophical presuppositions of that craft dare not be overlooked, for they will be present nonetheless and, examined or not, will shape his work. The theological implications of history of doctrine pervade every area of Christian thought, and, as a theologian, he has the obligation to consider them. But since these implications and presuppositions are the business of all scholars in theology, not only of the historical theologian, he must concentrate on the special issues of his own field.

Among all the theological implications of history of doctrine, the most far-reaching is the question of doctrinal change, and it is with this that the first section of this study deals. The setting for a consideration of this question is the universality of the phenomenon of change and the professional attention that historians must give to this phenomenon. Whatever its prominence in general historical thought, however, the question of change raises special difficulties for Christian theology, as we have already indicated. Attention will be devoted to the origin of these difficulties, to show how the very definition of Christian theological orthodoxy, as epitomized in the Vincentian canon of dogmatic consensus, was bound to make the admission of change in doctrine exceedingly problematical. This study will then turn to two of the ways for coping with the phenomenon of doctrinal change: the dogmatic at work in the condemnation of Origen in the 6th century, and the dialectical at work in the *Sic et non* of Peter Abelard. Chapter One concludes with an examination of the method of handling the questions that appears in the writings of St. Thomas Aquinas, particularly as he dealt with the theology of the Church Fathers.

Although Chapter One does not attempt a chronological account of how the question of doctrinal change was treated by Christian thought before the Reformation, Chapter Two uses a narrative of its treatment since the Reformation as an explanation of how it was that the historical became the chief perspective for viewing the question. This is not intended to be a complete history of historical theology, desirable though such a full treatment would be. Nor is it a catalogue of the books on history of dogma, although the appended bibliography includes such a catalogue.[46] Instead, it is an attempt to show how the new theological climate created by the Reformation made the historical way of looking at the Church and its doctrine an unavoidable element of theological thought. Once it had been invoked polemically, it remained to undermine many of the foundations of polemics. At the hands of the thinkers of the Enlightenment, most brilliantly represented by Edward Gibbon, history became a weapon in their campaign against the claims of traditional religion. Professional theologians, too, learned to wield the weapon, setting historical studies free from control by dogmatic theology. It was at this point that the history of dogma, as one of these historical studies, became the object of scholarly attention in its own right. The flowering of historical research during the 19th century helped to make the history of doctrine increasingly prominent, until at the end of that century Adolf von Harnack gave it its most distinguished expression. Chapter Two closes with an analysis of his work as a historical theologian.

Yet even Harnack's interpretation of the history of dogma must be subjected to critical examination, and the task of the discipline today must be reformulated. Chapter Three is an effort to develop such a reformulation. It proceeds on the basis of an analysis of certain trends in theological scholarship since Harnack that give new stimulus to historical theology. Although he relied upon this discipline as a means of extricating the true and original message of the gospel from its dogmatic confinement, any such reliance must be shaken by the discoveries of biblical research regarding the churchly context of the New Testament and its message. Special attention must also be given to the thesis of 'consistent eschatology' for its bearing upon the definition of the task of history of doctrine. Other results of theological study are also examined as they affect this definition, especially the rediscovery of Syrian Christianity and the recovery of an ecumenical outlook. All of this means that the history of doctrine must carry on its work in close association with 'secular' disciplines. It also means that the scope and the subject matter of the field dare not be prescribed as Harnack and his predecessors defined them. It cannot deal exclusively with dogma, especially not in the sense in which Harnack interpreted the word, but must put the dogma into the framework in which it developed. Chapter Three therefore concludes with a working definition of Christian doctrine as that which the Church believes, teaches, and confesses on the basis of the word of God, and it proposes that this be the object of research by the historical theologian.

Chapter Four is addressed to several of the technical and procedural questions that the historical theologian must answer as he takes up the writing of history of doctrine; each of them is discussed on the basis of specific historical problems. Historical method is a matter of acute sensitivity for any historian. But when his subject is Christian doctrine, he must intensify that sensitivity; for in the selection and arrangement of his sources he runs the danger of imposing his theological preconceptions, whether personal or confessional, upon the material. At the same time, that danger dare not be exaggerated in such a way as to overlook its presence in the work of other historians or in such a way as to relieve the historical theologian of the moral obligation to seek objectivity even if it eludes him. Several resolutions of the methodological dilemma are summarized and evaluated. The second problem of procedure for the historian of doctrine is the determination of the proper context for the interpretation of the teachings of the Church. By a consideration of how historians have employed various contexts to make sense of particular doctrines, this chapter seeks to put this question itself into its proper context. It tries to do the same for the question of periodization, which vexes the historian of doctrine at least as much as it does his colleagues in other branches of historical study. With the recognition that any scheme of historical periods is arbitrary and may be misleading, Chapter Four suggests a division into five major epochs that is based upon an awareness of the problem but also upon the study of source material from the history of doctrine as a whole rather than merely from one period or one doctrine or one tradition.

On the basis of the considerations surveyed in the first four chapters, Chapter Five essays to identify the locus of historical theology within the theological enterprise. Three traditional components of that enterprise are considered: biblical study, church history, and systematic theology. The connection between biblical theology and historical theology is guaranteed both by their intrinsic affinities and by the strong accent upon biblical research in the work of most historians of dogma. It must, however, be asserted that the connection is mutual and that neither of these disciplines can carry out its work today without an awareness of the other, so that even so apparently untheological an aspect of biblical study as textual criticism must pay attention to the history of doctrine if it is to evaluate properly the evidence of manuscripts, versions, and quotations. Church history has traditionally been the discipline that has trained historians of doctrine in their work. But the relation between church history and the history of doctrine is more subtle than this pedagogical affiliation would indicate. When both are honest, neither of them can do the work of the other, nor can either of them do its own work apart from the other; for church history is more than the history of doctrine, but it is never less. Similarly, systematic theology after the rise of historical theology will never be the same as it was before the 17th century. As church history has been a major component of the training of historical theologians, so the history of dogma has helped to discipline dogmaticians. Yet the integrity of historical theology as a scholarly field is violated if it is made merely an ancillary discipline to these other subjects. It has earned the right to be taken seriously in its own name.

The special vocation of the historical theologian is to study the history of doctrine, not to analyze its theological or methodological assumptions. There are certainly 'principles' of historical knowledge; there may even be 'lessons' of historical development. If the historian, including the historian of doctrine, is insensitive to any of these, he may well overlook part of his job. But if he is so paralyzed by reflection upon how anyone can know the past that he balks at the effort, he has betrayed his vocation. And if he is so intent upon the 'lessons,' especially upon the theological lessons, of his material that he moves toward them with unseemly speed, he has lost both his own craft and whatever lessons it may bring. Theological relevance and even methodological clarity may well be among the things that will be 'added unto us' if we seek first the integrity of historical scholarship. This is, finally, what historical theology is about.

HISTORICAL THEOLOGY

CONTINUITY AND CHANGE
IN CHRISTIAN DOCTRINE

CHAPTER ONE

The Problem of Doctrinal Change

One of the wisest men of the 20th century, Alfred North Whitehead, wrote in his *Adventures of Ideas*: 'I hazard the prophecy that that religion will conquer which can render clear to popular understanding some eternal greatness incarnate in the passage of temporal fact.'[1] Reiterating this need to deal with the awesome reality of change throughout our social, intellectual, and religious life, he declared later in the same work:

> Our sociological theories, our political philosophy, our practical maxims of business, our political economy, and our doctrines of education are derived from an unbroken tradition of great thinkers and of practical examples, from the age of Plato in the fifth century before Christ to the end of the last century. The whole of this tradition is warped by the vicious assumption that each generation will substantially live amid the conditions governing the lives of its fathers and will transmit those conditions to mold with equal force the lives of its children. We are living in the first period of human history for which this assumption is false.[2]

Although historians, philosophers, and theologians might want to quarrel with one or another aspect of this blanket generalization, its central thesis is one that all would be obliged to accept. *Adventures of Ideas* was published in 1933, at the end of the first third of the 20th century. The events of the second third of this century have thrust the fact of change in every area of human life into the center of consciousness with ever-increasing force.

Neither responsible action nor sound reflection can escape the impact of this fact. Those who deal with the affairs of men and of nations must be prepared for the demise of ideas and institutions that once seemed to have come down from time immemorial. Those who reflect on the meaning of human existence must likewise disabuse themselves of the illusion that there are certain clear and unchanging principles whose truth may incontrovertibly be derived from a consideration of nature and history. A man who combined political action with historical reflection in a unique way,[3] Winston Churchill may perhaps serve as a spokesman for this obligation to come to terms with the reality of change. As a historian, he well realized that the perspectives of history were anything but constant. For 'history with its flickering lamp stumbles along the trail of the past, trying to reconstruct its scenes, to revive its echoes, and kindle with pale gleams the passion of former days.'[4] He also realized that the historian was apt to ascribe far more rapid and radical changes to the events of the past than the contemporaries of those events themselves could have recognized.[5] It was therefore hazardous in the extreme to look for patterns in history; for these emerged into view only occasionally, and even then there were many facts that did not fit the pattern.[6]

One pattern, however, was clear, both in the present and also (though with the cautions just stated) in the past.[7] That pattern was 'the pervading mutability of all human affairs.' In a remarkable and eloquent passage, Churchill summarized the awareness of this mutability as he had learned it from his career as a statesman as well as from his research as a historian:

> Combinations long abhorred become the order of the day. Ideas last year deemed inadmissible form the pavement of daily routine. Political antagonists make common cause and, abandoning old friends, find new. Bonds of union die with the dangers that created them. Enthusiasm and success give place to resentment and reaction. The popularity of Governments departs as the too bright hopes on which it was founded fade into normal and general disappointment. But all this seems natural to those who live through a period of change. All men and all events are moving forward together in a throng. Each individual decision is the result of all the forces at work at any given moment.[8]

Like Whitehead, Churchill was born in the Victorian era,

when one could assume 'that each generation will substantially live amid the conditions governing the lives of its fathers.' But the events of the 20th century and the study of earlier centuries combined to convince them both that change, not continuity, was the law of history. A similar conviction has also become part of the theological climate of opinion. The assumption of dogmatic continuity has given way to an awareness of doctrinal change. Therefore the history of Christian doctrine is both a problem and a resource for theology, for it compels Christian thought to come to terms with the phenomenon of change within its own evolution.

In a sense, of course, the phenomenon of change in the history of ideas is an issue to which most creative thinkers have been obliged to address themselves. To cite only the most illustrious example, Aristotle devoted Book I of the *Metaphysics*, as well as portions of other writings,[9] to the history of philosophy that had preceded him, thus bequeathing to posterity a large part of the fragments of the pre-Socratics that have survived.[10] This made him, in Werner Jaeger's words, 'the inventor of the notion of intellectual development in time.'[11] Aristotle's interest in this development was philosophical rather than historical: he used the thoughts and writings of his predecessors both as a foil to set off his own views and as evidence for the ancestry of those views.[12] Aristotle's pupil, Eudemus of Rhodes, composed a treatise whose title could well be translated as *History of Theology*;[13] only fragments of this have survived, but they are enough to qualify him for the title that Jaeger has given him elsewhere, 'the first man to write a history of theology.'[14] For Hesiod's *Theogony* is the history of the gods themselves, not of beliefs and speculations about them.[15] More recent thinkers, too, have concerned themselves with change and development in intellectual history as an issue for philosophical and theological reflection. Even Wagner, the famulus in Goethe's *Faust*, found it a source of great satisfaction:

> To enter in the spirit of the ages and to see
> How once a sage before us thought and then how we
> Have brought things on at last to such a splendid height.[16]

Less superciliously stated, this view of the past as prologue has been the tacit assumption in many treatments of the history of doctrine.

Christian Doctrine as Unchangeable

With the coming of Christian doctrine, however, a new perspective on the problem of theological change was introduced. The eschatological consciousness of Christians expressed itself in the conviction that, although the speaking of God in the doctrines of the prophets could be said to have taken place 'in many and various ways,' now that He had spoken 'in these last days,' any further change or novelty was precluded by the finality of the revelation given in Christ.[17] Knowing itself to possess this revelation, the Church could recognize the variations on the theme that had been heard throughout the history of Israel as well as beyond the confines of the covenant people, but it could not envisage the possibility of a similarly contrapuntal development of the theme during whatever time remained between the first and the second coming of Christ. For the theology of the early Church, therefore, theological change could only distort, it could not enhance, what was already the pure truth and the perfect doctrine. The classic formulation of this view, which Harnack calls 'unique because here the question of tradition is handled *ex professo*,'[18] was the *Commonitorium* of St. Vincent of Lérins, written in 434.[19] His well-known canon of Catholicity, that 'one must take the greatest possible care to believe what has been believed everywhere, ever, by everyone,'[20] did not assume its present place as a theological axiom until the controversies of the Reformation.[21] It became even more an issue during the 19th century, as a result of the Tractarian movement in England and the work of Möhler and Johann Evangelist Kuhn on the Continent.[22] Nevertheless, it summarizes in succinct form what may be identified as the conventional answer of Christian orthodoxy to the question of doctrinal change.

The true faith was one that was believed everywhere. In the context of St. Vincent's own theological position, this criterion may partly have been intended as a polemic against the Augustinian doctrines of original sin and predestination;[23] for it was the persistent contention of St. Augustine's critics, also in the West, that his theology was not shared by the great doctors of the Christian Orient[24]—a contention that is still reiterated by Eastern Orthodox writers on St. Augustine.[25] Therefore, according to the Vincentian canon of universality, such a doctrine could not claim to be Catholic truth. But quite apart from its possible polemical intent, the canon does speak for the standard understanding of authentic theology as a given and established doctrine that does not change from one portion of the Church to another. One was to 'confess that one faith to be the true one which the entire Church throughout the world confesses.'[26] Translated into a theory about the history of theology, this could be taken to mean that in all the various cultures within which Christian doctrine was being confessed by St. Vincent's day— which included the Syriac, the Hellenistic, the North African, the Roman, the Celtic, and already to some degree the Germanic— the history of theological thought must have moved in the same direction and at the same speed. St. Vincent foresaw the possibility that 'a city or even a province' would dissent from the others, but believed that a comparison of the beliefs of others would establish the consensus of Catholic truth in spite of a minority opinion by one segment of Christendom.

To obtain such a consensus, however, it was essential that one compare and consult the beliefs not only of one's own contemporaries but of ancient teachers as well; 'everywhere' was to be qualified by 'ever.' Here, too, a theory of historical theology was at work. For it was evidently assumed that theological opinions from various centuries could be collated across the differences of language and emphasis in such a way that one could discern the lines of agreement and of disagreement. During the debates over the Vincentian canon in the 19th century, this criterion came to be identified as the most important and was placed first in the series.[27] At least some justification for this can be found in St. Vincent's emphasis upon 'those interpretations that obviously were maintained by our saintly forebears and fathers.'[28] Within the 'ever' there were evidently some eras more normative than the others; in general, the more ancient the belief, the greater the weight it carried. But that was not a simply chronological test; the true doctrine was the most ancient because it was true, it was not true merely because it was ancient. Therefore it was also the most contemporary, for it went on being confessed from generation to generation, all of whom were embraced in the 'ever.' The history of right belief, then, would seem to be devoid of change or even of movement. The differences of time would appear to be no more important than the differences of nation and culture in shaping varieties of Christian teaching. Right doctrine was ever and everywhere the same.

To these two criteria was added a third, in some ways the most problematical for the question of doctrinal change: 'by everyone.' Obviously, St. Vincent did not intend this in any purely statistical sense. He knew that in the preceding century the Arian heresy had poisoned 'not some insignificant portion of the Church, but almost the entire world.'[29] As an Occidental Catholic, moreover, he was aware that 'almost all the Latin-speaking bishops' had been infected by it.[30] If at such a time the meaning of orthodoxy were to have been determined by a theological public opinion poll, at least of the hierarchy,[31] Catholic truth would have gone down to defeat before Arian heresy.[32] But 'by everyone' is qualified, indeed defined, by 'ever.' Because the history of pure doctrine is assumed to be unilinear, the voices of the Fathers must be given preponderance over those of the brethren in determining what has been believed and taught 'by everyone.' This seems to preclude even more decisively the possibility of genuine change in the history of theology. If truth is one in all ages as well as in all cultures, the formula 'everywhere, ever, by everyone,' thus understood, would imply a rejection of the notion of change in doctrines as repugnant to the oneness of truth.

Such an application of the Vincentian canon to the issues of historical theology is, however, a considerable oversimplification even of its own intent. The author of the *Commonitorium* was well aware of variations within the history of theology. Nor did he simply write off all such variations by consigning them to the sects and heresies, such as Arianism and Donatism.[33] The two instances of variation that he analyzed at some length both involved theologians of great learning and devotion, men justly revered for their enduring contributions to the cause of orthodoxy: Origen and Tertullian. He was especially ardent in his admiration for Origen—his piety, his erudition, his literary productivity, his eloquence.[34] But none of these qualities protected Origen from going astray in his doctrine, from supposing that he knew more than anyone else, and from 'despising the traditions of the Church and the determinations of the ancients, interpreting certain passages of Scripture in a novel way.'[35] This judgment shows again what weight St. Vincent assigned to antiquity as a norm of Catholic doctrine.[36] But it also proves that he was not so naïve about the fact of theological variation as a simple division of all so-called Christians into orthodox and heretics would suggest. And this, in turn, reinforced the tacit polemic against Augustinianism. St. Augustine, too, was a man of great piety, learning, and genius, an ornament of the Church; but even an ornament such as he could fall into error. Theological change was a fact of theological history, with which one had to come to terms. But this coming to terms was achieved by an even more rigorous application of the threefold canon to both the great and the near-great of the history of theology.

The oversimplification of St. Vincent's canon must be qualified by yet another theme, the admission and acceptance of a genuine 'progress in religion.'[37] Sensing that his defense of theological antiquity might be interpreted as no more than archaism —as indeed it has been interpreted—St. Vincent sought to allow room for some kind of movement in the history of theology. But no such movement was to be understood as in any way altering the content of the received faith. It was to take place, he insisted in an apparent echo of the creation story in Genesis, 'in its own kind,'[38] that is, by organic growth rather than by increment or change. Therefore the metaphors he invoked in defense of his theory were organic. An infant and a young man differed significantly in the size and shape of their bodies, yet they were the same. As the young man was merely carrying out into actuality the potential that had already been placed into the child by the Creator, so any progress in religious doctrine was no more than the actualization of possibilities that had been there all along. Similarly, a seed planted in the ground would mature and grow; it was not an expression of loyalty to that seed if one harvested tares rather than wheat.[39] Thus true growth in doctrine entailed 'the same laws of progress, so as to be consolidated by years, enlarged by time, refined by age, and yet, withal, to continue uncorrupt and unadulterate . . . admitting no change.'[40]

Growth there could be, then, but not change: here was the understanding of historical theology to which Christian orthodoxy seemed to be committed. A premise thus formulated in polemical theology was also documented in church history. As Ferdinand Christian Baur observed:

> What the object of historical study in dogma might be cannot be seen if the dogma that in dogma nothing changes, that dogma therefore has no history, is regarded as basic. . . . In contrast to the objectivity of dogma, which remains unchanged throughout all ages, the source of such endeavors [at change] could only have been the mania for innovation, the self-conceit, the subjective arbitrariness of heretics (as they are customarily called for this reason) who opposed their own self-chosen opinions to the universal tradition. . . . While dogma remains always the same and represents in its whole temporal manifestation only the pure apostolic tradition, the heresies form a self-composed sequence of continually changing phenomena, which in their continual reaction to dogma only serve to place the eternal, unshakable truth of the latter in a vivid light.[41]

This assumption that orthodox dogma was unchanging and that innovation was automatically heretical was shared by theologians of widely divergent viewpoints. For instance, the two diametrically opposed adversaries in the christological controversies before Chalcedon, Theodore of Mopsuestia and St. Cyril of Alexandria, were at one in affirming this assumption. Theodore took the words of Gal 1.15–17 to mean: 'Perish the thought that any novelty or any human invention be mistaken for the kerygma!'[42] St. Cyril, on the other hand, described heretics as those who 'corrupt the faith that has been handed down to us by tradition, making use of the recently discovered inventions of the Dragon.'[43] Consequently, each was willing to concede to the other a far greater degree of inventiveness than he himself possessed, because inventiveness was characteristic of heresy. The truth did not have a history in the same sense of the word, because the truth did not change.

This principle becomes evident in the way Eusebius and his successors in ecclesiastical history handled the materials of historical theology. In the introduction to his work, Eusebius stated as the proper subject matter for such an investigation, first of all, the positive and constructive elements that had helped to assure an authentic series of legitimate successions, summarized in the opening words: 'The successions from the holy Apostles, together with the times that have elapsed from our Saviour's day down to our own; the important affairs that are said to have been transacted in the history of the Church, and those who took a prominent place in that history as leaders and presidents in such communities as were especially famous.'[44] But when one examines his actual narrative, it becomes evident that these 'successions' and 'important affairs' have themselves been selected as a means of stopping the mouths of the gainsayers, viz, 'those who through love of innovation fell into the most grievous error.'[45] For in response to the claim of Gnostics to possess a secret tradition,[46] or to the claim of Montanists to receive private revelations,[47] Eusebius points to the centers of genuine and reliable apostolic succession, where the old faith has been preserved against all the changes and chances of fluctuating heresy.

One result of this approach—and a result with far-reaching consequences for the entire history of historical theology—is that we are much better informed about the vagaries of sectarianism and heresy in the 2d and 3d centuries than about the historical development of the mainstream of Christian doctrine. If one were to expunge from modern histories of that period all the information that has been supplied by Eusebius, the remaining body of data, especially for the East, would be a scattered set of fragments.[48] Being so completely dependent upon one single source for their knowledge of this crucial era, historians have followed their source in paying attention to change at the expense of continuity—even though, ironically, it was the guiding purpose of the *Ecclesiastical History* to accentuate the change as a means of documenting the continuity. The successors of Eusebius as ecclesiastical historians, notably Socrates Scholasticus and Sozomen, were, if anything, even more zealous to document the apostolic succession not only of dioceses but especially of dogmas. Therefore Socrates, for example, citing the authority of Eusebius, solemnly affirms that the bishops at Nicea were 'unanimous in expression and sentiment' and therefore subscribed the confession adopted there.[49] Already at the time of Socrates it was known, or could have been known, that the controversies that broke out after Nicea were not a violation of that supposed unanimity, but a continuation of fundamental differences that had been papered over at Nicea because of imperial pressure; and, for that matter, that a prime agent in these controversies had been Eusebius himself.[50] Nevertheless, the religious commitment to succession and continuity was so overriding that Socrates, too, seems to take the Catholic faith largely for granted and to concentrate in his narrative on the various deviations from that norm.

This concentration of historians such as Eusebius on the history of heresy has its counterpart in a genre of Christian literature that arose in the 2d century and established itself as a permanent form of theological work, the treatise with the title *Against Heresies* or something similar.[51] Although many of these works, especially the early ones, have been lost,[52] the character of this literature may be discerned from those that have been preserved. Almost all such catalogues were written by orthodox churchmen, who identified themselves enthusiastically with the conquest of the heresies. Therefore it is extremely difficult to piece together enough evidence from their partisan accounts to file a minority report in absentia on behalf of the maligned heretics, but this is an inadequacy for which modern historians of dogma, as friends of the court, have done their best to compensate. In addition, the discovery during the 19th and 20th centuries of long-lost works by various heretics and heretical groups has provided a control against which to check the reports of the Church Fathers;[53] out of this process, many of those reports have been shown to be more objective than had often been thought.[54] But amid this effort to recover the actual intent of Gnostic and other heresies, it is sometimes overlooked that in many ways orthodox doctrine, prior to its being challenged from one or another 'heresy,' is almost as difficult to reconstruct as is heretical doctrine. There is much truth in Whitehead's epigram that 'wherever there is a creed, there is a heretic round the corner or in his grave,'[55] but sometimes the identity of the heretic is more evident than is the ancestry of the orthodox creed. For example, as we shall note in somewhat more detail later,[56] the first full-scale controversy on the Real Presence was that between Ratramnus and St. Paschasius Radbertus in the 9th century. The history of the doctrine of the Eucharist during the preceding centuries is therefore compelled to draw upon various brief quotations from the writings of the Church Fathers and upon the more or less evident theological implications of liturgical language and practice.[57]

The debates over this evidence are an index to the historical difficulty of putting to an ancient text a question that, at least in our formulation, had not occurred to its author. Perhaps the best example of these debates is the controversy that has raged over an explanation of the Eucharist introduced by St. Irenaeus into his defense of the goodness of the creation against its denigration at the hands of the Gnostics. If created things are good enough to serve as a medium for the Divine, they dare not be disparaged. The Eucharist, therefore, is a well-pleasing sacrifice: 'Giving directions to His disciples to offer to God the first-fruits of His own created things . . . [Christ] took that created thing, bread, and gave thanks, and said, "This is My body." And the cup likewise, which is part of that creation to which we belong, He confessed to be His blood, and taught the new oblation of the new covenant.'[58] This passage has seemed to the defenders of the sacrificial understanding of the Mass to be a clear statement of Roman Catholic doctrine against the Protestant contention that the only 'new oblation' was the unrepeatable death of Christ on Calvary.[59]

According to the apologists for this view of the Mass, the doctrine that corresponds to it is transubstantiation. That doctrine seems difficult to find in such a formulation as the following, which comes a few paragraphs after the passage just quoted: 'As the bread, which is produced from the earth, when it receives the invocation of God, is no longer common bread, but the Eucharist, consisting of two realities, earthly and heavenly; so also our bodies, when they receive the Eucharist, are no longer corruptible, having the hope of resurrection to eternity.'[60] In the Wittenberg Concord of 1536, this formula of the 'two realities' became the common ground on which Luther and Bucer could join in opposition to Roman Catholicism.[61] The same passage has been subjected to careful, in fact tortuous, examination by its editors and by other scholars, all in an effort to show that it supports a Protestant view of the Eucharist.[62] For our present purposes, these two passages are relevant as an indication of the difficulty inherent in any reconstruction of the doctrine of the Eucharist on the basis of the sparse evidence available in the writings of the Fathers. Thus the historical attempt to describe the development of the doctrine of the Eucharist founders on the orthodox assumption that there has been no change in true doctrine except insofar as heretics have presumed to attack and to revise it.

Although that assumption was almost universally shared by

all theologians who called themselves orthodox, it did not go unchallenged. The most dramatic challenge to it came in the work of Peter Abelard.[63] Proposing a series of 150 questions in doctrinal theology, Abelard lined up quotations from the Fathers in support both of a Yes and of a No to the questions. It was, he said in his preface, altogether understandable that 'in such a multitude of words some statements even of the saints should seem to be not only diverse from one another, but even adverse to one another.'[64] And in the event, the passages he quoted were mutually exclusive. Whatever may have been Abelard's intentions in producing such a compilation (of which more later), there is no question that his researches had discovered unresolved contradictions within what was blithely accepted as the consensus of the Fathers. Anyone who took all these texts at face value simply could not maintain a theory of 'everywhere, ever, by everyone' in the presence of such obvious diversity. Thus it belongs to Abelard's achievement, even though neither he nor his defenders nor his detractors could recognize it at the time, that he did ask the question about the emperor's clothes and make the fact of doctrinal difference—and hence, inevitably, of doctrinal change—an issue for theological reflection.

Abelard's own reflection on the issue did not lead to any reconsideration of the historical theory that had come down from the heresiologists of the ancient Church. He proposed several possible solutions for an apparent contradiction in the dogmatic proof texts from the Fathers; but, with one possible exception, none of these solutions suggested any new theory about the history of doctrinal change. Each of the solutions had, in one way or another, been attempted before Abelard, and each was to play a role long after him.[65] He urged, first of all, that one should investigate whether a writing attributed to a particular Church Father was actually his work; for there were 'many apocryphal works bearing the names of saints in order to give them authority.'[66] Indeed, even in the writings assembled in the Old and New Testament there were scribal errors.[67] A second resolution of contradictions within the patristic consensus was suggested by the *Retractations* of St. Augustine: 'Nor do I regard it as less important to consider whether the matters that are cited from the writings of the saints are of the kind that were retracted by them themselves elsewhere and corrected, once they had recognized the truth.'[68] Another version of this solution was to see that certain opinions had been set forth by the Fathers, not as their own teaching, but as 'questions that they settled by a precise definition.'[69]

It was in the course of articulating his third principle of resolution that Abelard came closest to a historical method for dealing with the dilemma of theological change. After setting down the principle that one must carefully distinguish between those moral or canonical regulations that are an absolute requirement incumbent upon everyone and those that apply only in certain special cases, he continued: 'One must also distinguish among times and causes of dispensations, because often what is permitted at one time is found to be forbidden at another.'[70] Although, as he added, 'it is particularly necessary that these matters be distinguished in the ordinances of ecclesiastical decrees or canons,' some analogous distinction could conceivably be applied also to the realm of doctrine. In his actual resolution of the apparent contradictions within traditional material, however, as Martin Grabmann has pointed out, 'because of the dogmatic character of the materials treated in the book *Sic et non*, this third rule of harmonization does not receive much attention.'[71] Grabmann notes: 'Abelard did not refer to the most important rule for the interpretation of difficult texts from the Fathers, namely, the explanation of such texts on the basis of the context, on the basis of the purpose and time of the writing, and by the reference to parallel passages.' Willing though Abelard was to recognize this factor in the treatment of the data of canon law, he does not seem to have envisaged an interpretation of doctrinal formulas that would 'distinguish among times and causes of dispensations, because often what is permitted at one time is found to be forbidden at another.'

The fourth and fifth methods of coping with contradictions in the tradition, however, did apply again both to the area of canon law and to the area of dogma. 'An easy solution of many controversies will be found,' he proposed, 'if we can defend the proposition that the same words have been used by various authors with various meanings.'[72] One was to determine whether the supposed univocity of such theological terms as 'grace' could be maintained. Abelard's own preference seems to have been for this method, which, as we shall note later, assigned to dialectics the task of identifying the diverse meanings of equivocal theological terms. The fifth and last method, to be invoked when all the others had proved unequal to the problem, was to admit that 'there is a manifest conflict of opinion, one that cannot be resolved by any reasoning.' Faced by the undeniable evidence of a genuine contradiction between two or more patristic authorities, the theologian had one final recourse: 'The authorities are to be compared, and the one that is more powerfully attested and has been more fully substantiated is to be preferred.'[73] This reference to attestation and confirmation as the criteria takes one back, in effect, to the Vincentian canon; for it would appear that the weight of tradition, in some sort of unspecified combination with the contemporary authority of the teaching power of the Church, would have to do the attesting or confirming. It seems then that, at least in this respect, Abelard's bold recognition of ambiguities in the dogmatic tradition led to an argument in a circle, leaving the historical relation between continuity and change unresolved—or, more precisely, resolving it by transposing it into a logical relation. Not change but contradiction was the key issue.

A theological change may involve a contradiction, but it does not always do so; likewise, a contradiction in theology may be due to a change in theology, but it need not be. The Abelardian way out of the problem, therefore, tends to foreshorten both the identification of the question and the specification of the answer, by de-temporalizing and de-historicizing the connections between opposing ideas. It is undeniable that many Church Fathers contradicted one another, and that more than a few of them contradicted themselves, even without being aware of doing so. So pervasive is the presence of the unseen contradiction and unexamined opposition in Christian doctrine that a distinguished historian of ideas, Arthur O. Lovejoy, was moved to assert:

> The term 'Christianity,' for example, is not the name for any single unit of the type for which the historian of specific ideas looks. I mean by this not merely the notorious fact that persons who have equally professed and called themselves Christians have, in the course of history, held all manner of distinct and conflicting beliefs under the one name, but also that any of these persons and sects has, as a rule, held under that name a very mixed collection of ideas, the combination

of which into a conglomerate bearing a single name and supposed to constitute a real unity was usually the result of historic processes of a highly complicated and curious sort. It is, of course, proper and necessary that ecclesiastical historians should write books on the history of Christianity; but in doing so they are writing of a series of facts which, taken as a whole, have almost nothing in common except the name; the part of the world in which they occurred; the reverence for a certain person, whose nature and teaching, however, have been most variously conceived, so that the unity here too is largely a unity of name; and the identity of a part of their historic antecedents, of certain causes or influences which, diversely combined with other causes, have made each of these systems of belief what it is. In the whole series of creeds and movements going under the one name, and in each of them separately, it is needful to go behind the superficial appearance of singleness and identity, to crack the shell which holds the mass together, if we are to see the real units, the effective working ideas, which, in any given case, are present.[74]

A radical nominalism of this sort about the universal themes of Christian theology would be regarded, not only by most systematic theologians but by most historians of theology, as a draconian solution of the problem of change and continuity. Yet it bears a curious resemblance to the more conventionally Christian theories that we have been examining; for, like them, it claims to be able to compare the data of theological history without investigating how one theology has grown out of its predecessors, or how the 'historic antecedents' have and have not shaped the development of the various ideas under examination. Lovejoy's own researches into the history of the Christian idea of God[75] or into the idea of 'nature' in Tertullian[76] go well beyond his definition of what the historian of Christian thought may or can undertake. To Abelard, the perplexing difficulty was the opposition between the teachings of various eminent authorities of the Church. At least some instances of such opposition, however, may be interpreted historically. To the historian, the issue is not opposition but change; he is less interested in contradiction than in innovation. Given the orthodox understanding of the relation between dogmatic truth and heretical novelty, however, the historical phenomenon of innovation becomes at the same time a theological question. The theologian whom the historian honors for creativity is liable to be condemned by the Church for heresy.

Although many instances of this could be selected from the history of theology—including the condemnation of Origen, to which we shall return—the controversies in which St. Augustine was involved during his lifetime are a particularly appropriate case. As a theologian of the Church, he strove throughout the literary works of his more mature years to think and speak in accordance with the authority of the Church's confession. Even in the most speculative of his major theological works, *On the Holy Trinity*, whose discussion of the 'vestiges of the Trinity' probed both the depths of the human personality and the outer reaches of the created world for evidences of the imprint of the Divine Triad, Augustine wanted to be understood as a spokesman for the public doctrine of the Catholic Church. Thus he concludes his summary of orthodox trinitarianism with the statement: 'This is also my faith, inasmuch as it is the Catholic faith.'[77] At the end of Book I he refers again to 'the right faith of the Catholic Church.'[78] Leaving aside for the present the question of whether the doctrine of Filioque proposed in *On the Holy Trinity* is integral to the tradition of this professedly Catholic faith, both the exegesis in the earlier books of the treatise and even the speculation in the later books make sense only on the assumption that the author felt himself bound by what the Church believed, taught, and confessed. Augustine's principle that (in Newman's translation) 'the universal Church is in its judgments secure of truth'[79] was the unassailable presupposition for whatever he taught on either faith or morals.

Yet the very Donatism in opposition to which St. Augustine enunciated those 'palmary words,'[80] writing against Parmenian, the Donatist bishop of Carthage, was also the occasion for the most far-reaching examination of the problem of doctrinal change anywhere in his writings. The substance of the Donatists' charge against St. Augustine's asseverations of loyalty to the unity of the Church can almost be reduced to two accusations: by continuing in fellowship with bishops who, either through betrayal during persecution or through personal immorality, had contaminated their office and their Sacraments, the Catholic Church had become schismatic; by rejecting this understanding of the relation between the holiness of the bishop and the unity of the

Church, Augustine had become guilty not only of separation from the true Church of his own time but also of apostasy from the teaching of the Catholic tradition as embodied in St. Cyprian.[81] The Donatists, for their part, saw themselves as the defenders of what had been believed 'everywhere [or, at least, in North Africa], ever, by everyone' about the doctrine of the Church. And the Church Father whose authority they invoked had, in fact, given more serious consideration to the nature of Christian unity than virtually anyone since the days of the Apostles. To this day St. Cyprian's views of unity and authority in the Church are a matter of continuing interest and lively controversy.[82]

Both in the modern literature and in the debates between Augustine and the Donatists, 'Cyprian's attitude in the Baptismal Dispute is not a matter of controversy, i.e., converted heretics need to be baptized.'[83] There was no denying that, according to St. Cyprian, Baptism depended for its validity on its being administered under the proper auspices. The principle for which St. Cyprian is perhaps best remembered is the axiom that 'outside the Church there is no salvation.' But the context of that axiom is a denial of the validity of heretical Baptism:

> If not even the Baptism of a public confession and blood [in martyrdom] can profit a heretic to salvation, because there is no salvation out of the Church, how much less shall it be of advantage to him, if in a hiding-place and a cave of robbers, stained with the contagion of adulterous water, he has not only not put off his old sins, but rather heaped up still newer and greater ones! Wherefore Baptism cannot be common to us and to heretics, to whom neither God the Father, nor Christ the Son, nor the Holy Ghost, nor the faith, nor the Church itself, is common. And therefore it behooves those to be baptized who come from heresy to the Church, that so they who are prepared, in the lawful, and true, and only Baptism of the holy Church, by divine regeneration, for the kingdom of God, may be born of both Sacraments, because it is written, 'Except a man be born of water and of the Spirit, he cannot enter into the kingdom of God.'[84]

As Willis has said, 'The Donatists founded their whole schism upon a rigid application of this principle in their own favour.'[85]

From St. Augustine's most important reply to the Donatist view of heretical Baptism, the treatise *On Baptism*, it is clear that he recognized the force of their accusation that his divergence from the tradition represented by St. Cyprian had made him guilty of doctrinal innovation. He himself said elsewhere of the Fathers of the Church, among whom he explicitly named St. Cyprian: 'What they found in the Church, that they maintained; what they learned, that they taught; what they received from their Fathers, that they passed on to their sons.'[86] Yet on this issue, what St. Cyprian had received from his fathers (presumably, from Tertullian, among others) and had passed on to his sons (among whom the Donatists claimed first place)—that St. Augustine seemed willing to reject. St. Augustine's defense against the accusation of having introduced a new theory about heretical Baptism, contrary to the authority of tradition, was to appeal from St. Cyprian's doctrine of Baptism to St. Cyprian's doctrine of the Church. St. Cyprian's primary concern had been to preserve the unity of the Church, and for the sake of this concern he had been quite willing to maintain communion even with those whose opinions about heretical Baptism he opposed. Thus the Donatists were guilty of two evils: of error on the doctrine of Baptism itself, and of schism by separating themselves from those who had the true doctrine of Baptism.[87] Who, then, was being the more faithful to the tradition of St. Cyprian? According to St. Augustine, there was a fundamental inconsistency between St. Cyprian's theory about the influence of a bishop's subjective status upon his conferral of sacramental grace and his views about the objective unity of the Church. Far from being a doctrinal innovation, then, the Catholic teaching was a fuller statement of the sacramental implication that had to be drawn from St. Cyprian's ecclesiology.

The fact remained, however, that the explicit statements of St. Cyprian on the baptismal question were different from St. Augustine's position in the controversy with the Donatists. He encountered a similar embarrassment in his controversy with the Pelagians. This is one of the very few points of contact between the two controversies. Apart from one or two attempts to draw a correlation between the two heresies on the ground that they both made divine grace dependent upon human worthiness,[88] the principal parallel between St. Augustine's two lines of argumentation is the prominence of St. Cyprian and of the doctrine of Baptism in both. But this time it was St. Augustine who identified himself with St. Cyprian's doctrine of Baptism, as set forth in St. Cyprian's defense of Infant Baptism in his Epistle 64,[89] which St. Augustine called St. Cyprian's 'book on the Baptism of infants.'[90] It was with good reason that he had fastened upon St. Cyprian, for St. Cyprian and St. Ambrose[91] were the chief authorities whom he could claim as antecedents of his position. Otherwise, the Fathers had been more intent upon defending the free will of man and his moral responsibility against the determinism of certain pagan thinkers, and especially against the Manicheans and other heretics, than upon specifying what man had lost through the fall of Adam. Therefore they appeared to be partisans of the Pelagian doctrine, and St. Augustine appeared to be an innovator in relation to them.[92] But the reason for this was that 'before this heresy [Pelagianism] arose, they did not have the necessity to deal with this question, so difficult of solution. They would undoubtedly have done so if they had been compelled to respond to such men. As a result, in their writings they only touched briefly and in passing upon their views of the grace of God.'[93] And so it was not St. Augustine but his Pelagian opponents who were guilty of introducing 'profane novelties' into Christian doctrine.[94] Although this may have satisfied the needs of the immediate controversy, the criticisms of St. Vincent of Lérins against the Augustinian doctrines[95] show that these doctrines continued to be regarded as the real 'profane novelties,' and that neither the anti-Donatist nor the anti-Pelagian explanation was adequate to resolve the problem of theological change.

The problem does, of course, acquire special shading after the doctrine at issue has been promulgated as the official dogma of the Church. For example, the eventual development of the Filioque in the Western text of the Nicene Creed and in Western Catholic dogma not only became a barrier between the Greek Church and the Latin Church; it also raised the question of continuity with the Church of earlier centuries. Reacting to that question, Newman—who, though still an Anglican, had already moved a long way toward his decisive step of 1845—declared in his sermon of 1843 on doctrinal development: 'The doctrine of the Double Procession was no Catholic dogma in the first ages, though it was more or less clearly stated by individual Fathers; yet if it is now to be received, as surely it must be, as part of the

Creed, it was really held everywhere from the beginning, and therefore, in a measure, held as a mere religious impression, and perhaps an unconscious one.'[96] The prominent echoes of the Vincentian canon in this statement suggest that, at least in the case of those teachings that have been canonized as creedal and dogmatic, Newman felt obliged to posit the existence of a continuity, however 'unconscious' it may have been. The debates over the definability of doctrine occasioned by the promulgation of the Assumption of the Blessed Virgin Mary in 1950[97] have thrust the problem of the development of dogma into the center both of interconfessional discussion and of the intramural reexamination of the several denominational traditions.[98] The question of development is therefore highly pertinent to the problematics of doctrinal change being discussed here.[99]

Yet the two questions are not identical. Despite the thickness of various textbooks on dogma, the actual number of doctrines defined officially as binding *de jure* upon all believers is relatively small as compared with the theological proposals and doctrines set forth by individual theologians or schools of theology. Even the official dogmas, moreover, must not be interpreted as having settled an issue in the sense of shutting off further theological discussion. As the history of the doctrine of the person of Christ demonstrates perhaps more fully than any other, conciliar and creedal definitions may be called precise only in the sense that they draw the lines of the perimeter beyond which devotion and speculation may not go without violating orthodoxy. Within the perimeter, however, there remains, if not an agreement to disagree, at least a great deal of room for further speculation, debate, and perhaps dogmatic development. But in the case of many doctrines, there has been little or no delineation of such perimeters. For example, in the related doctrine of the work of Christ as Redeemer, the Nicene Creed, after reciting a series of predicates intended to specify the relation between the Father and the Son, goes on to state that the Incarnation happened 'for the sake of us men and for the purpose of our salvation.'[100] But what the content of that salvation is and how the life, death, and resurrection of the Son of God brought it about—these and similar questions the Creed leaves for the liturgy to celebrate and for theology to investigate. Save for an occasional condemnation of a theory of the atonement that appeared to deny the soteriological significance of the events of Redemption (for example, Abelard's speculations about the purpose of the Incarnation[101]), the doctrinal declarations of the various denominations have been quite chary of codifying any particular metaphor for the content and method of salvation. Even the doctrine of the death of Christ as vicarious satisfaction, while the common property of most Western theologians regardless of denomination, has never attained the dogmatic status of the doctrine of two natures in Christ.[102]

The problem of doctrinal change is, however, not resolved by any theory about the development of dogma. Most of the changes in the history of doctrine have not become, and could not have become, dogmatic developments. Yet they were a fact with which subsequent generations had somehow to come to terms. To account for the phenomenon of doctrinal change, theologians have resorted to a variety of theological methods. Two of these have predominated throughout most of the history of Christian thought, the dogmatic and the dialectical.

The Dogmatic Solution

By a dogmatic method in the present context is meant a treatment of the theologians and theologies of the past that measures them against criteria of orthodoxy formulated after their own time. Identifying those criteria of orthodoxy as a summary of what, according to the Vincentian canon, must also have been in force during an earlier age, this method feels competent to adopt as Fathers those who were the ancestors of orthodoxy and to condemn as heretics those who deviated from these later norms.[103] Unfortunately, the ancestors of orthodoxy were in many instances also the thinkers who were found to have deviated from a later definition of orthodoxy. Thus an orthodoxy that, humanly speaking, could not have come into existence without them takes it upon itself to charge them with false doctrine.

The outstanding instance of such an anomaly, at least in patristic theology, was the condemnation of Origen. The *Panegyric to Origen* written by St. Gregory the Wonder-Worker[104] is a personally moving, if rhetorically cloying, testimony by a former pupil to the learning and the kindness, but also to the doctrinal and ecclesiastical fidelity, of his master, 'this sacred personage, who stands alone among all men.'[105] Although St. Gregory's language may have been more extravagant than that of most other tributes, the regard for Origen that it bespoke was widely, almost universally, shared. Thus, for example, although St. Athanasius and Eusebius of Caesarea never came to an agreement about the supposed Sabellianism of 'Nicene' theology, both were devoted admirers of Origen: Athanasius called him 'the industrious one'[106] and used him to prove the continuity of his own doctrine,[107] while Eusebius devoted most of the sixth book of his *Ecclesiastical History* to a loving account of the life and influence of the Alexandrian scholar, whose father, already during Origen's youth, 'gave profound thanks to God, the Author of all good things, that He had deemed him worthy to be the father of such a boy.'[108] It was not only Origen's piety, which was profound, nor only his erudition, which was enormous, but his loyalty to the Church and to her tradition that so deeply impressed both his own contemporaries and the theologians of later generations. During the Arian controversies, therefore, almost all parties laid claim to the heritage of Origen—and almost all of them with at least some justification, for, in Harnack's trenchant phrase, 'every conceivable heresy is touched upon'[109] somewhere in Origen's writings. Particularly in this the case if one includes those teachings that Origen, either out of tentativeness or out of timidity, put forward, not as definite opinions, but as questions and hypotheses. The condemnation of Arianism at Nicea could, therefore, also be regarded as a condemnation of Origenism.[110] Epiphanius was expressing a widespread belief among the orthodox when he identified Lucian and Origen as the teachers of the Arians;[111] but he should, for the sake of completeness, have given some explanation of how Origen had also managed to be the teacher of such orthodox stalwarts as the Cappadocian Fathers.

This attack was the opening gun of an assault upon Origen's orthodoxy. Epiphanius listed a long catalogue of Origen's errors,[112] from which it was clear that Origen was not only a heretic himself but the originator of many later heresies. A sermon against Origen, delivered by Epiphanius at Jerusalem,[113] was important both as part of his own campaign against Origenism and as the occasion for converting to this cause the learned and polemical St. Jerome, who had previously been an ardent devotee of Origenist theology.[114] Taking up the crusade, St. Jerome became involved in a memorable quarrel with Rufinus, in which Origen's *On First Principles* was one of the chief issues: Rufinus had tampered with the text of the treatise in his translation, maintaining that the doctrinally questionable passages were the interpolation of heretics, and St. Jerome responded with an accurate translation of the Greek (which has, unfortunately, since been lost), to prove that Origen was himself responsible for these erroneous teachings.[115] According to Rufinus, St. Jerome was attacking a dead man unfairly: 'After this repentance of his, and after he has been dead a hundred and fifty years, you drag him into court and call for his condemnation.'[116] St. Jerome replied:

> Your Origen allows himself to treat of the transmigration of souls, to introduce the belief in an infinite number of worlds, to clothe rational creatures in one body after another, to say that Christ has often suffered, and will often suffer again, it being always profitable to undertake what has once been profitable. You also yourself assume such an authority as to turn a heretic into a martyr, and to invent a heretical falsification of the books of Origen.[117]

Such attacks by St. Jerome and others upon Origen's orthodoxy are based partly upon authentic citations from Origen, partly upon opinions that Origen may have been quoting from others without expressing his own judgment, partly upon oversimplification, and partly upon slander. The outcome was, however, the repeated condemnation of Origen and Origenism, during the 5th century and again in the 6th. The epistle of Pope Anastasius I to Venerius of Milan, written probably in 401, was directed against Origenism, including the Latin translations of the books of Origen by Rufinus.[118] A council held in Origen's own city, Alexandria, in 400, was directed by Theophilus, patriarch of Alexandria, to condemn Origenistic doctrine.[119] Theophilus himself attacked Origen as 'a many-headed monster of heresies' and condemned his adherents.[120] A century later these anathemas were reiterated and reinforced, first of all by the Emperor Justinian, whose epistle to the patriarch of Constantinople, Mennas, was to a large degree a diatribe against Origen. This polemic received official ecclesiastical endorsement at a regional synod held in Constantinople in 543, where various false doctrines associated with Origenism were proscribed,[121] and then at an ecumenical council, also held at Constantinople, in 553, now commonly designated as the Second Council of Constantinople and the Fifth Ecumenical Council.[122] (It should, however, be noted that the explicit reference to Origen in the 11th anathema of this Council may be a later interpolation.[123]) In any case, both the theologians of the 5th century and the churchmen of the 6th believed themselves to be in a position to pass dogmatic judgment upon a theologian of the 3d century—and not only *a* theologian but *the* theologian without whom the subsequent development even of their own orthodoxy is historically inconceivable.

So confident an expression of the right to judge not only the quick but also the dead was not, of course, peculiar to the opponents of Origenism. Repeatedly in Christian history, the defenders of a newly formulated orthodoxy have taken it upon themselves to require that their theological ancestors pass in review so that the changes brought on by the passage of time might be evaluated in the light of what was now being set forth as timeless truth. Nor was this procedure confined to the patristic development. The bitter conflict over the theology of Philipp Melanchthon during the generation that followed the death of Martin Luther in 1546 was—with due allowance for the differences between Origen and Melanchthon, which are in many ways more decisive than the analogies—another case of a thinker's being condemned by those who owed him much, but apparently not their gratitude.[124] In the Roman Catholic theology of the 20th century, a somewhat similar position was occupied by Modernism, which had asked many of the most important and embarrassing questions (including many of the central questions with which this study is concerned).[125] Because of its antitraditional excesses, Modernism earned the condemnation of Pope St. Pius X in *Lamentabili* and in *Pascendi gregis*,[126] and no one can acknowledge it as an ancestor.[127] Thus the phenomenon of doctrinal change is called to judgment before a dogmatic tribunal that finds in the recent doctrinal legislation of the Church a proper yardstick for measuring the history of all previously existing theology. There is no convincing reason to believe that later generations will not continue to assess the past in the light of the present, even as they inevitably (though often unconsciously) take a part in the present only because someone was willing to take a risk in the past.

The historical theologian must, perhaps inevitably, treat such a procedure with a considerable degree of ambivalence. If he takes seriously the requirement that the theologian be found a faithful steward of what is entrusted to him,[128] he will acknowledge, at least in principle, the need for doctrinal discipline in the Church. The condemnatory clauses of the Nicene formula,[129] or for that matter of the Augsburg Confession,[130] are an expression of the Church's responsibility to identify forms of teaching that, consistently carried out, threaten the truth of divine revelation. Nor is that responsibility being faithfully discharged unless the vigilance of the Church extends also to those theologies from the past that continue to exercise a baneful influence. It is, in fact, often impossible to determine just how baneful a theology is until long after its founder is dead; the good is sometimes interred with his bones. If there are, moreover, perennial errors—or, as Schleiermacher termed them, 'natural heresies'[131]—which, in various configurations, continue to appear within Christian theology, the teaching authority of the Church would seem to have a special duty to point these out and to warn against them. 'Do not speak evil of the dead,' whatever its validity as a maxim of moral theology, cannot be called a principle regulating dogmatic or polemical theology. When a theologian dies, his theology often lives on after him, for good or ill; it cannot be ignored or its errors condoned simply because he is no longer living.

When one has said all of this, however, the execution of the responsibility to assess the theology of the past requires careful scrutiny; for it, too, must be evaluated as a method for coming to terms with doctrinal change. It cannot be denied, for example, that these condemnations of the dead—as well as many condemnations of the living—have frequently been brought about more by political than by theological considerations. So it was, for example, with the condemnation of Origen by Justinian. But a more serious objection to the dogmatic method is that it does not take the fact of doctrinal change seriously. Reduced to its essence, it seems to be largely indifferent to time and to history. This indifference is evident also in the positive application of the dogmatic method. Quotations from various centuries and various traditions are lumped together, with little or no consideration of the historical contexts in which they were originally formulated.[132] A 'consensus of the Fathers' is assumed, and changes from one Father to the next are blunted by the belief that, if they are orthodox, they will display the consensus. The working assumption behind the compilation of patristic florilegia[133] was to 'bring together all possible doctrines and errors'; but while the purpose of such a collection was to serve as 'an arsenal of weapons for orthodoxy, for us it is above all one of the most important sources for the knowledge of earlier theologians.'[134] Absent even from so eminent a florilegium as the *Sacra parallela*, traditionally ascribed to St. John of Damascus,[135] is a sense of the historical dimension, which would regard the chronological relation between the sources of the tradition as decisive for their interpretation and even for their evaluation. Once again, change is regarded as something that can happen only to heretical doctrine; true doctrine is a constant, and it is immune to change. Conversely, what there is in the history of doctrine that changes may be regarded as heretical, what remains the same as orthodox.

Unfortunately for the simplicity of such a criterion, the closer one studies the various texts, the more evident does change become, with the result that none of the Fathers appears to have been exempt from the inexorable reality of change. By a strange but not unique irony, the dogmatic method of treating the phenomenon of theological change can move with great rapidity into the very relativism it seeks to avoid.

The Dialectical Interpretation of Change

Neither relativism nor the dogmatic method seems able to distinguish between theological difference and theological change; each, in its own way, tends to identify the two. The dialectical method of dealing with theological change depends for its validity upon a refinement of the tools for measuring theological difference, so that not every difference is automatically seen as a question of truth against error. The word 'dialectical' as used here refers to a methodology by which, to adapt Aristotle's words, 'through a process of criticism, the opinions generally held on the particular points that have to be discussed'[136] are classified, distinguished from one another, and related to the general principles of theological science. Although it does not deny the possibility of genuine theological opposition, a dialectical method will inquire whether seemingly antithetical propositions may not represent complementary rather than contradictory views of the matter. It begins, as the definition of Aristotle indicates, by gathering 'the opinions generally held' on the theological issue in question. Within the present context, this means the various opinions and propositions set down in Scripture, the creeds, the Councils, the Fathers, and the other documents of the tradition of the Church. With these data in hand, it seeks, by analysis and definition, to identify the kinds and the degrees of difference among them.[137]

Some such aim seems to underlie Abelard's compilation of patristic opinions. It is in keeping with the vulgar understanding of 'dialectics' as synonymous with 'sophistry' that Abelard has so often been interpreted as either a rationalist or a sceptic or both. For in his work, as Henry Osborn Taylor has said,

> ... the duality of method becomes explicit, and is, if one may say so, set by the ears. On the one hand, he advances in his constructive theological treatises toward a portentous application of reason to explain the contents of the Christian Faith; on the other, somewhat sardonically, he devises a scheme for the employment and presentation of authorities upon these sacred matters, a scheme so obviously apt that, once made known, it could not but be followed and perfected. ... Abaelard was a reasoner, more specifically speaking, a dialectician according to the ways of Aristotelian logic.[138]

As we have pointed out earlier,[139] Abelard seems to have had special confidence in the method by which it could be demonstrated that various Church Fathers had used the same word in different senses; therefore the apparent antinomy between two propositions, equally well attested as authoritative expressions of the one true faith, might simply be due to differences of meaning. Even Grabmann, who seeks to exculpate Abelard of the charge of rationalism, concludes that 'in the emphasis on the fourth rule of harmonization lies the inadequacy of the *Sic-et-non* method,' for it could so easily lead to a situation where dialectics, introduced as a means, becomes an end in itself.[140]

It is, in addition, easy for the dialectical method to treat its proof texts from the Fathers as atomistically as do the florilegia.

Abelard's own procedure is a good illustration. The evident conflict between two or more such proof texts is usually not resolved by identifying the polemical target of a statement or by specifying its place in the personal and theological history of the writer, but by examining the several possible meanings of the key terms; if these meanings can be related to one another in a concordant manner, the contradiction is resolved.[141] Yet the suspicion of Abelard's orthodox detractors,[142] curiously reinforced by the praise of his rationalistic devotees,[143] leads to the charge that his dialectical method consisted in the manipulation of equivocal terms as a means of undercutting confidence in the dogmatic tradition. Even if one does not accept this imputation of motives, Abelard's very selection of patristic quotations, as well as his adjudication of the conflicts between them, frequently fails to grasp either the most profound divergences or the most important continuities between them.[144] Thus it is a matter of general agreement among historians of medieval thought that Abelard is more important for the questions that he raised, in part by indirection, than for any of the answers he proposed. As we have mentioned earlier, Abelard's method of interpreting theological change did not make use of historical criteria; he could write a *Historia calamitatum* but not a *Historia dogmatum*.

The Method of St. Thomas

But even when measured by its own criteria rather than by those of historical theology, Abelard's version of the dialectical method fell short of its assignment. For there is a theologically defensible and a methodologically valid use of dialectics in the study of theological change. This is not the place for an extended analysis of the theological method of St. Thomas Aquinas, but one way to characterize that method would be to see in it the refinement of Abelard's *Sic et non*. On the one hand, the quotations from the Fathers, which figure so prominently in the consideration of alternatives in the *Summa theologiae*, call attention to many of the same disharmonies with which Abelard had been engaged.[145] There is likewise a parallel between the defenses of the role of dialectics in theology advanced by the two men with the support of certain patristic passages.[146] On the other hand, the Victorine tradition made its contribution to the

Thomistic method by its scrupulous orthodoxy.[147] Thus, in the words of Maurice de Wulf, 'the two currents that issued from the school of St. Victor and from that of Abelard united in the great theological works of the princes of scholasticism.'[148] Drawing these two lines of development together, St. Thomas assigned to dialectics the function not of exaggerating the contradictions but of resolving them, and thus of clarifying the terms of the orthodox tradition.

Among the many examples that could be selected from the writings of St. Thomas, his discussion of the applicability of the term 'person' to the Godhead is particularly relevant because of its echoes of the development of the dogma of the Trinity.[149] Each of the patristic quotations introduced into the debate carried connotations from its historical origins. As was his wont, St. Thomas introduced his dissertation on 'person' with several quotations from the Fathers that suggest that the answer to the question of the applicability of 'person' ought to be in the negative.

Pseudo-Dionysius had maintained that the only titles that should be predicated of 'the supersubstantial and hidden Divinity' were those handed down by Sacred Scripture.[150] Even though the title 'the supersubstantial and hidden Divinity' had not been handed down in this way itself, the argument was clear. As part of his apophatic theology,[151] the author of *On the Divine Names* was arguing that positive assertions about God that went beyond the statements of Scripture were illicit; 'supersubstantial' and 'hidden,' while affirmative in grammar, were basically negative in signification, telling us only what God is not. Because 'person,' whatever its authority, was a positive term lacking in biblical warrant, the testimony of this supposedly subapostolic writer would seem to exclude it from orthodox usage.

A second voice of the tradition that seemed to be opposed to the use of the term 'person' was that of Boethius. Sometime between 1257 and 1259,[152] St. Thomas had composed his commentary on the treatise of Boethius *On the Trinity*, clarifying both his own trinitarian thought and his epistemology on the basis of this text.[153] Now that he had to treat of the technical terms of trinitarian doctrine, the study of Boethius stood him in good stead. For as both a careful student of classical languages, Greek as well as Latin,[154] and an expositor of the orthodox dogmas of the Trinity and the two natures in Christ,[155] Boethius was uniquely qualified to relate dogmatic terminology to pre-Christian and non-Christian usage. This he did for the term 'person.'

From this background Boethius commented: 'The term person seems to be taken from the masks which represented men in comedies and tragedies. For "person" comes from "sounding through" [*personando*], since a greater volume of sound is produced through the cavity in the mask. These "persons" or masks the Greeks called *prosōpa*, as they were placed on the face and covered the features from the eyes of the spectators.'[156] Even if the definition of person as mask did not connote Sabellianism to St. Thomas, it could be argued that the term was not a fitting name for God except in a metaphorical sense. Yet the trinitarian dogma did not mean to apply it to Him only metaphorically. Therefore that dogma appeared to be in conflict with yet another authoritative voice from the tradition of the Church.

Also from Boethius came a second objection based upon a comparison of the Greek and the Latin Fathers.[157] The term person was tantamount to hypostasis. On the basis both of etymology and of usage, however, hypostasis meant that which is 'the substance of accidents,' that of which accidents may be predicated. So it had been employed in part of the Greek tradition, both philosophical and theological. Depending upon whether one derived it from the middle voice or from the active voice, it could 'mean either that which underlies, or that which gives support.'[158] In one sense, therefore, it referred to that which lay beneath and behind the accidents and changes of sense experience. But this could not be applied to God, for there are no accidents in Him. Moreover, the only major Church Father who could be called Boethius's peer as a student of both Latin and Greek usage, St. Jerome, had also warned against the term hypostasis.

In a letter to Pope St. Damasus, written perhaps in 376,[159] he had addressed himself to the confusion arising from the fact that hypostasis, which had been used in Latin as a synonym for substance and therefore as a term for the One in God, was now being used for the Three in God. After listing his reasons for opposing this usage, St. Jerome stated his position: 'I do not object, but believe me, poison lies concealed under the honey.

An angel of Satan has transformed himself into an angel of light.'[160] Quoting these words about the poison and the honey, St. Thomas cited St. Jerome's hesitancy as yet another reason why the term 'person' seemed not to be proper in Christian language about God. All these authorities, then, seemed to rule out the use of the term in theology.

Responding to them, St. Thomas maintained that a novelty of terms was not heretical, and that for this reason it was permissible to use words besides those of Sacred Scripture. The origins of person in the language of plays did not forever determine its meaning for Christian theology. As for the warning of St. Jerome, it was based on the well-known confusion in Latin between hypostasis as substance and hypostasis as person. Therefore it was fitting to use person of God. St. Thomas thus employed several of the methods suggested in the prologue to Abelard's *Sic et non*, but the result of the method was to confirm orthodox usage.

In the terms that we have been using here, St. Thomas made use of the dialectics in the service of dogmatics. But it must also be pointed out that he did not make use of history as such to account for the changes that he was attempting to explain. The Latin confusion about hypostasis, for example, was not described in its historical development, as we would now describe it, but analyzed philologically and dialectically. And explicit in the discussion is the assumption that the only innovation permitted in theology is a novelty that 'finds new words to express the ancient faith about God.'[161] When St. Thomas corrected the Fathers, he usually did so in an implicit way, without calling attention to the changes in theology either between one Father and another or between one of the Fathers, e.g., St. Augustine, and himself.[162]

Although the Thomistic method represents a significant advance over both the Vincentian and the Abelardian as a way of coming to terms with the fact of doctrinal change, all three of these are much closer to one another than any of them is to the method most characteristic of 20th-century theological scholarship. Separating the great bulk of modern theological thought from its predecessors is the intervention of a new temper and thus of a new method, which causes theologians to view the phenomenon of change differently. This new method, which is itself a change of the greatest importance, seeks to account for doctrinal change on historical grounds. Even if a theologian still evaluates the change dogmatically or analyzes it dialectically, he first tries to understand it historically—and many historical theologians claim to stop at this. How this new temper and method arose and what role it has come to play in the history of modern theology will be the subject of our second chapter.

CHAPTER TWO

The Evolution of the Historical

Although the various methods described above for dealing with the phenomenon of doctrinal change were all appropriate within their particular frameworks, the study and interpretation of this phenomenon has now become the special work of historical theology. So dominant has history become as a way of understanding man and his world that modern men need to be reminded, also by history, that the category of the historical has itself developed and changed. This is true both of historical study in general and of historical theology in particular. The study of the history of Christian doctrine has its origins in the development of the historical outlook. Both as an introduction to the place that historical theology has come to occupy in the modern interpretation of the problem of doctrinal change and as an example of the very innovation that history purports to describe, the evolution of the historical merits scholarly consideration.

Renaissance and Reformation

G. P. Gooch once said that democracy was a product of the Reformation, but not of the Reformers.[1] He meant that it was far from the minds of Luther, Zwingli, and Calvin to allow popular sovereignty to prevail within those territories over which Protestantism gained control, but that democratic ideas arose out of the conditions that the Reformation, quite against the will of the Reformers, brought about.[2] Some similar epigram could be coined about the development of historical theology, which was in many ways a by-product rather than a product of Reformation theology. Gooch himself described the situation well in another place:

> Historical study begins with the humanists of the Italian and German Renaissance. . . . For a brief period the European mind devoted itself to secular learning; but the Renaissance was destroyed by the Reformation. History became the expression of confessional animosities, and remained enveloped in an ecclesiastical atmosphere till the opening of the 18th century. In this long struggle there is little to choose between Protestant and Catholic controversialists, but in its course many documents were brought to light and valuable materials were accumulated.[3]

As Gooch's comments suggest, the principal contribution of Renaissance humanism to historiography was probably in the domain of secular history. Unavoidably, the great Italian historians of the 15th and 16th centuries had to deal in their narratives also with ecclesiastical history, though not very often with the history of doctrine; but their primary interest did not lie in the Church or in theology. Jacob Burckhardt's judgment, that 'the Italians were the first of all European nations who displayed any remarkable power and inclination accurately to describe man as shown in history, according to his inward and outward characteristics,'[4] would, with some qualification, still be accepted by historians of historical writing. Flavius Blondus has been called 'far the greatest historical scholar that Italian Humanism produced.'[5] In several distinguished works devoted to the history of classical Rome, he made use not only of the literary sources that were being revived in his own time, but also of archeological investigations.[6] Even more impressive was his historical work on the Middle Ages, which many scholars adjudge a new departure in the interpretation of the relation between classical and medieval times.[7] The history of Florence written by Francesco Guicciardini in his early years was not published until 1859,[8] but his history of Italy has long been recognized as a basic work of historical analysis.[9] Although the reputation of Niccolò Machiavelli as a political thinker has sometimes overshadowed his historical interests, especially because his commentary on

Livy was more political than historical in its orientation,[10] his history of Florence, despite its flaws as a work of research, helped to lay the foundations of modern critical history.[11]

Lorenzo Valla, a younger contemporary of Blondus, is considerably more important for the beginnings of historical theology than any of these scholars.[12] The work that has gained him the greatest notoriety is his critical examination of the Donation of Constantine, which he wrote in 1439.[13] His refutation of its claim to have been written by the emperor Constantine was based in part upon linguistic anachronisms, which proved that the Latin of the document was to be dated later than the 4th century, and in part upon certain historical allusions in the text, which likewise betrayed an origin closer to the time of the emperor Charlemagne than to that of the emperor Constantine.[14] Although it was neither so erudite nor even so original as has sometimes been supposed,[15] Valla's treatise on the Donation did serve to call attention to the vulnerability of the Church's historical traditions. He applied similar methods of analysis to the purported correspondence of Christ with Abgar of Edessa.[16] Eusebius had quoted it, presumably on the basis of documents, as genuine evidence,[17] and with various interpolations it had established itself not only in the legends of the Church[18] but also in its iconographic tradition. The icon of Himself that Christ had reputedly sent to Abgar was preserved in Edessa until the 10th century, when it was taken to Constantinople.[19] There were so many false copies of the icon that a 'true icon [*vera icon*]' had to be identified; this may be the origin of the name of St. Veronica.[20] Valla showed in this case, too, that cherished elements of the Church's life were not a part of original Christianity, but a result of later accretion.

Another cherished element to which Valla's criticism turned was more important for the history of doctrine than either the Donation of Constantine or the letter of Christ to Abgar. From its origins at least as far back as the 2d century, the Apostles' Creed had evolved, both in its text and in its authority, into an official creed of the Western Church.[21] Rufinus repeats a story, on the basis of earlier tradition,[22] that just before departing for their several missionary assignments the Apostles 'assembled in one spot and, being filled with the Holy Spirit, drafted this short summary . . . of their future preaching, each contributing the clause he judged fitting.'[23] Suitably elaborated, this legend became the standard account of the apostolic composition of the symbol.[24] At the Council of Basel (actually during its sessions at Ferrara), the supposed apostolic authority of the Apostles' Creed was denied by the spokesmen for the Greeks.[25] Thus the doubts about its claims to antiquity had already been voiced earlier in the 15th century. But it was Valla's analysis of the Creed that precipitated what Monrad has called 'the first controversy over the origin of the Apostles' Creed.'[26] He showed that the accepted account of its composition had to be a legend, and that, far from having been put together all at once by the Apostles, the Creed had been the subject of historical evolution.[27] It is a mistake to exaggerate Valla's impact upon Christian thought.[28] As Roland Bainton has said, 'the Church was sufficiently entrenched that the loss of a few documents did not unsettle her foundations.'[29] Yet the implications of Valla's critique of the Apostles' Creed for the continuity of doctrine did seem to be dangerous, and Valla eventually recanted.[30] Nevertheless, so formidable a polemical weapon as the historical criticism of dogma could not long be banned from theological warfare.

When the warfare broke out 60 years after Valla's death, the weapon came into use on both sides. During the Leipzig debate of 1519 between Martin Luther and Johann Eck, questions about the history of doctrine were vigorously argued.[31] Eck spoke as a defender of the continuity of the one, unchangeable Catholic faith, from which the church at Jerusalem and the church in Bohemia had apostatized.[32] By his reference to Bohemia he was accusing Luther of adherence to Hussite doctrine, which had been condemned at the Council of Constance in 1415.[33] When pressed on this point, Luther admitted that among the teachings of Jan Hus anathematized by the council some were 'most Christian and evangelical.'[34] Thus he identified himself with the heretics and broke with the doctrinal authority of the Church. If Constance had been mistaken in its doctrine as formulated against the heresies of Hus, other church councils could err also. Such a conclusion jeopardized the fundamental tenet that orthodox doctrine, as unanimously defined by the ecumenical councils and by other constituted authorities in the Church, represented the one, holy, Catholic, and apostolic faith.[35] (This was, among other things, to assume that Constance had the full authority of an ecumenical council—an assumption that was, and still is, a matter of some debate.[36]) Eck and Luther shared the presupposition that there was only one true doctrine and that it was immutable. If it could be shown that Luther diverged from this true doctrine, as defined at Constance, he was a false teacher; if it could be shown that Constance itself had diverged from this true doctrine, it was not the notion of an immutable truth, but the notion of an unbroken transmission of it through the history of the Latin Church, that had to be revised.

This use of earlier heresy to attack one's theological opponents was nothing new. Ever since the ancient Church, as Runciman has noted, 'the average orthodox Christian, when faced with any sign of dualism, would cry out "Manichaean," and everyone would know that here was rank heresy,'[37] even though there might be no lineal connection with historic Manicheism. Luther's doctrine of the bondage of the will was denounced as Manichean by his Roman Catholic opponents;[38] and the teachings of Matthias Flacius Illyricus on original sin were accused by his fellow Lutherans of the same heresy.[39] The response of Luther and his followers to this accusation of Manicheism was to assert that the real analogy between the 16th century and ancient heresy lay in the identity of the teaching of men like Eck and his colleagues with the Pelagianism refuted by St. Augustine.[40] Yet another heresy whose recrudescence the critics of the Reformation professed to recognize in the theology of Luther was Arianism.[41] Luther did make a few negative comments about the language of orthodox trinitarianism,[42] notably one in his treatise of 1521 *Against Latomus*: 'Even if my soul hated this word, *homoousion*, and I refused to use it, still I would not be a heretic. For who compels me to use the word, providing I hold to the fact defined by the council on the basis of Scripture?'[43] Such criticism of the formulations of the dogma of the Trinity, to which it would be possible to find parallels in the Church Fathers,[44] prompted one opponent after another to accuse the Reformation of Arianism. The accusation may in part have been based on the conviction that if the authority of the papacy were to be surrendered, the dogmatic tradition would disappear with it.[45] For whatever reason, this situation also prompted Luther to give rather careful study not only to the text of the Nicene Creed as transmitted—which he, of course, attributed verbatim to the

Council—but to the historical circumstances under which it had originally been adopted.[46]

Luther's study of the history of Nicea found its most substantial scholarly result in his work of 1539 *On the Councils and the Church*.[47] The immediate provocation for this careful examination of the history of the first several ecumenical councils was the prospect that, after decades of postponement, the papacy might finally be willing to convoke a reform council to deal with the issues raised by Luther and his associates.[48] Now it became necessary to come to terms not only with the individual doctrines formulated at councils, such as the doctrine of the Church at Constance, but with the very doctrine of councils, viz, what constitutes a true council of the Church and what authority it may be said to possess. Luther recognized that to answer this question he had to look at the early councils historically as well as theologically. On the basis of the source material available to him, including an edition of the acts of the councils that had just been published in 1538,[49] he therefore set about to interpret the history of the first four ecumenical councils. Some of his historical judgments were extraordinarily acute, for example, his intuitive insight into the combination of factors at work in the condemnation of Nestorius at Ephesus in 431.[50] More noteworthy, however, is the evident conclusion that even in this, his most historical writing, Luther continued to share the common assumption about the immutability and continuity of the true doctrine. Except for some occasional comments challenging traditional historical ideas,[51] such as the one just mentioned, Luther's work did not produce a radically new approach to the phenomenon of theological change; it did produce a radically different evaluation of certain specific changes.

Perhaps the most palpable documentary proof of change in the history of dogma to emerge from the controversies of the age of the Reformation arose, not in the debates between Roman Catholicism and Protestantism, but in the exchanges between the various species of Protestantism. Johannes Oecolampadius, the Basel reformer, was profoundly concerned to maintain doctrinal continuity with the Church of the preceding centuries.[52] For example, in 1530, long after he had forsworn any allegiance to the Pope, he could still dedicate his commentary on the Book of Daniel with this formula: 'To the Catholic Church of Christ, the Mother most to be obeyed, Johannes Oecolampadius, her most devoted son in Christ.'[53] To document his opposition to Luther's doctrine of the Real Presence, he published a treatise on the meaning of the words of institution, '... in accordance with the most ancient authors.'[54] Here he sought to show that, properly interpreted, the patristic consensus was on the side of a 'spiritual' interpretation of the words 'This is my body.'[55] Luther wanted, if possible, to have the Church Fathers on his side, also in this debate.[56] But Melanchthon was much more eager to align the Reformation doctrine with what could, by careful philological study, be proved to be patristic teaching; therefore he was more exercised than Luther over this thesis of Oecolampadius, and he endeavored to reply to it.[57] In this eucharistic controversy the question of the proper relation to the history of the doctrine of the Eucharist was confronted in a new way. The answers that were found to the question were still not historical in the strict sense, but they do suggest the direction of future scholarship.

Nevertheless, the separation between Roman Catholicism and Protestantism was the stubborn new fact with which any interpretation of the history of doctrine now had to come to terms. There had now arisen within Western Christendom an articulate theological position whose central thesis was the cleavage between primitive Christianity and the Catholic tradition. Historical scholarship was being invoked to prove that such a cleavage did exist in the doctrine of the Church or the doctrine of the Eucharist or, above all, in the doctrine of justification. Neither side would admit that doctrinal change could be anything but pernicious innovation, and therefore both claimed to stand for the unchangeable teaching of the first several centuries —just how many centuries was itself part of the problem for all sides. Yet by introducing the historical argument, even in this highly limited form, the controversies of the Reformation assured to the history of doctrine a new place in theological discussion. Whenever a doctrine came up for debate on either side— even, for example, the controversy on the descent into hell provoked within Lutheran theology by Johannes Aepinus[58]—the history of the doctrine almost inevitably occupied an important place in the theological literature. The individual dissertations on various doctrines that were elicited by such controversies needed to be set into the framework of a more comprehensive view of the history of the Church, with special emphasis on the history of the Church's doctrines.[59]

That need was satisfied neither by Luther nor by his opponents nor by his colleagues, but by his epigones and their opponents. Of these epigones the most influential in the history of historical theology was Matthias Flacius Illyricus.[60] Flacius is best remembered for the controversy he precipitated over the relation between original sin and the essence of man,[61] and for his *Clavis scripturae sacrae*, which laid the foundations for Protestant hermeneutics.[62] Applying to historical study some of the same methodological thoroughness evident in the *Clavis*, as well as some of the polemical zeal evident in the controversy about original sin, he was the principal architect of the monumental *Centuries*, usually called the *Magdeburg Centuries* because of their association with that city.[63] The work appeared from 1559 to 1574, but was not completed; various efforts to finish the job in later years proved unsuccessful. The purpose of the *Centuries* was to demonstrate, century by century, that Roman Catholicism was not identical with the orthodox Christianity of the early Church, and that therefore the theological changes that had taken place in later times were a departure from the patristic consensus. In support of this theological brief, the *Centuries* assembled many documents, some of which have since been lost and are therefore preserved only here.[64]

Both the thoroughness and the bias of the *Centuries* can be seen from the set of rubrics under which the church history of each century was arranged.[65] There were 16 such rubrics in all, beginning with a general characterization of the century and of the state of the Church in its external and internal life and concluding with the state of non-Christian religions, especially Judaism, and the political history of the time. Within these 16 subheads by far the most important were those that dealt with the history of doctrine. The fourth chapter, which often bulked larger than several of the others put together, was explicitly devoted to this subject, but it was also predominant in other chapters, as in the fifth (heresies), the ninth (church councils), and the eleventh (heretics). The condition of doctrine in a particular century was the criterion by which its church polity, the lives of the saints and martyrs, its missionary expansion, and the relation of the Church to the State were all evaluated. As Baur has pointed out, 'the Centuriators differ from the historians of the Catholic Church only insofar as they must, from their Protestant point of view, give the history of dogma an even higher and greater significance for the general history of the Christian Church.'[66] It was to doctrine that the reader was to give his primary attention, for doctrine was 'as it were, the light and the very sun of sacred history.'[67] This referred, of course, to the right doctrine, which was the teaching of Sacred Scripture as it had now been restored in all its truth and purity by Luther's Reformation.

In its execution, this elevation of right doctrine to normative status gave a preponderant authority to the doctrine of justification by grace through faith alone and to the doctrine of the sole authority of Scripture—*sola fide* and *sola Scriptura*—which orthodox Lutheranism later interpreted as the 'material principle' and the 'formal principle.'[68] Applied not only to the formal theology but to the practice and life of the Church, the *sola fide* was the real touchstone by which the history of the Church and of its doctrine was to be evaluated. On this basis, for example, both the rise of the papacy and the growth of monasticism could be attributed to an 'obscuring of the doctrine of justification.' As Preger notes, moreover, the *sola Scriptura* serves to distinguish the view of historical theology at work in the *Centuries* from that which animated Eusebius.[69] His leitmotiv, as has been seen, was the stress on legitimate succession sounded in the very first words of the *Ecclesiastical History*; in the apt formulation of Gustave Bardy, 'The history itself takes the form of a succession, *diadochē*, and the place that this word occupies in the opening phrase of the work aptly indicates its importance.'[70] By contrast, the authors of the *Centuries* undertook 'the critique of the individual centuries on the basis of the knowledge of Scripture that they had achieved.'[71] Hence it is understandable that present-day estimates of the historical scholarship of the *Centuries* are so often colored by confessional judgments, with Protestant scholars such as Karl Heussi[72] seeing them as an anticipation of modern historiography and Roman Catholic scholars such as Pontien Polman[73] emphasizing the methodological shortcomings of the work.

Those shortcomings were the object of attack already in the 16th century. The *Annales ecclesiastici* of Caesar Baronius were intended as a response to the *Centuries*, although usually without referring to them by name.[74] Refuting the charge that various distinctive teachings and practices of Roman Catholicism were innovations without warrant in the early Church, Baronius sought to vindicate the identity between apostolic Christianity and Roman Catholicism. This led him, for example, to ascribe to the rule of celibacy a greater antiquity than most historians do.[75] He also sought to prove, in an anticipation of recent historical arguments, that it was an unwarranted historical assumption to maintain that early Christianity had retained the Jewish opposition to the use of graven images; the worship of icons could, he insisted, claim very early support.[76] The apostolic and orthodox character of Roman Catholic doctrine meant that the condemnation of Pope Honorius I at the Third Council of Constantinople in 681 must be false.[77] Baronius charged[78] that both the letter of Honorius to Sergius, patriarch of Constantinople, with its fateful reference to 'one will' in Christ,[79] and the anathema pronounced upon the Pope by the Council[80] were forgeries. At the same time, he corrected many of the egregious textual mistakes of the *Centuries* and supplied other documents that the Centuriators could not, or in some cases would not, have published themselves.[81]

Implicit both in the historical polemic of the *Centuries* and in the historical defense of the *Annales* is the assumption that Christian truth is unchanging, so that the presence of change would be evidence of false teaching. Each side used historical research to demonstrate its loyalty to that unchanging truth, but especially to prove that its opponents had changed from it and were therefore heretical. Because of the continuing prevalence of this assumption in the polemics of the Reformation period and of the age of Protestant Orthodoxy, it is a misreading of intellectual history to interpret the Reformation as the line of demarcation between medieval and modern views of history.[82] In this respect as in so many others, the distinction between medieval and modern is itself subject to serious question; but whatever validity it may have, the outlook of the Reformers is closer to the former than to the latter.[83] Nevertheless, the Reformation did help to make possible or even necessary a new attitude toward the phenomenon of doctrinal change. The religious pluralism that came out of the Reformation helped to expose the illusion of a monolithic and unchanging truth either in the past or in the present: the more one knew about the past, the more pluralistic it was seen to be. And therefore one had eventually to come to terms with the presence both of variety and of change within the history of Christian doctrine.

The Enlightenment

Not the Reformation, but the Enlightenment, was the intellectual movement under whose aegis this recognition of the fact of change came to be widely, if not universally, shared. No work of Enlightenment scholarship gave more eloquent expression to this recognition, or won wider circulation for it, than *The History of the Decline and Fall of the Roman Empire* by Edward Gibbon, 'the most learned of the philosophic historians.'[84] Its treatment of Christian history represents the conscious effort of an Enlightenment thinker to account for the internal and external development of the Church in a natural and rational way. As Gibbon himself phrased it, with his usual dry wit, 'The theologian may indulge the pleasing task of describing Religion as she descended from Heaven, arrayed in her native purity. A more melancholy duty is imposed on the historian. He must discover the inevitable mixture of error and corruption which she contracted in a long residence upon earth, among a weak and degenerate race of beings.'[85]

In the performance of this 'melancholy duty' Gibbon dismissed, as outside the purview of the historian, a causal explanation of the development of Christianity that would account for it on supernatural grounds. He contented himself instead with enumerating, 'with becoming submission . . . the secondary causes of the rapid growth of the Christian church.'[86] The five secondary causes were:

1. The inflexible, and, if we may use the expression, the intolerant zeal of the Christians, derived, it is true, from the Jewish religion, but purified from the narrow and unsocial spirit which, instead of inviting, had deterred the Gentiles from embracing the law of Moses.
2. The doctrine of a future life, improved by every additional circumstance which could give weight and efficacy to that important truth.

3. The miraculous powers ascribed to the primitive Church.
4. The pure and austere morals of the Christians.
5. The union and discipline of the Christian republic, which gradually formed an independent and increasing state in the heart of the Roman Empire.

A recurring theme in this discussion is an emphasis upon the changes that took place within Christianity after the apostolic age. Both the Christianity that conquered the Roman Empire and the Christianity that attacked Gibbon could thus be shown to be different from the primitive Church, whose authority they both acknowledged.

The contrast between primitive Christianity and later ages was especially obvious in the second of the causes cited by Gibbon for the expansion of Christianity. 'The ancient Christians,' he writes, 'were animated by a contempt for their present existence, and by a just confidence of immortality, of which the doubtful and imperfect faith of modern ages cannot give us any adequate notion.'[87] Significantly, he does not distinguish as sharply between the doctrine of the immortality of the soul and the doctrine of the resurrection of the body as he does between earlier and later Christian doctrines of immortality.[88] Perhaps even sharper is the contrast he draws between later theology and the eschatological context of the doctrine of immortality in primitive Christianity. In the early Church the doctrine of immortality 'was very powerfully strengthened by an opinion which, however it may deserve respect for its usefulness and antiquity, has not been found agreeable to experience. It was universally believed that the end of the world and the kingdom of Heaven were at hand.'[89] And although this supposition had to be labeled an 'error,' it had nevertheless had a salutary effect on the faith and life of Christians, who stood in expectation of the second coming of Christ. Useful, indeed indispensable, though this expectation was for the preservation of primitive Christian belief, it was no longer viable; for 'the revolution of seventeen centuries has instructed us not to press too closely the mysterious language of prophecy and revelation,' that is to say, not to believe any longer in a literal end. In the course of his disquisition upon the de-eschatologization of the Christian message Gibbon managed to identify other points of discontinuity that he claimed to discern, such as, for example, the canonization of the Apocalypse.[90]

Yet none of these points of discontinuity was as prominent in his mind as that associated with miracles. The dissertation on this subject in chapter 15 of the *Decline and Fall*[91] reveals not only the sarcasm of the rationalist but the bitterness of the disillusioned convert. For it had been in connection with a study of the problem of miracles that Gibbon, as a boy of 16, had become convinced that the continuity of Christian history with the primitive Church lay in Roman Catholicism, not in Protestantism. Anticipating some of the key arguments of Newman's *Essay on Development*, Gibbon had come to the conclusion that most of the distinctive doctrines of Roman Catholicism, which he had been taught to regard as later accretions to the deposit of apostolic teaching, were already present in the first centuries of the Church. To this conclusion he was led, first, by a study of Conyers Middleton's *A Free Inquiry into the miraculous powers which are supposed to have subsisted in the Christian church from the earliest age, through several successive centuries.*[92] This essay compelled him to face the question of change and continuity. To the reading of Middleton was added the study of Bossuet's *Exposition of the Catholic Doctrine* and of his *History of Protestant Variations*, both in English translation.[93] 'I read; I applauded; I believed. . . . [These works] achieved my conversion, and I surely fell by a noble hand.'[94] Middleton's purpose had not been to raise questions merely about the miracles of the early Church. As Owen Chadwick has said, 'He was not trying to discredit the supernatural: he was trying to discredit the authority of the primitive Church.'[95]

Although Gibbon forsook the communion of the Roman Catholic Church less than two years after his conversion, the impact made upon his youthful mind by Middleton's explosion of the miracle narratives continued to be visible long afterwards; more than 20 years later he still called the book 'a very free and ingenious inquiry; which, though it has met with the most favourable reception from the Public, appears to have excited a general scandal among the divines of our own as well as of the other Protestant churches of Europe.'[96] What impressed Gibbon about the claims of the early Church to possess miraculous powers was their virtually unbroken continuity. They extended 'from the first of the fathers to the last of the popes, a succession of bishops, of saints, of martyrs, of miracles . . . without interruption.'[97] Despite the continuity of these claims, however, no thoughtful person could credit an uninterrupted succession of supernatural feats; for 'every friend of revelation is persuaded of the reality, and every reasonable man is convinced of the cessation, of miraculous powers.'[98] There must have been a point in history at which the miracles stopped. Of the primitive miracles themselves Gibbon asks with ironic rhetoric, 'But how shall we excuse the supine inattention of the Pagan and philosophic world to those evidences which were presented by the hand of Omnipotence, not to their reason, but to their senses?'[99] Regardless of the matter of credibility, however, there was discontinuity also in the matter of credulity. Even those who in Gibbon's day claimed to stand in the succession of apostolic faith took a different attitude toward miracles from the one evident in the early centuries; 'their admission of supernatural truths is much less an active consent than a cold and passive acquiescence. . . . But, in the first ages of Christianity, the situation of mankind was extremely different.'[100]

Primitive Christianity and later Christianity were 'extremely different' from each other in other ways as well. There was a great difference, for example, in their attitude toward the world. On the basis of the *Pedagogue* of Clement of Alexandria[101] and of some of the works of Tertullian,[102] Gibbon recounted the strictures of the early Fathers upon personal adornment, self-indulgence, loose talk, and other kinds of worldly behavior.[103] Especially detailed is his description of their asceticism in matters of sex and marriage, 'the chaste severity of the fathers, in whatever related to the commerce of the two sexes.'[104] But on both counts, the study of subsequent Christian history led to the conclusion that there had been a break between earlier and later doctrine. 'When Christianity was introduced among the rich and the polite,' Gibbon coolly noted, 'the observation of these singular laws was left, as it would be at present, to the few who were ambitious of superior sanctity.' A particular instance of this adaptation to the form of the world was the withering away of the primitive communism described in the early chapters of the Book of Acts, a 'generous institution' that 'the progress of the Christian religion relaxed, and gradually abolished.'[105] At least by implication, Gibbon was saying that in this respect also no present-day Christian denomination could claim to be identical with the Christianity of the 1st century. In a footnote he cited the 'patient principles' of the peace churches, 'the Socinians, the modern Anabaptists, and the Quakers,' who did follow the pattern of the primitive Church and who thus served to reinforce the difference between the great body of modern Christians and their apostolic forebears.[106]

As we have noted, the question of change and discontinuity was not equally prominent in all five of Gibbon's 'secondary causes' for the success of Christianity, although it played at least some role in each. The fifth and last cause, 'the union and discipline of the Christian republic,' was in many ways the most visible sign of discontinuity between the first generation of Christian believers and their successors. Gibbon's statement of the contrast is typically sapient:

> But the human character, however it may be exalted or depressed by a temporary enthusiasm, will return, by degrees, to its proper and natural level, and will resume those passions that seem the most adapted to its present condition. The primitive Christians were dead to the business and pleasure of the world; but their love of action, which could never be entirely extinguished, soon revived, and found a new occupation in the government of the church.[107]

Within the grand design of the *Decline and Fall* this observation had a special place, for it substantiated Gibbon's charge that, by siphoning off the moral power of a large part of the Roman citizenry, Christianity helped to weaken the empire and thus hastened 'the triumph of barbarism and religion.'[108] But it also enabled him to ridicule the attempts by theologians of various traditions, 'the hostile disputants of Rome, of Paris, of Oxford and of Geneva to reduce the primitive and apostolic model to the respective standards of their own policy.' Objective scholarship, however, disclosed that 'the apostles declined the office of legislation' and that therefore 'the Christians of a future age' were equally justified in claiming apostolic authority for their various doctrines of church polity.[109]

Gibbon was not a church historian, much less a historian of doctrine. In his interpretation of these fields, as Peter Gay has put it, 'he exploited [theological scholarship] with his characteristic respect for learning mixed with his equally characteristic irony: he conducted his forays with almost courtly elegance, diverted from objectivity only by his feline malice and his unrelieved disdain for religion.'[110] Yet this emphasis upon Gibbon's pirating of the scholarship of Tillemont[111] and of the great Benedictine compilers,[112] valid though it is, may obscure the extent to which his analysis of the discontinuity in Christian history itself stood in continuity with large parts of the scholarship of his own time, not only the scholarship of other rationalists and philosophers but also and especially the scholarship of men working in theological disciplines, particularly in the various branches of church history. Both on the Continent and in Great Britain, the 18th century was the time for the scholarly study of church history to emancipate itself from its ecclesiastical sponsorship and to define itself as an academic discipline. The scholar with whose work this emancipation is usually associated is Johann Lorenz von Mosheim,[113] whom Gibbon found 'ingenious and candid,'[114] 'learned and candid,'[115] and again 'full, rational, correct, and moderate'[116] in his scholarship.

As Hirsch has said of Mosheim, 'He deliberately extricated church history from theology.'[117] This he did by declaring it to be the purpose of church historical scholarship to avoid fanaticism and dogmatic partisanship. For the achievement of this objective, church history had to be based upon a careful study of the sources, including an evaluation of their biases or their rhetorical exaggerations.[118] Drawing upon the writings of historical scholars of other lands, he sought to set himself free of both national and confessional limitations. In his treatment of questions that had become an issue between the major confessions, he claimed to be speaking historically rather than dogmatically; but his performance fell considerably short of these intentions. Much closer to his ideal of a nonpartisan account of church history, especially of the history of doctrine, is his way of handling heresy. There had not been, he charged, any history of heresy before him worthy of the name 'history.'[119] The writings of the orthodox manipulated history for the sake of polemics; and even though the effort of Gottfried Arnold to write a 'nonpartisan history of the Church and of heresy' had been slandered by its orthodox critics, it was true that 'no one was less fitted to write history than he.'[120] Examining the accounts of the Church Fathers about Gnostics and other heretics, Mosheim attempted to reconstruct the historical facts. He insisted: '[It is] of no matter to me whether the heretics seem lovely and fair or ugly and deformed. The only thing I care about is, if I can, to show them as they actually were.'[121] Mosheim's works enjoyed international acclaim. They were translated into French,[122] and in various English translations they had a wide readership not only in Great Britain but also in the United States.[123] Although Mosheim's accounts covered the history of the Church as a whole, it seems clear that his historical approach to doctrine, especially his unpolemical account of the heretics, meant the most for the progress of historical theology.

Reference has already been made to another historical account of the heretics that had become notable, or notorious, by the time Mosheim undertook his own works on the subject, that of Gottfried Arnold.[124] Here the Reformation theory of a fall of the Church[125] achieved the status of an organizing principle. When the second birth of conversion and regeneration was replaced as a requirement for being a Christian by simple external membership in the institutional Church, the continuity with apostolic Christianity was broken. According to Arnold, therefore, continuity was not to be found in the succession, as Eusebius had sought to prove, nor in pure doctrine, as the *Centuries* had maintained. Rather it was the threefold purpose of Christianity to purge worship of ritualism, to order social life through the proper use of temporal things, and to give the individual a peaceful heart.[126] In this understanding of the nature of Christianity and the history of the Church, doctrine could not be identified with dogma. 'Doctrine was the one true mystical theology, which was transmitted from generation to generation through the oral tradition; it unites man with God in humility, and it sanctifies his life in "practice." '[127] The dogmatic decrees of the councils had been dictated by a majority of bishops, with the aim of crushing diversity, rather than by the Holy Spirit. The creeds, including the symbolical books of the Lutheran Reformation, had used the pretext of pure doctrine to foist rationalistic formulas upon true believers.[128] Therefore 'a heretic is not one who errs in his understanding and deviates from the rational dogma, but one who has no experience of God and who lives worse than a heathen.'[129] It became customary for later historians of heresy and of doctrine to dismiss this brilliant but bizarre narrative,[130] but even Mosheim's comments represent a grudging acknowledgment of his debt to Gottfried Arnold.

The debt of Johann Salomo Semler[131] to Arnold is even more evident. Usually, Semler's scholarship is discussed as one of the early chapters in the history of the rise of the historical-critical study of the Bible,[132] but he also wrote extensively on church history and the history of doctrine.[133] It was Semler's insistence that 'the rise and continuation of a learned theology, a systematic arrangement [of doctrine] . . . must be evaluated in view of those times and their particular style.'[134] Therefore it was 'detrimental and unjust . . . to elevate and urge any teacher and any form of doctrine as the continuing and eternal model for the presentation and form of doctrine in dogmatic theology, because all the factors that must be considered here arise out of a particular time.'[135] The proper method for the interpretation not only of heresy (as Arnold and Mosheim had shown) but of all doctrine was the historical method. It could not impair true faith, nor imperil authentic continuity; for these lay in the heart, not in the intellect. As Erich Seeberg puts it, 'Above all, Semler regarded piety as the heart of church history, and his conviction about the reality and the central importance of religious experience leads him to a recognition of the relativity of the dogmas and of historical Christianity in general.'[136] With the widespread acceptance of this elevation of piety and feeling over dogma and theology, the way was prepared for the development of the history of doctrine as a theological discipline.

This development took place shortly after Semler's death. There has been some controversy about who most deserves the title 'father of the history of dogma.'[137] Without entering into the dispute over that title, we can identify Wilhelm Münscher[138] as the author of 'the first complete presentation of our discipline'[139] and therefore as its 'real founder.'[140] Münscher proceeded from the assumption that 'since their origin Christian doctrines have gone through innumerable changes, which have to do either with their content or with the way they are defined and proved or with the estimate of their importance or with their order and presentation.'[141] Dividing the history of dogma into three periods —1–600; 600–1517; since 1517—Münscher arranged the material within each period under doctrinal headings, such as 'the doctrine of the kingdom of Christ,' 'the doctrine of angels,' and the like.[142] For the second period, he divided the doctrines into those whose content had already been fixed by the first 6 centuries, such as the Trinity and the person of Christ, and those that became the subject of change during the Middle Ages, such as the Filioque and the Sacraments.[143] Preceding these summaries of each period doctrine by doctrine was a general characterization of the history of dogma during those centuries. Later editions of the work amplified it with bibliographical information and with apposite quotations from the sources.[144] The advantages and the shortcomings of this method, as practiced by Münscher and others, were to engage historical theologians throughout the 19th century.[145]

One of Münscher's concerns, even as the history of dogma was beginning to establish itself, was with the problem of source material, both with the selection of what was pertinent to the subject and with the availability of the material in reliable texts.[146] On the latter score, the generations preceding Münscher had served historical theology well; as David Knowles says, 'The 17th century, or more exactly the period from about 1630 to 1730, was a golden age of scholarship.'[147] Although this description refers to the great editions of European sources, it applies no less to the production of the standard texts for the history of doctrine.[148] During the 18th century Giovanni Mansi had assembled his collection of the acts and decrees of the Councils.[149] Much more thorough and careful was the publication of patristic texts by the Maurists, such as their monumental but controversial edition of St. Augustine.[150] By the time scholars were ready to undertake the study of the history of dogma, there were in existence compilations of the principal documents with which they had to work, although many of these had not been critically edited, but only reprinted from earlier, unsatisfactory collections. Preparation of critical editions of these sources and research into their meaning for the history of doctrine were to go hand in hand throughout the 19th century.

The 19th Century

For the history of historical theology, the 19th century would certainly have to qualify as the golden age. Not only the history of Christian doctrine but most other historical disciplines achieved their most impressive form during the century before the First World War. Beginning with Gustav Hugo, the historical study of the law became a dominant method in jurisprudence;[151] and in the works of Friedrich Karl von Savigny this school of legal thought not only opened up the meaning of the Roman law on such controverted questions as the meaning of possession but showed the possibilities and the limits of a contemporary adaptation of historical precedent.[152] At the hands of Georg Wilhelm Friedrich Hegel, the history of philosophy became a way of coming to terms with the fundamental issues of philosophical thought, such as its relation to religion;[153] and so, in Windelband's words, 'it was . . . through Hegel that the history of philosophy was first made an independent science.'[154] The histories of the various national literatures now were subjects to be investigated in their own right, and it was to the historians of the various peoples that one looked for a clarification and definition of their national identity.[155] This preoccupation with history, which was both scholarly and romantic—and rarely either of these without the other—created the conditions under which the history of Christian doctrine came of age. The words of Karl Barth are critical but wistful:

> In the history of Protestant theology the 19th century brought with it the none too worthy spectacle of a general flight, of those heads that were wisest, into the study of history. From the safe, distant regions of the history of religion, church history, the history of dogma, and intellectual history, one can theologize with a vengeance if one has the necessary equipment. . . . [But] what decides whether theology is possible as a science is not whether theologians read sources, observe historical facts as such, and uncover the nature of historical relationships, but whether they can think dogmatically.[156]

Be that as it may, what Barth regards as a liability is for our present purposes an asset.

In the 19th century, when study and research in Christian theology, Roman Catholic and Protestant, came to be dominated by the modern historical method, and especially by the historical investigation of the New Testament and of the development of dogma, no historical theologian was more eminent than Ferdinand Christian Baur.[157] His fame as a scholar is due largely to his application of Hegel's dialectics to the stuff of Christian theological history.[158] In 1835 he published a radical examination of the Pastoral Epistles, in which he employed Hegelian analysis to explain the development of early Christianity. That development was viewed as the outcome of a conflict between Jewish Christianity and Gentile Christianity. According to the Hegelian categories, Jewish Christianity was the thesis, to which Gentile Christianity then provided the antithesis. What emerged from the conflict to determine the history of early Christian doctrine was neither Jewish nor Gentile Christianity, thus neither the thesis nor the antithesis, but a synthesis, the Catholic Christianity whose workings Baur discerned in the Pastoral Epistles. He therefore assigned the Pastoral Epistles to the 2d century and denied their Pauline authorship, as Schleiermacher already had in 1807, although on other grounds.[159]

Despite this apparent captivity to Hegelian categories, Baur was a hard-working historian of genuine independence and creativity; and it is ironic that this craftsman of historical scholarship has acquired a reputation in the textbooks as the man who trimmed the facts of Christian history and theology to fit the Procrustean bed of Hegelian dialectics. In his later years, as his research carried him into the history of the Church since the New Testament, he manifested an ever greater independence of Hegelian philosophy. On the central doctrines of Christian theology he wrote historical-theological monographs: on the doctrine of reconciliation and atonement in 1838;[160] and on the dogmas of the Trinity and the Incarnation in 1841–43.[161] His lectures on the history of dogma were published posthumously by his son in 1865–67.[162] These works show that all three of the traditional fields of theological scholarship—the biblical, the systematic, and the church-historical—became for Baur functions of his research and writing as a historical theologian. Although he is sometimes dismissed as little more than a philosopher in the cloak of a historical theologian, Baur formulated many of the questions with which every historical theologian since his time has been compelled to come to terms.[163] He also recognized, with greater clarity than most historical theologians have, that the history of dogma must be understood both in relation to church history and in relation to dogmatics.

This implied, on the one hand, a delineation of the place of the history of dogma within church history. A recent monograph on Baur has summarized his view as follows: 'While Church history concerns itself with the external side of the life of the Church, history of dogma turns itself toward the internal side. . . . "It is therefore history of dogma which allows us to see into this inner aspect of the life of the Church and which acquaints us with the course of this spiritual movement, to which the outward manifestations are led back as to their ultimate foundation."'[164] On the other hand, the history of dogma had to be seen in its intimate connections with systematic theology. As only the latest chapter in a long series of attempts to interpret Christian doctrine, any dogmatics was by definition a part of the history of doctrine; and it had to be aware of its tentative character. But the systematic theologian was also obliged to 'extract the steady and enduring from the constantly changing and moving. This can be done only when the dogmatician understands the entire process of dogmatic development which lies behind him.'[165] To perform this function for both church history and systematic theology, the history of dogma had a twofold assignment. It sought to comprehend the historical development of the central dogmas of the Church in their unity,[166] but it also gave attention to the special place occupied by certain dogmas in certain periods of church history.[167] Ernst Troeltsch maintained that in this comprehensive understanding of historical theology as both a science and a part of intellectual history, Ferdinand Christian Baur met his peer only in Adolf von Harnack. 'I am persuaded,' Troeltsch wrote, 'that in a review of the strictly scholarly achievements of Protestant theology in the 19th century, the names of Baur and Harnack will be in the foreground. . . . Baur and Harnack: they represent the aristocracy of scholarship.'[168]

Throughout the period from Baur to Harnack, as in the preceding period, the history of dogma was, according to Baur's slightly defensive explanation,[169] an almost exclusively Protestant science—in fact, a German Protestant science. As Baur himself acknowledged elsewhere, this was due at least in part to the difference between two radically opposite conceptions of the history of Christianity.[170] Although the *Magdeburg Centuries* and Caesar Baronius shared the Eusebian understanding of the immutability of truth, the centrality of the Reformation in the Protestant interpretation of the history of the Church and of doctrine compelled Protestant historiography to move in the direction of acknowledging the reality of change as a historical force. Significantly, it was with the historical interpretation of ancient heresy that this shift in direction took place; and it was with an examination of the rise of Catholic Christianity that Baur set the pattern for the historical theology of the generations that followed him. These same issues, the beginnings of Catholicism and the origins of the opposition between heresy and orthodoxy, were exercising Roman Catholic historians and theologians in the 19th century, both in Baur's Germany (in fact, in his own university of Tübingen) and elsewhere. While history of dogma was not the usual title for their dissertations on these issues,[171] they helped to give historical theology the form it now has.

Baur's sometime colleague at Tübingen, Johann Adam Möhler,[172] saw a fundamental divergence between Protestantism and Roman Catholicism in their attitudes toward the history of doctrine. The very formulation of the question indicated the divergence, for Möhler spoke of tradition rather than of history of dogma. In his *Symbolics* of 1832[173]—the work that called forth Baur's vigorous reaction in 1834,[174] while they were both at Tübingen—he developed his view of tradition in relation to the history of doctrine. The word 'tradition' was to be understood in both a subjective and an objective sense:

> This collective understanding, this consciousness of the Church, is tradition in the subjective sense of the word. What, then, is tradition? The peculiar Christian sense that is present in the Church and that is transmitted through the Church's instruction. This is, however, not to be thought of apart from its content. . . . Tradition in the objective sense is the collective faith of the Church throughout all the centuries, which is present in outward historical testimonies; it is in this sense that tradition is usually called the norm, the criterion for the interpretation of Scripture, the rule of faith.[175]

The determination of the content of tradition was therefore a historical assignment, at least initially; eventually, other criteria must be introduced to separate the wheat from the chaff and thus to find, within the 'outward historical testimonies' of the Church Fathers, what is truly the 'collective understanding' and 'collective faith of the Church throughout all the centuries.'

An earlier work dealing with this question, Möhler's youthful and romantic *Unity in the Church* of 1825,[176] had been considerably less specific about the historical locus of the Church's tradition. The work had been written, its subtitle declared, 'in the spirit of the Church Fathers of the first three centuries.' Interpreting the Fathers as 'generations of ancestors in the Church,' he posited a mystical identification of present-day believers with those who had gone before.[177] One factor that moved him from the romanticism of 1825 to his more specific view of the patristic tradition was his own historical study. 'What was actually taught by Christ and the Apostles,' he said in his lectures on church history during the following years, 'can be transmitted only historically.'[178] In his last years he went even further toward identifying tradition with the external authority of the teaching Church.[179] Even this could not resolve all the ambiguities in his view of the history of doctrine; for the ambiguities were present not only in his view but in the history as well. Yet his scholarship in historical theology enabled him to 'take his position in relation to the problems of his own time by way of the history of dogma,' for the various movements of thought and teaching in the ancient Church became for him 'types of the intellectual currents of his own day.'[180] This is especially evident in his biography of St. Athanasius, published in 1827, where Arianism becomes the type of modern deism and Sabellianism the type of modern pantheism.[181]

This biography was not the only attempt to use the life and thought of St. Athanasius to meet the theological crisis of the first third of the 19th century. At about the same time, John Henry Newman,[182] an Anglican priest and scholar, was developing a deep interest in the same Church Father. In spite of his generous comment that 'several distinguished writers of the Continent, such as De Maistre and Möhler,'[183] were giving attention to the same concerns that agitated him, it seems clear that there is no genealogical connection between Newman's thought and Möhler's.[184] Nor, for that matter, does there appear to be even that much basis to posit any scholarly commerce between Newman and Baur.[185] One may, of course, surmise that certain common origins—it is both an identification of the *Zeitgeist* and an evasion of responsibility for identifying this more precisely when one uses the term 'romanticism'[186]—prompted a wide variety of thinkers from England through Continental Europe to Russia to develop organic metaphors for their language about the Church and its history. There was also a deepening awareness of the fact of secularization, as well as a growing recognition that individualism was spiritually and intellectually bankrupt. But more precise pedigrees of theological doctrine are extremely difficult to document. What we are obliged to note, in any event, is that during the first half of the 19th century men like Möhler and Newman—together with Alexei Khomyakov in Russia,[187] John Nevin and Philip Schaff in the United States,[188] and Nikolai F. S. Grundtvig in Denmark[189]—came to an understanding of the Church and its history that stressed the organic character of its development rather than the organizational continuity of its structure.

Newman never wrote a book under any such title as *The History of Dogma*. He did not read German,[190] and the Germans did not read him. But his scholarly work did strike many of the very points and problems with which, in its own ways, the German history of dogma was also concerned. The patristic essays eventually collected in *The Church of the Fathers*[191] are an illuminating introduction to the relation between historical scholarship and theological-ecclesiastical commitment in his thought. For here the lives and struggles of several Church Fathers are set forth with consummate skill and impressive erudition, all for the purpose of evoking a genuine identification from the reader. Perhaps because he himself was aware of how tenuous the hold of English culture on the Christian tradition had become,[192] Newman found it possible to portray the apologetic struggles of a minority Church in the most moving language. Even more, the Church Fathers moved from the past to the present, from the dead pages of history to a living confrontation with Englishmen of the 19th century. A more scholarly exposition of the relevance of the Fathers was spread before the critical reader in Newman's brilliant translation of the writings of St. Athanasius with learned commentary.[193] Although German historians of dogma in their isolation managed to ignore this work for decades, Newman's insights into the evolution of trinitarian creeds[194] and into the variety of patristic theology[195] would have enlightened even the most erudite among them. These works alone would qualify their author as a historical theologian who must be taken seriously.

Yet all of this scholarship has been overshadowed, with both good and evil results, by Newman's *An Essay on the Development of Christian Doctrine* of 1845.[196] The immense complexities of the problem of development of doctrine, both theological and historical, belong to another study;[197] but Newman's *Essay on Development* has generated research in the history of doctrine with a fecundity matched only by Harnack's *History of Dogma*. Not even Baur's brilliant insights into the patterns of dogmatic change can vie with Newman's theses as provocative attempts to make some sense of the plethora of historical detail. The seven tests by which authentic development may be distinguished from false accretion are anything but invulnerable, not only on dogmatic grounds but on historical ones as well. Dogma has not been as predictable or as obedient to the rule book as Newman's peremptory legislation would suggest. Nevertheless, the very vigor of the replies to the *Essay on Development* is testimony to its power.[198] Members of the charmed circle of German Lutheran historians of dogma relegated Newman to a footnote[199] or treated him as nothing more than the ancestor of a doomed Roman Catholic Modernism.[200] But the *Essay on Development* anticipated later generations of scholars by being the first to ask some of the questions about tradition, development, and continuity with which the history of doctrine must deal today. Curiously, then, any student of historical theology is obliged by the facts of historical development—even though both of them would be shocked by the conjunction—to link the names of John Henry Newman and Adolf von Harnack.

The Work of Adolf von Harnack

In Adolf von Harnack historical theology acquired its most erudite and eloquent spokesman.[201] Before he was 30 years old, Harnack had already begun to assume a stature in the field that he held for the remaining 50 years of his life. His inaugural dissertation[202] and his first treatise as a university lecturer[203] dealt with Gnosticism, seeking to replace both the dogmatic polemics of the Church Fathers and the antidogmatic polemics of men like Gottfried Arnold with sober textual study and sound historical analysis. The critical edition of the Apostolic Fathers on which he collaborated in 1875[204] was the first of hundreds of patristic texts that, in several series, he either edited himself or supervised. And his conjectures of 1878 about the chronology of the early bishops of Antioch and the date of the composition of the Ignatian epistles[205]—conjectures that he himself was to reconsider as a result of his ongoing research[206]—were so arresting that 2 years later an encyclopedia article on St. Ignatius by Gerhard Uhlhorn closed with the sentence: 'Further investigations, of which there will be no lack also in the future, will have to come to terms with the possibility that Harnack has opened up.'[207] The bibliography of his works, compiled by Max Christlieb for his 60th birthday and published in 1912, listed over 1,000 items;[208] Friedrich Smend's continuation of it, prepared for Harnack's 75th birthday and published in 1927, added 400 more;[209] and a posthumously published supplement included a list of the works dedicated to him.[210] He admitted, on the occasion of the presentation of Smend's bibliography, that he had 'long since lost the rudder in the flood that he himself had conjured up.'[211]

With very few exceptions[212] these books, monographs, articles, editions, and reviews dealt, directly or indirectly, with the history of Christian doctrine. Even those that were intent primarily on making a constructive theological point, such as the best-selling *What Is Christianity?*, professed to be setting forth the results of the author's historical investigation. Much of Harnack's work, of course, discussed church history rather than merely the history of doctrine. But when in *The Mission and Expansion of Christianity in the First Three Centuries*, first published in 1902,[213] he examined the geography of early Christian expansion, he related the entire history of the missions in that period to the message of the gospel and to the distinctiveness of Christian teaching. He was describing the guiding principles of his entire scholarship when, in the fourth edition of this book, he declared: 'I can boast of this work that it contains virtually no hypotheses, but [only] assembles facts. . . . I hope that this book will contribute to the strengthening of interest in the history of the Church, in opposition to dilettantism and romanticism, with their predilection for the "Christian" trivia of all sorts that history provides.'[214] Together with his trenchant essay on monasticism[215] (which went through seven or eight editions and was translated into six languages) and his several publications on church polity,[216] this provided much of the church-historical foundation for Harnack's concentration on historical theology.

The principal foundation, however, was laid not in the institutional history of the Church, for all his expertise in that field and contribution to it, but in the history of early Christian literature. Historical study meant above all textual study, and the 'facts' of which Harnack boasted were facts verified by the documentary evidence. We have already referred to Harnack's lifelong concentration on the preparation of critical editions of the principal literary sources of early Christianity. His annual reports to the Prussian Academy of Sciences on the progress of the work of the commission charged with editing the Greek Church Fathers spanned a third of a century, from 1893 to 1927.[217] Related to this enterprise was the series of texts and studies, many of which were Harnack's own work.[218] He synthesized both his own research and that of many other scholars in a work of more than 2,000 pages, a three-volume history of Christian literature before Eusebius,[219] by which he sought to substitute the history of literature for patrology as a more reliable and objective method of treating the documents. Beyond this vast output of literary history, Harnack's method in his works on the history of doctrine was that of a documentary historian. Perhaps the outstanding example is his *Marcion*,[220] on which he worked intermittently for most of his scholarly life. The work did not actually appear until 1921, although Harnack noted in the preface that he had first taken up the subject in his prize-winning essay of Dec. 12, 1870, on Marcion's doctrine according to Tertullian.[221] In the interim he had ransacked not only the five books of Tertullian, our principal source of knowledge about Marcion, but hundreds of other documents for any scrap of information or gossip relevant to the assignment.[222] The result was a storehouse of quotations so rich that even those interpreters of Gnosticism who disagree with Harnack's assessment of Marcion must still rely almost completely on his compilation of the source material.[223]

Although *Marcion* was in some ways Harnack's own favorite among his books[224] and *What Is Christianity?* was the one that earned him the greatest notoriety, most students of the history of doctrine would concur with the judgment of a distinguished historical theologian of the present, himself Harnack's student at Berlin, that 'among Harnack's books, the *History of Dogma* is the clearest expression of this basic conception of the historian's task. It shows concretely how and to what extent he tried to carry out his historical principles in his own field of study.'[225] The first volume of the *History of Dogma* appeared in 1886, the second in 1887, and the third in 1890.[226] The work underwent three revisions; the final edition, the fourth, was published in 1909 and 1910.[227] When volume 1 was finished, Harnack wrote to his former student Friedrich Loofs:

> I thank my God and Lord that, as a part of my vocation, I have had the opportunity in this book to say without pretense what I think about crucial questions, without anyone being able to cast in my teeth the charge that I have sought opportunity for expression. Some of the joy that Luther had when, after his testimony at Worms, he joyfully exclaimed, 'I am through, I am through!' seized me when my book lay before me completed. . . . It has been such a high joy that I have been privileged to say what I think, and not to appear to be other than I am, that in the strength of this joy all the tortures with which I have been wracked will vanish.[228]

It is interesting to note that Loofs, himself the author of a history of doctrine (which, even when in its fourth edition it reached 1,000 pages, he went on calling a 'syllabus'),[229] was also most penetrating in his criticism of Harnack's views about the scope of the history of dogma. Despite its title, Harnack's *History of Dogma* was, Loofs said, 'a monograph on the rise and development of the dogma of the fourth century, written with genius and placed into a large context.'[230] By restricting his definition of dogma essentially to the Trinity and the Incarnation, Harnack had excluded from consideration large bodies of Christian teaching that, in Loofs's judgment, belonged in any history of dogma. For dogma did not mean only these two officially formulated teachings. So narrow a definition also obliged Harnack to treat most of the history of doctrine after the 4th or 5th century as a long epilogue, whose final stage was the 'threefold outcome of dogma'[231] in modern Roman Catholicism, the conservative Reformation of Luther and Calvin, and the radical Reformation. In his search for a restrictive principle by which to hold the subject matter of historical theology within some manageable bounds,[232] Harnack identified dogma in the official sense as the phenomenon whose history he would study.[233] Neither the doctrinal confessions of Protestantism nor the theological systems of Catholicism belonged to this history except insofar as they continued to reflect the authority of the dogmas formulated in the 4th and 5th centuries.

In addition to this special definition of dogma, there was another factor at work in Harnack's concentration on the early Church: his conviction, as stated in 1888, that 'the center of gravity of church history as a scholarly field lies in the church history and history of dogma of the first six centuries.'[234] When he voiced this conviction, he insisted, he was not speaking *pro domo* as a patristic scholar, but identifying that area of church history in which every student of the field, regardless of his other interests and special subjects of concentration, had to be something of an authority. Writing at a time when other periods of church history, above all the Reformation, were becoming the chief preoccupation of a growing body of scholars,[235] Harnack warned that, without a strong grasp upon the data and documents of the epoch when Catholic Christianity arose, a church historian concentrating on the Middle Ages or the Reformation would have nothing better than 'a certain common sense' to apply to the crucial questions. This judgment applied to many areas of the life of the Church—for example, to polity or to the relation between Church and State—but it was especially important for dogma. Here was an authoritative force even in 19th-century Christianity that could not be understood in any other way than by sound patristic study. Loofs's description of Harnack's *History of Dogma* as essentially a monograph on the ancient Church was an apt one; but considering Harnack's presuppositions about the centrality of the history of the ancient Church in any study of church history, and especially in the study of historical theology, the description, intended as a criticism, was one that Harnack would have accepted as a compliment.

Harnack's claim that a thorough acquaintance with the church history and history of dogma of the first centuries equipped a scholar to deal competently with later periods was substantiated not only in the work of his student and then junior colleague Karl Holl, a patristic scholar who changed the direction of Luther research,[236] but also in his own interpretations of Luther and the Reformation.[237] His principal interest in the Reformation as a chapter in the history of dogma was in its ambiguous position as simultaneously the 'shattering of dogma'[238] and the proof of the 'tenacity of dogma.'[239] This ambiguity led

Harnack to exclaim: 'What an amazing concatenation of affairs! The same man who delivered the gospel of Jesus Christ from ecclesiasticism and moralism *reinforced its authority in the forms of ancient Catholic theology. In fact, after centuries of their quiescence, he was the first to give them meaning and importance for faith again.*'[240] At a time when Roman Catholic scholars were still condemning Luther as the revolutionary who had subverted the authority of Church and dogma[241] and when Protestant scholars were claiming him for their own programs of completing the Reformation, Harnack's historical insight enabled him to point out both the partial validity and the inadequacy of each interpretation. He, too, wanted to identify his constructive theological proposals as a legitimate continuation of Luther's reformatory work, but as a historian he had to make sense also of those aspects of Luther's thought—and of all the history of doctrine—that he did not find congenial.

The need to be able to interpret, critically but sympathetically, theological positions distant from his own[242] applied even to that aspect of the history of dogma with which Harnack's name is so often associated, the Hellenization of Christianity. As an issue in the identification of the relation between Christian doctrine and its cultural context, the question of Hellenization is one that no study of historical theology can avoid.[243] But it was more than this in Harnack's *History of Dogma*; it was a major theme, perhaps even *the* major theme. At the very outset of the work he described dogma as 'in its conception and in its development a work of the Greek spirit on the soil of the gospel.'[244] This has been vulgarized by some of its critics and by some of its advocates into the notion that, according to Harnack, the gospel had disappeared into dogma; but such a version does an injustice to the subtlety both of Harnack's mind and of the process of Hellenization. The process took place 'on the soil of the gospel': Harnack knew as well as any other historian that the teachings and deeds of Jesus Christ continued to be the center of Christian worship and preaching even after the trinitarian and christological dogmas had been enthroned.[245] Nor did he identify dogma with all the speculation that attached itself to dogma. What he did attack as the Hellenization of Christianity through dogma was ' . . . the fact that, from the beginning, Christian dogmatic thought was combined with Greek philosophy of religion and with the intellectualism characteristic of this philosophy. The result was not only that the Christian faith came to be dependent upon metaphysics but also—and this was an observation which Harnack thought was amazing and shocking—that "a fancied Christ was put in the place of the real one." '[246] The discovery of this fact was, Harnack believed, the result of his work as a historian of doctrine. Having discovered it, he felt obliged, as a historian and as a theologian, to transcend it.

This he undertook to do in the 16 public lectures he delivered during the winter semester of the academic year 1899–1900 at Berlin on 'What Is Christianity?'[247] The published version of the lectures went through 14 printings and 71,000 copies in German by 1927,[248] was translated into 14 languages,[249] and called forth replies from all over the world.[250] Here Harnack proposed to identify what lay within and beyond (or, perhaps more precisely, behind) the variations of the history he had studied. To this he felt impelled by the alienation of large segments of the youth from the evangelical faith of their fathers. Unconvinced by the older apologetics, they needed to be told the answer to the question 'What is Christianity?' Only a historian was in a position to handle this question: 'It is solely in its historical sense that we shall try to answer this question here; that is to say, we shall employ the methods of historical science and the experience of life which is earned by witnessing history. We thus exclude the view of the question taken by the apologist and the philosopher.'[251] Although it has become customary for writers on Harnack, both friendly and critical, to stress the theological presuppositions of the *History of Dogma* and to find these spelled out in *What Is Christianity?*, it would be no less justified—and far closer to Harnack's stated intent—if one were to see in the lectures of 1899–1900 a distillate of the historical knowledge that had already filled so many thousands of pages of his works by the turn of the century.[252]

For Harnack took seriously the apologetic function of the historian's vocation, and precisely for that reason he did not want to debase the vocation by manipulating the historical materials to suit a preconceived theological position. After quoting a recent comparison between Harnack's situation and the present,[253] G. Wayne Glick observed: 'Harnack faced in his time all of the vicissitudes [of theological change]. . . . His response was to continue with that historical research which alone, he thought, could redeem the time.'[254] Not only would historical research redeem the time; it would, or at least could, make the Christian faith intelligible to modern men, as Harnack tried to do in *What Is Christianity?* Yet the apologetic significance of historical research lay deeper. In a remarkable letter, written while he was still in his teens and a student in secondary school, Harnack had already charted this course: 'As you will have heard, I am going to study theology. I do not know whether you are also one of those who look down with contempt or at least with indifference at everything that goes by the name of religion and theology. In any case, one may look at Christianity in any way one pleases, yes, even grant that it is an error. Yet is it not a matter of the greatest interest to investigate the history of this "error"?'[255] Since Schleiermacher and Johann August Neander, the only theologian to be elected to the Prussian Academy of Sciences had been Christian Dillman, the Orientalist and Old Testament scholar.[256] In 1890 this honor was conferred upon Harnack,[257] not because he was a theologian, but because he was a historian; and for the next 40 years he found in such associations the fulfillment of his boyhood expectation, the recognition by his fellow scholars in other disciplines that the historical investigation of Christianity, one's personal commitments aside, was 'a matter of the greatest interest.'

A significant index of the hold that Harnack's account of the history of dogma has established upon theologians is the fact that, even amid a drastic repudiation of his theological position as stated in *What Is Christianity?*, much of the historical analysis developed in the *History of Dogma* has continued to stand as the standard interpretation of the development of the doctrines of the Trinity and the Incarnation. The dogmatic cleavage between Harnack and his former student Karl Barth was publicized in the pages of the German theological press,[258] but the continuity between them in the history of dogma has been far less widely noticed. For example, Harnack's insistence that the history of Christian liturgy is irrelevant to the development of Christian dogma[259] is very close to Barth's dismissal of liturgy as 'religion' within Christianity.[260] Similarly, the hostility of Harnack and other Ritschlians to the positive role of mysticism in the history of Christian doctrine[261] has found a strong echo in the

Barthian treatment of various mystics, both Roman Catholic and Protestant.[262] Positively, too, Harnack as a historian of dogma has helped to shape the dogmatics of those who have gone on to make the dogma of the Trinity fundamental to systematic theology. A striking illustration of the subtler affinities beneath the evident conflict was Barth's rather surprised acknowledgment, in the second edition of *The Epistle to the Romans* in 1921, of some apparent parallels with the theology of Marcion as interpreted by Harnack.[263]

In the realm of historical theology, meanwhile, the continuing influence of Harnack can be measured by the absence of any real alternative. The few historians of early dogma who have come out of the Barthian school, such as Felix Flückiger,[264] demonstrate their continuity with Harnack despite significant points of difference. Critics of the theology of Barth have long prophesied that if his position were to be taken as normative, the history of doctrine would once more become a part of dogmatics rather than of history.[265] More by default than by performance, this prophecy has been vindicated. In one of Harnack's major areas of scholarly work, the preparation of critical editions of the Church Fathers, those who have opposed his theology have not made many significant contributions, and other series have preempted much of the position of his editions.[266] Barth's affirmative statement of the dogma of the Trinity in the *Church Dogmatics* is, despite its surface divergence from Harnack's position, based largely upon Harnack's account of how the dogma emerged from the primitive biblical witness.[267] Both in its reprinted editions[268] and in the other manuals of the history of doctrine,[269] Harnack's *History of Dogma* is probably still the most influential account of the genesis and evolution of Christian doctrine. Although Harnack's version of one or another chapter in the history of doctrine, even his interpretation of the Apostles' Creed or of Marcion, has been superseded in the monographic literature, it is still to his overall account of historical theology that readers of all theological persuasions continue to turn.

More important than any of these considerations, as the remaining discussion will attempt to show, is the continuing validity of Harnack's commitment to the historical method as the means for analyzing Christian doctrine. During his half-century of work as a scholar and teacher, Harnack found many of his favorite hypotheses questioned by his students, and with very few exceptions he welcomed their independence as a tribute to this commitment. When their divergence from him was based on dogmatic judgments, however, his patience was quite limited. It did not matter a great deal whether their dogmatism was on his right (as was that of men like Erik Peterson[270]) or on his left (as was that of the protagonists in the controversy over the Apostles' Creed[271]). What did matter was whether historical research was assigned the primary responsibility or whether it was to be subordinated to other norms. Thus Harnack brought together in his own work much of the history of the development of historical theology. With the polemical histories of the period of the Reformation he shared a concern for the 'restoration of the pure gospel'; with the historians of the Enlightenment he shared a commitment to a 'nonpartisan' reading of the sources, including the sources on heresy; and with his predecessors in the 19th century he shared an interest in going beyond the bare facts of the history of doctrine to an understanding of the processes by which the doctrine had developed.

CHAPTER THREE

The Present Task of the History of Dogma

The development of historical theology, sketched briefly above, makes it clear that the nature and the purpose of the field have not always been understood in the same way. No student of the subject dare overlook the work of his predecessors, but he may not permit that work to prescribe the limits and procedures of his own research. This means that he must, at one and the same time, pay attention to the new situation of theological scholarship in his own time and examine the history of historical theology with a view toward reconceiving its assignment. In an effort to determine the present task of the history of dogma, this study first will consider the general state of theological scholarship and assess its significance. In the light of this assessment it will be possible to reopen the question of the proper scope and subject matter of the field, considering and criticizing various alternatives that have been produced in the course of its history and proposing a definition of Christian doctrine, and therefore of the history of Christian doctrine.

The New Situation of Theological Scholarship

As the careers of men like Baur and Harnack demonstrate, the history of dogma, which is charged with a specialized responsibility for the study of the past, isnevertheless involved very deeply in the questions and conflicts of its own time as well. It not only examines history; it fashions history and is fashioned by it. This is true above all because historical theology is an equal partner with its sister disciplines in the theological conversation, a partner without whose presence both that conversation and the individual disciplines would be impoverished.[1] But historical theology participates in its own present also because the problematics of the Church and of theology at a given point in history will and should affect the definition of the task to which the historical theologian addresses himself.

The situation of the Church and of theology in the final third of the 20th century needs to be analyzed for its pertinence to the present assignment and future prospects of historical theology. Of course, historical theology dare not take all of its cues from the contemporary state of the theological enterprise, merely supplying precedents from history for questions that are now in fashion; for one of its principal functions is to counter-balance momentary fashions with the weight of tradition. Nevertheless, such fashions do make available hitherto neglected resources for the historian, who can thus correct the oversimplifications imposed upon his discipline by the fashions of an earlier time. An analogy from secular historiography may illustrate this point.[2] The racial crisis of the 20th century in the United States has not only called into question many widely held prejudices in the present. It has also precipitated a searching reexamination of how those prejudices have affected the interpretation of the past.[3] African history and Afro-American history are being fundamentally recast. What is more, all the other history books—including the textbooks of church history[4]—must be revised in the light of this reexamination. Despite the obvious dangers of overcompensating and of trimming the past to suit the present, such a reconstruction of the conventional wisdom about history can bring about a correction and an enrichment of scholarship by paying attention to the new insights coming out of current social trends. Similarly, so long as historical theology does not abdicate its responsibility for the interpretation of the past, it, too, can be stimulated in its understanding of its task by current theological trends. To the evaluation of these trends, then, it brings a criterion different from the usual ones. It asks about any position or school: Does it provide its adherents—in Harnack's phrase—with an adequate 'antenna'[5] for picking up the signals of the past? Measured by this criterion, some otherwise impressive theological systems prove to be quite inadequate.

There has always been a close connection between historical theology and biblical exegesis, especially between New Testament study and the investigation of the origins of creed and dogma. For example, Baur's research into the importance of Marcion for the stabilization of the Church's New Testament canon[6] not only made the interpretation of Marcion a prime issue for historical theologians of his and succeeding generations; it also formulated the problem of Luke–Acts within the framework of the conflict between Jewish and Hellenistic Christianity, or between St. Peter and St. Paul, and thus prescribed the terms for the debate over the Third Gospel for generations.[7] Harnack, too, believed that the interpretation of the New Testament was too important a matter to be left only to exegetes, and he made substantial contributions to the New Testament field, including the study of Luke–Acts.[8] In a letter to Karl Holl, Harnack insisted that 'church historians whose special interest lies in early church history' should, as a matter of principle, undertake exegetical assignments from time to time, if only to dispel the superstitious notion that the New Testament is beyond the reach of historical study.[9] A demonstration of Harnack's thesis was provided by his student Hans Lietzmann, whose work in early Christian archeology and in liturgical history gave special illumination to his New Testament scholarship.[10]

This long-standing cooperation of historical theology with New Testament scholarship is, if anything, intensified by developments in the biblical field. In his search for an essential gospel behind ancient dogma, Harnack tried to isolate the authentic teachings of Jesus out of which the 'Greek spirit' created dogma 'on the soil of the gospel.' New Testament study no longer finds it either useful or possible to assume such a disjunction. Instead, it attempts to identify the particular situation of the primitive Christian community that will help to explain how a saying of Jesus or a miracle story became part of the proclamation.[11] Such a method does not, or at least it need not, imply the kind of radical scepticism about the life and message of Jesus that is sometimes inferred from it;[12] but it does imply an understanding of the communal setting within which, from the very beginning, that life and message were perceived. Nor are its implications confined to the study of the Gospels, even though it was developed principally through research into the history of the Synoptic tradition.[13] Applied to the Epistles, this method reads them as addressed not only *to* the Church but also *from* the Church. For example, the statements of St. Paul to the Corinthians that he had 'received from the Lord' the account of the institution of the Eucharist (1 Cor 11.23) and had also 'received' the Easter message (1 Cor 15.3) were almost uniformly interpreted by earlier exegetes as claims of direct inspiration from God;[14] today they are almost unanimously[15] seen as reflections of what was being taught, celebrated, and commemorated in the Christian community. The Apostle had indeed received these things 'from the Lord,' but from the Lord through the Church.

When the New Testament is interpreted on the basis of assumptions such as these, historical theology is presented with a whole new set of issues and opportunities, both formal and material. It is, for example, no longer possible to separate the process of creed-building from the development of the books of the New Testament. Valla's study of the Apostles' Creed exploded the artificial theory of its supposed composition by the 12 Apostles,[16] but in the aftermath of his work the composition of the creed was explained as a compilation from the New Testament of the fundamental doctrines of the gospel.[17] In many ways that explanation fell further short of history than had the legend of apostolic authorship; for there was a creed—or, to put it perhaps more accurately, there were creeds—before any of the books of the New Testament had been written.[18] No interpreter of the Bible can relegate the history of the creeds to an unimportant position in his work, for he must be alert to their presence even in passages that on their face do not seem especially creedal.[19] Conversely, no interpreter of the history of creeds can begin his study of the evolution of the Christian confession with the Apostolic Fathers, Tertullian and Hippolytus, as earlier scholars sometimes did;[20] to do so would be to neglect evidence that is intertwined with the data supplied by the Church Fathers. The creedal-liturgical phrases of the Didache,[21] which go back to the 1st century even if the Didache itself does not,[22] are certainly older than portions of the New Testament, some of which were probably written early in the 2d century.[23] Even on formal literary grounds, then, the New Testament is indispensable to the history of Christian doctrine.

On material grounds the connection is even more intimate. A simplistic evolutionism thought it possible to contrast the Jesus of the Gospels with the Christ of faith and to trace the growth of the doctrine of the person of Christ as succeeding generations of Christian apologists, in conflict first with Judaism and then with philosophy, gradually promoted Jesus to a divine status.[24] More careful study of the New Testament makes the theory of a unilinear movement from a low Christology to a high Christology untenable. Exegetes such as Lohmeyer have posited the existence of a 'Christ hymn' behind the words of St. Paul in Phil 2.5–11.[25] Even though the provenance of the 'hymn' is widely debated, its ascription to Christ Jesus both of 'equality with God' and, after the Resurrection, of a 'name' at which heaven, earth, and hell must bow would suggest that by the time this epistle was written, perhaps A.D. 54–55, Christians had already been speaking of their Lord in such 'titles of majesty'[26] for some time. It is likewise untenable simply to contrast the high Christology of the Fourth Gospel with the less exalted conceptions of the Synoptics; for in some of the earliest strata of the Gospel of Mark, Jesus appears as an exorcist and wonder-worker whose uniqueness is confessed by the demons even before it has been recognized by His own Disciples.[27] This does not necessarily imply that the development of doctrine within the New Testament must be incorporated into the history of doctrine. What it does imply is that the history of doctrine, even if for practical and substantive reasons it begins after the New Testament, must constantly relate its narrative to the New Testament. What the New Testament may originally have meant is less important to the history of doctrine than what it eventually came to mean.

One implication of New Testament study with extensive ramifications for historical theology is the theory of consistent eschatology, set forth by Johannes Weiss, Albert Schweitzer, and others.[28] The antithesis of the Jesus of history and the Christ of faith here becomes a contrast between His own apocalyptic understanding of His mission in relation to the coming kingdom of God and the developing view of Him as Messiah and Son of God. No aspect of 1st-century Christianity remains unaffected by this thesis, and every problem of Christian history during the following 2 or 3 centuries takes on a different significance if the thesis holds. The rise of monasticism, whose impact upon early church history Harnack tried to measure,[29] means something quite different from what he supposed if the absolute moral demands of the Sermon on the Mount, out of which the counsels of perfection evolved,[30] had originally been intended as an interim ethic for the messianic community as it awaited the imminent dawn of the kingdom.[31] Harnack's polemic against Roman Catholicism made it clear that the constitution of the early Church, which provided the organizational machinery for creating and enforcing dogma, must be seen in a different light if Jesus did not intend to found a Church;[32] but Harnack's own interpretation of early polity must itself be revised if the message of Jesus was consistently eschatological and if the Disciples were being constituted as the 'friends of the Messiah.'[33]

The bearing of the Weiss-Schweitzer hypothesis upon the task of historical theology is the subject of Martin Werner's provocative monograph, *The Formation of Christian Dogma*, first published in 1941.[34] It seems safe to say that Werner laid down one of the most serious challenges ever addressed to Harnack's idea of the history of dogma, and that the paralysis brought on by this challenge has helped to prevent most historical theologians since Harnack from undertaking the task anew. Werner reopened the case by moving the previous question.[35] It is, he maintained, illegitimate to inquire how dogma grew until one has asked first about the starting point.[36] This Werner professed to find in the delay of the parousia, which eventually rendered many sayings and stories of the Gospels meaningless because they had originally carried an apocalyptic meaning. The report of the miracles attending the death of Jesus was part of the depiction of the advent of Jesus as the end of the aeon.[37] But when that view had ceased to make sense to Christians because the promised second advent failed to materialize, such passages became proof texts for the trinitarian and christological dogmas.[38] Christian thought had to find ontological language to give an account of the relation of Jesus to God when the original language for describing that relation was vitiated by the disappointment of the eschatological hope.

The strictly exegetical issues underlying Werner's theses are of concern to us here only insofar as they impinge on the rise of dogma, but the reductionism evident in his handling of patristic texts would seem to have affected his biblical interpretations as well.[39] Tertullian is generally recognized as the source for much of the trinitarian thought and language of the West,[40] even though the present state of the evidence does not permit a definitive answer to the question of his originality. Tertullian is also a test case for Werner's concept of the de-eschatologization of Christian thought. His declaration that Christians 'pray for the delay of the end'[41] provides Werner with clinching proof that, although Christians went on, in creed and liturgy, reciting the formulas of their apocalyptic tradition, their hearts were no longer in this hope.[42] Upon detailed examination, however, the eschatology of Tertullian appears to be more complex.[43] Alongside such statements as that about the delay of the end there continue to appear vividly apocalyptic sighs and exhortations.[44] The relation of the two kinds of language to each other cannot be accounted for either on the basis of chronology or by reference to Tertullian's acceptance of Montanism.[45] There is, rather, reason to believe that both the 'already' and the 'not yet' were meaningful elements of his eschatology, so that the elimination of either one would lose in historical accuracy what it would achieve in logical consistency. Yet this very response to Werner's account of the first 3 centuries is a tribute to the centrality of the issues he has raised and to the boldness with which he has handled them. The history of doctrine after Werner cannot simply repeat Harnack's answers, nor even go on asking Harnack's questions.

One such question is Hellenization.[46] Werner deliberately formulated his concept of de-eschatologization as a modification of Harnack's definition of dogma as a product of the Greek spirit on the soil of the gospel,[47] but both biblical scholarship and historical research would seem to demand an even more drastic modification of it. To an extent that neither Harnack nor even Werner acknowledged, the doctrines of the early Church were first articulated in a Jewish setting. Word study in the Greek New Testament, for all its limitations as a method,[48] has disclosed that one technical term after another was borrowed and adapted by the early Christians from Jewish sources.[49] As the interpretation of Philo's doctrine of the Logos has clarified his relation to rabbinical theology,[50] so New Testament study has established the connection of the Logos idea not only with Philo and with the Memra of the synagogue fathers but with the Wisdom of the Old Testament and particularly with the hypostatized Wisdom of the eighth chapter of the Book of Proverbs, thus confirming the exegesis of such Church Fathers as Athanasius.[51] There continues to be much controversy about the Jewish provenance of other Christian terms, especially about the equation of Kyrios as a title for Christ with Yahweh.[52] But historical theology dare not treat the question of Hellenization without a deeper feeling for the Jewishness of the New Testament.

Nor dare it ignore the continuing role of Judaism in the history of the Church long after the New Testament. Harnack's examination of the historicity of St. Justin's *Dialogue with Trypho*[53] needs to be broadened to include what must have been a great variety of contacts between Jews and Christians at different centers in the Mediterranean world and even beyond. Although the literary and archeological evidence from these centers is still quite scanty, it has become clear that long after the fall of Jerusalem in A.D. 70 and even after the conversion of Constantine, vigorous Jewish communities were still a force for Christian churches to consider.[54] In 4th-century Alexandria, for example, the presence of such a Jewish community was a major factor in the theological work of St. Cyril, whose picture of Christ as Second Adam owed at least as much to his controversy with Judaism as it did to the controversy with Nestorianism, to which it is usually related.[55] Even at Hippo Regius, the preaching of St. Augustine confronted Jews in sufficient number to require attention.[56] And in Antioch of Syria at about the same time, the fulminations of St. John Chrysostom against the Jews[57] are an unintentional testimony to the continuing vitality of Judaism long after, according to St. Chrysostom and most other Christians, it had outlived its role in the divine economy. From other sources, too, we know that Judaism in Antioch and its environs had by no means disappeared from sight,[58] and that therefore Syrian Christians—even when, as in the case of St. Chrysostom, they spoke only Greek—never became so 'Hellenized' that they could overlook the presence of the synagogue.

Syrian Christianity provides another refutation of any simple notion of Hellenization.[59] Beginning some time before the days of the Greek-speaking Chrysostom, a succession of Syriac-speaking theologians, poets, and masters of the spiritual life at least in retrospect, how a loyalty to the person of Jesus Christ could lead someone into such devious and labyrinthine ways. Greater effort still is required for the attempt to appreciate that this loyalty may be present not only where there is a wrong answer to the question, but where there is a blindness even to the question itself. The infusion of this appreciation into the ecumenical discussion is principally, though not exclusively, the vocation of historical theology. The question of the relation between divine grace and human responsibility, once it had been asked in the controversy between Augustine and his Pelagian opponents, proved to be so ineluctable that for more than a millennium it was to draw the lines of the theological map in the West. Reformation debates both before and after Luther's *The Bondage of the Will* of 1525[78] operated with 'Pelagianism' as a doctrinal position whose views were thought to be understood by both sides: Victorinus Strigel[79] or Jacobus Arminius[80] could be denounced as a Pelagian, without any further examination of what this epithet implied. Yet historical investigation has not only compelled examination of whether Pelagius was truly guilty of the heresies attributed to him;[81] it has also gone behind the Pelagian debate, with all its possible alternatives, to come to terms with 'a doctrine which cannot properly be called either Augustinian or Pelagian.'[82] Only historical theology can ensure an ecumenicity in time as well as an ecumenicity in space,[83] so that the present boundaries of theological debate do not determine the range of its issues and resources.

Part of the present task of any theology is to ensure that the boundaries of theological debate be even broader than the boundaries of the entire institutional Church. Historical theology can make its contribution above all by pointing out that this has always been the case, and that even those dogmatic positions most cherished by churchly theologians could not have achieved their present clarity and force without the benefit of secular and even pagan thought.[84] In the great crisis of trinitarian orthodoxy, which came after the Council of Nicea rather than before it, the formulas of St. Athanasius, for all their soteriological and religious validity, proved inadequate to the challenge.[85] To safeguard the oneness of the divine essence without relapsing into the Sabellian heresy, some device had to be found that would simultaneously affirm the distinctness of each of the Three and preserve the reality of the One. One such device that helped to carry the day for Nicene orthodoxy was the suggestion, put forth by the Cappadocian Fathers, that Father, Son, and Holy Spirit were the three members of a class, and that not only the members but also the class as such possessed reality.[86] Thus a Platonizing version of the relation between the three persons and the divine essence became an explanation of the dogma of the Trinity. It was never the only explanation, even in the thought of St. Basil, St. Gregory of Nyssa, and St. Gregory of Nazianzus.[87] Nevertheless, the presence of this theory within the corpus of trinitarian theology stands as a refutation of any overly fastidious rejection of the role of philosophy in the articulation even of the mysteries of the faith. From the history of theology it is also evident that the champions of this antiphilosophical theologism have themselves been unable to avoid involvement in the problems of philosophy. Tertullian is usually remembered for having asked the rhetorical question 'What has Athens to do with Jerusalem?'[88] But historical research has made clear that, in his case at least, the vocabulary of Athens (in the form of such pagan thinkers as Soranus of Ephesus) had contributed much to the language of Zion.[89]

The contribution has, however, moved in both directions, and historical theology reminds the heirs and adherents of secular thought that they owe much to the language of Zion. As a result of the dichotomy between the study of theology and the study of arts and sciences, brought on by the isolation of the seminary from the university, humanistic scholarship is often unable to probe the origin and development of fundamental concepts in the history of ideas. The literature of the Bible,[90] the forms of the liturgy,[91] and the vocabulary of dogma[92] have been a part of the equipment of the literate man of the West for so long that their atrophy threatens to make history unintelligible to the historian. Without access to the history of the development of the notion of covenant from the Old Testament to the federal theology of 17th- and 18th-century Calvinism, the student of political thought may misread the evolution of democratic theory.[93] A grasp of Christian doctrine is indispensable to an understanding of the intellectual and institutional history out of which the contemporary world has come. The scholarly investigation of the history of Christian doctrine, in addition to having become a proper branch of theology, is also a legitimate area of scientific concern because of its involvement with the intellectual history of the West.

The secular assignment of historical theology is not confined to such investigations of the mutual influences between Christian doctrine and philosophy or other nontheological disciplines. As the subject that was, for more than 1,000 years, the principal interest for some of the best minds of Europe and Asia Minor, Christian doctrine deserves scholarly attention in its own name. To understand a culture, it is essential to identify those presuppositions in its thought and language that are so obvious to all that they are only rarely raised to the level of formal statement. As Whitehead once observed:

> When you are criticising the philosophy of an epoch, do not chiefly direct your attention to those intellectual positions which its exponents feel it necessary explicitly to defend. There will be some fundamental assumptions which adherents of all the variant systems within the epoch unconsciously presuppose. Such assumptions appear so obvious that people do not know what they are assuming because no other way of putting things has ever occurred to them. With these assumptions a certain limited number of types of philosophic systems are possible, and this group of systems constitutes the philosophy of the epoch.[94]

This observation would apply even more to theology than to philosophy, for many of the assumptions of theology involve the life and worship of the Church. The warning is especially pertinent when such assumptions are basically alien to the observer and to his culture. To a degree that is alarming for their historical expertise (whatever it may or may not mean for their existential situation), historians have lost the ability to resonate to the religious convictions of previous ages, which they therefore feel obliged to explain away in terms of political, economic, or psychological factors. Only if historical theology is prepared to deal with these factors in relation to the beliefs and doctrines that have animated Christians may it claim a right to be heard in the councils of the secular historians. But it has the right, in turn, to require that these historians attend to the history of Christian faith and doctrine as part of the record. Exploitation of the history of doctrine for apologetic and evangelistic purposes, even if it were by some chance to be effective, is an injustice to the nature of the sources and to their cultural setting; they deserve to be read historically whether or not they are evaluated theologically.

It remains true, nevertheless, that by their very content these sources raise questions that cannot be answered through objective historical inquiry. Or, to put it more directly, authentic historical inquiry into such sources demands that the historian include their truth-claims in his study. Schooled in the law rather than in the theology that had occupied his grandfather's attention,[95] Oliver Wendell Holmes, Jr., once expressed this demand in a colorful way. After commenting upon Aristotle's *Metaphysics* as 'a compound of profound verities and the discussion of sophisms no longer worth understanding' and upon Hegel's *Logic* as 'the strikingest book in the world for the mixture of prophetic insight and charlatan word juggling,' he exclaimed: 'Oh how it bores me to read books that long since have ceased to be revelations and that are now important only in the history of thought. Yet I should have been unwilling to die leaving their rotten bones ungnawed.'[96] We have already pointed to the dangers of a cryptopolemical method in the history of doctrine, to which we shall return in a later chapter. Those dangers do not justify the opposite error, that of trivializing the seriousness of the documents by ignoring their claim to be speaking about an ultimate and universal truth that affects every man. Particularly when this claim is no longer being addressed to thoughtful men in the name of the dominant ideology of their culture, the history of Christian doctrine, rather than the preaching of Christian doctrine, may be their first and only exposure to the message of the gospel in any form. No theory of historiography dare be so antiseptic in its definition of scholarly objectivity that it rules out the possibility of an existential reaction to the message announced in the sources. Conversely, the discovery of the historical conditionedness even of the most cherished of those sources has sometimes been the occasion, if not also the cause, for a believer to lose his trust in their claims of truth.[97] As already noted, the documentation of this discovery was the leitmotiv for much of the development of historical theology during the 18th and 19th centuries.

While it was carrying out this negative role with devastating effectiveness, however, historical study was also providing some men with a bridge to the Christian tradition. Mosheim, for instance, did not intend his publications for clergy or prospective clergy only; he addressed them to interested laymen also—to those 'whom it will help, even without a teacher, to learn the history of matters Christian.'[98] Although this meant readers who were church members, it included those who had lost most forms of connection with the Church and its doctrines. Elsewhere, too, 'the history of matters Christian' was called upon to serve this purpose. Thus when Ezra Stiles was appointed president of Yale in 1778, 'it was arranged that he should be professor of ecclesiastical history as well as president. . . . At a time of religious decline, with the college under attack for clerical domination, Stiles may have seen ecclesiastical history, in part, as a way of resuscitating interest in religion.'[99]

Even the radical historical scholarship of Harnack served as such a bridge to the tradition. The negative effects of his works were often deplored by his critics, who blamed his *History of Dogma*, but even more his popular *What Is Christianity?*, for widespread apostasy among German Protestants.[100] The actual situation was considerably more complex, as even the brief canvass of his students in his daughter's biography shows.[101] The testimony of Otto Dibelius, who was to become the Lutheran bishop of Berlin-Brandenburg, is positive evidence about Harnack's capacity to make the Christian tradition a living thing for his students.[102] In the same vein was the farewell of his students when his seminar in church history adjourned after 54 years of uninterrupted work.[103] It was spoken by Dietrich Bonhoeffer, who also delivered a eulogy in the name of the students at Harnack's memorial on June 15, 1930.[104] In that same year one of Harnack's students, Erik Peterson,[105] professor of New Testament and ancient church history at Bonn, converted to Roman Catholicism. Peterson's correspondence with his former teacher reveals what a shock it was to Harnack whenever one of his students took this step.[106] For his part, Peterson found in this action a logical outcome of what he had learned from Harnack, for 'this same Harnack who declares that a return to Catholicism is not possible for us because of the historical knowledge which we possess, has opened a way for a return to the Catholic tradition as no other person has done.'[107] As we have seen, Harnack did not want, even in *What Is Christianity?*, to present an apologetic case for Christianity, but only to describe it as it is in essence. Yet he hoped that when he did so, his hearers and readers would respond to his conviction that 'it is religion, the love of God and neighbour, which gives life a meaning; knowledge cannot do it.' And he spoke 'as one who for thirty years has taken an interest in these things,' that is, in historical knowledge.[108]

One part of the present task of the history of Christian doctrine, therefore, is to describe its material in a way that enables the secular mind to appreciate how it is that otherwise intelligent and critical thinkers of another age could ever have entertained such beliefs as the doctrines of the Trinity and the Incarnation. Within the Christian community, it can introduce those who are already believers to dimensions of the tradition that their own denomination has overlooked. The interrelation of historical research and theological conviction in the thought of Newman is too complex to justify the theory of a unilateral causal connection in either direction,[109] but one may take him at his word that his reading of the Church Fathers compelled him to ask questions about the adequacy of the Anglican *via media*,[110] just as these questions in turn drove him to deeper patristic study.

But this survey of the situation of theological scholarship as it bears upon the task of historical theology would be incomplete without a basic reconsideration of that task. Not only the traditional presuppositions and conclusions but the very definition of the field must be examined and revised. The present task of the history of dogma compels a broader and deeper definition of its scope and subject matter, as well as a more comprehensive definition of the very meaning of Christian doctrine.

Scope and Subject Matter

An influential little volume by Gustav Krüger, published in 1895, asked the question, 'What is the history of dogma, and why does one study it?'[111] In addition to the methodological issues, which had been raised with such acuteness by Albrecht Ritschl in 1871,[112] Krüger's examination served to precipitate a discussion that is still going on over the scope and subject matter of historical theology. Among the most important statements in this discussion were the profound and erudite articles on the history of dogma that Friedrich Loofs wrote for two theological encyclopedias.[113] Each successive author of a manual in the field has been obliged to shatter a lance in the conflict.[114] It has sometimes been difficult for the historical theologian to explain how his theory diverged from that of his predecessors on this question, and frequently even more difficult to prove that his own practice did not diverge from his theory.

According to its original conception in the 18th century, the history of dogma defined its subject matter to include at least the chief doctrines of the Christian faith as these were interpreted by the Christian confession to which it was addressed, which usually meant a mildly rationalistic species of Lutheranism. Rationalistic or not, the theological matrix for dogmatic history was dogmatic theology, which meant a systematic presentation of Christian doctrine under the rubric of *loci communes* or *loci theologici*.[115] By arranging the material theologically rather than only chronologically, such a procedure made the results of the investigation of the history of doctrine readily applicable to the exposition of each doctrine; but in the process it stood in danger of losing sight both of the sequential nature of doctrinal development and of the connection between one doctrine and another in a particular period or thinker.[116] In its delimitation of the scope of historical theology, moreover, it could hardly have avoided the tendency to measure the importance of a doctrine in Christian history on the basis of its importance in Lutheran theology. The doctrine of justification by faith was central to the theological discussions of the period of the Reformation, as well as to those of the Protestant scholasticism that followed it, and its history before the 16th century was an important component of those discussions.[117] But the effort to elicit from the early centuries of doctrinal history[118] a detailed answer to questions that were not raised in their present form until considerably later is bad theology—and worse history.[119] Moreover, the steady decline of Marian doctrine in Protestant theology after the Reformation[120] meant that, by the time historical theology came along, the primary treatment of Mariology was polemical rather than positive, and historical theology reflected this reorientation by the place it assigned, for example, to the designation of the Blessed Virgin as Theotokos at the Council of Ephesus in 431.[121]

Clearly there had to be some other arrangement of material for the sake of historical adequacy. Abandonment of the *loci* in

The Present Task of the History of Dogma

systematic theology[122] made substitution of some other concept that much easier also in historical theology. Yet if the proximity of a doctrine to the center of the Christian message, however this might be conceived, was not to decide its place in the historical presentation, perhaps the history of doctrine itself could suggest another set of criteria. These criteria came in part from the practice of employing the dates of ecumenical councils, together with the dates of prominent pontificates, as markers for periods of the historical narrative.[123] Dogma was the doctrine acknowledged at these councils, and the history of dogma was therefore the account of the conflicts in doctrine that led up to them. For a Lutheran historian of doctrine, of course, the so-called ecumenical councils, with or without Trent, could not be the sole landmarks. But there was an equivalent in the history of the Lutheran Reformation. As the conflict between Alexandrian and Antiochene theology had led up to the Councils of Ephesus and Chalcedon, so the controversies between Luther and his opponents, both Roman Catholic and Protestant, formed the backdrop to the Augsburg Confession of 1530, and the internal debates among his followers issued in the Formula of Concord of 1577 and finally in the Book of Concord of 1580.[124] Calvinist Protestantism also had its counterparts to the ecumenical councils in the various confessional statements adopted by national Reformed churches, such as the Belgic Confession of 1561,[125] but above all in the doctrinal decrees of the Synod of Dort of 1619.[126] The chronological proximity of the Council of Trent (1545–63), the Book of Concord (1580), and the Synod of Dort (1619) made that half-century or so an ideal *terminus ad quem* for the history of dogma.

To these historical conclusions there were added theological considerations as well. Gottfried Thomasius may not have been the first, but he was probably the ablest, exponent of a view of doctrinal history that saw in the theology of the Lutheran Reformation, as this was definitively formulated in the Book of Concord, the logical outcome of the preceding centuries. Here previous antitheses were resolved, overemphases surmounted, neglects rectified.[127] Roman Catholicism had veered off in one direction at Trent, while the several types of non-Lutheran Protestantism had gone to various degrees of the opposite extreme. The christological position to which Thomasius himself came as a systematician is a reflection of his scholarly work in historical theology,[128] and there are more than a few traces of this position in his account of the way various doctrines developed, especially the christological. But measured by the criterion enunciated earlier,[129] the theology of Thomasius had fitted him well for his historical work, for it enabled him to treat with genuine sympathy an impressive range of viewpoints.[130] It had also predisposed him to a particular definition of the scope of the history of dogma, one that was to set the rules for the discipline, at least officially, even for historical theologians who no longer shared the confessionalism of Thomasius and the Erlangen school.

The widely influential manual of the history of dogma by Reinhold Seeberg[131] reflected the continuing hold of Thomasius' definition of scope and subject matter upon later historians. In Seeberg's case, this is understandable, for his maiden effort at a history of dogma was the revised edition of Thomasius that he and Nathanael Bonwetsch published in 1886-89.[132] Each successive edition of Seeberg's own history of dogma provided further evidence of a restiveness with the arbitrary limitations imposed by a rigid understanding both of dogma and of its history.[133] Eventually Seeberg even hazarded this prophecy about the study of the history of dogma:

> The sources of the history of dogma are: the decisions, decrees, bulls, and confessions; the minutes of the deliberations out of which those emerged; the writings of the theologians who had a part in their rise, whether positive or negative, direct or indirect; but also the evidences of the belief of the Christian community in sermons, hymns, liturgies, morals, customs, etc., as well as the literature of canon law. These latter come into consideration because they teach us to recognize the actual understanding and the significance of the dogmas, sometimes also their ultimate motivation. The history of dogma in the future will perhaps emphasize this democratic element even more than is being done in the present work.[134]

No less pertinent to the problem of scope and subject matter is the disparity between his formal delineation of the task in his first volume and the attention devoted to the theology of Luther in the fourth volume.[135] Assigning less than 200 pages to St. Augustine and almost 500 pages to Martin Luther[136] would be difficult to justify on the grounds either of Luther's treatment of the received dogmas of the Church (which, especially in Seeberg's account, is fairly bland) or of his bearing upon the subsequent formulations of dogma in the sense defined by Seeberg's prolegomena (which, even in Seeberg's accounts of the Council of Trent and of the Book of Concord, cannot be called so constitutive as to justify such prominence). Even in the succession of Thomasius and the Erlangen school, therefore, it proved impossible to uphold with any consistency their concept of the scope of the history of dogma.

Whether or not he ought to be called a scion of the Erlangen school,[137] Harnack did put forth a somewhat idiosyncratic version of this concept. He was stricter than either Thomasius or Seeberg in confining his presentation of theological trends in the 2d and 3d centuries to those that belonged to the presuppositions of the trinitarian and christological dogmas, such as the theories of salvation that helped to shape the doctrine of the Incarnation.[138] Like Seeberg, Harnack found the theology of Luther interesting in its own right;[139] but instead of incorporating in his history a full-length systematic monograph on the subject, he concentrated his attention on Luther's relation to the received norms of church dogma and on the unresolved tension in Luther's thought between what was old in the dogma and what was new in the Reformation.[140] Nevertheless, his treatment of Eastern Christianity,[141] specifically of the refinements of the dogma of the person of Christ after the Council of Chalcedon,[142] does not square with the stated intent to organize the historical account on the basis of the teachings that the Church eventually accepted as binding upon all its members. There is also some merit to the criticism that Harnack permitted his concentration on this intent to be diverted by his lifelong interest in Marcion.[143] Subsequent research has not only challenged Harnack's attempt to dissociate Marcion from Gnosticism[144] and to make him a 'pre-reformer'; it has also questioned the importance assigned to him and his movement in the creation of the fixed norms of church doctrine, especially the New Testament canon.[145] Even more fundamentally, Harnack's concentration on the first 3 or 4 centuries and his arrangement of material merit the criticism quoted earlier from Loofs,[146] that his *History of Dogma* is, in effect, a monograph on the early Church and a plea for radical reconsideration of both the idea and the content of dogma.

This criticism should, if anything, be sharpened even further. Harnack's conception of dogma was in some ways an uncritical acceptance of the very system against which he was protesting. He could not follow Thomasius in determining the scope of his history on the basis of Lutheran confessional orthodoxy,[147] but he may be accused of having substituted an essentially juridical understanding of dogma for the theological one. Canon law turns out to be a more prominent force in Harnack's understanding of dogma than it is in that of many Roman Catholic historians and theologians.[148] At the same time, Harnack was quite cavalier in brushing off the liturgical component in dogma. An appendix to the third edition of the first volume of the *History of Dogma* put the matter quite baldly:

> It may seem surprising that I have made so little reference to liturgy in my description of the origin of dogma. For according to the most modern ideas about the history of religion and the origin of theology,[149] the development of both may be traced in the ritual. Without any desire to criticize these notions, I think I am justified in asserting that this is another instance of the exceptional nature of Christianity. For quite a time it possessed no ritual at all. . . . The history of dogma during the first three centuries is not reflected in the liturgy.[150]

He later qualified this by inserting into the fourth and final edition 'the full acknowledgment of the thought that the common worship of Christ was the genuine expression of the community's understanding of itself and the foundation of its existence, including its consciousness of faith.'[151] But the fundamental thesis still stood. The dogmatic expression of liturgy was alien enough, but he was even more hostile to the liturgical expression of dogma, particularly in the history of Greek theology after the 4th century.[152] What he had called 'second-class Christianity' in his description of folk piety[153] applied also to the Greek idea of 'deification.'[154] The critics of the *History of Dogma* among Eastern Orthodox and Roman Catholic scholars showed that Harnack's definition of the scope and subject matter of his discipline needed careful reconsideration and drastic revision.[155]

The revision came, however, not principally from patrology, where most of these criticisms were based, but from the other end of the history of dogma, the history of Protestant doctrine. Otto Ritschl published a four-volume account of the 16th and

17th centuries, dealing especially with such doctrinal issues as tradition and biblical inspiration; the work was dedicated to Adolf von Harnack.[156] In an introductory essay, justifying the subject and the title, the author took issue with Harnack's limitation of the history of dogma to the trinitarian and christological dogmas.[157] There was, Ritschl insisted, a history of dogma also within Protestantism, but it had to be understood within the distinctive framework created by Lutheran and Reformed dogmatics. According to Harnack's nomenclature, this was history of theology, not history of dogma, but even this distinction seemed strained and artificial to Otto Ritschl.[158] Another of Harnack's pupils also sought to extend the scope and subject matter of historical theology to post-Reformation developments. A. C. McGiffert was an accomplished patristic scholar, thus living up to the dictum, quoted earlier from Harnack,[159] that the church historian or historian of doctrine must be an authority in the early Church and in his own period of specialization; he published a two-volume *History of Christian Thought*,[160] several monographs on various aspects of the history of dogma,[161] and an annotated translation of the *Ecclesiastical History* of Eusebius.[162] His *Protestant Thought before Kant*, published in 1911, was dedicated to Harnack,[163] just as Otto Ritschl's work was; and while McGiffert did not as explicitly argue against his teacher's definition of dogma, his choice of subject matter made his divergence from it unmistakable.

The concentration of historical theology upon dogma has been regarded as vulnerable on other grounds as well. It seemed anomalous that Harnack, whose reduction of Christianity to its 'essence' was often called moralistic,[164] single-mindedly and regretfully excluded from his account any detailed presentation of the history of Christian morals.[165] Most of his occasional references to this area, moreover, applied to individual rather than social ethics.[166] To rectify this imbalance, Ernst Troeltsch undertook a history of *The Social Teaching of the Christian Churches and Groups*, which appeared in 1911.[167] Troeltsch made no effort to conceal his dependence on Harnack in this book,[168] as in his thought generally.[169] What he was proposing was to be a counterpart to Harnack's *History of Dogma*. The very nature of Christian social teachings made it obligatory upon the narrator of their history to pay attention not only to social theory but also, at least in passing, to social institutions—both the institutions of secular society, such as the family, with which the social teachings of the Church have dealt, and the institutions of the Church, such as monasticism, by which the Church has shaped the social thought of its members.[170] Pioneer that he was in this field, Troeltsch formulated many of the issues that still dominate research and discussion.[171] The role of natural law in the development of Christian ethical theory, a problem that has been prominent in both Roman Catholic and Protestant histories;[172] the capitulation of the conservative Reformers, especially of Luther, to the forces of social and political reaction, a question that has been revived in the encounter between Marxism and Christianity;[173] the radicalism of the social theories of the Anabaptists, a major theme in the burgeoning literature on the left wing of the Reformation[174]—these and other topics attest the enormous enrichment of historical theology through Troeltsch's work. Yet it was an enrichment achieved at the price of a deep confusion about scope and subject matter. For if one were to follow Troeltsch, the history of Christian doctrine would be absorbed into the history of Christian thought, which would in turn be absorbed into the general history of ideas. No subject matter less comprehensive than this would do justice to the scope of Troeltsch's own thought and research.[175]

Almost all of the discussion we have been summarizing took place within Protestant theology, which has set the terms for most of the development of historical theology. Nevertheless, the revision of previous ideas about scope and subject matter has also been prompted by Roman Catholic work in the field. Noteworthy though often unnoticed was Joseph Bach's history of medieval dogma, which came out in 1873–75.[176] Despite some difference of emphasis, Bach seems largely to have taken over the conception of dogma, and therefore the definition of the scope for the history of dogma, current among his Protestant contemporaries.[177] But even within that conception he supplied a sorely needed counterweight to their antimedieval prejudices. Far from being as barren of creative work in dogmatic theology as the Reformers of the 16th century and the Protestant historians of the 19th century supposed, the Middle Ages produced some work of a very high order, not only in philosophical theology but also in the area of pure dogma. It was the merit of Bach's history to have called attention to the christological development of the Scholastic period. To say, as Harnack does, that 'almost everything that Bach has described in the second volume of his history of dogma in the Middle Ages . . . belongs exclusively to the history of theology and is irrelevant to the history of dogma,'[178] seems, even on the basis of Harnack's own position, evasive and 'irrelevant.' Recent studies of the history of the doctrine of the hypostatic union in the medieval West,[179] while they have corrected and supplemented Bach's work in many ways, also give testimony to the new estimate of the crucial importance of the Middle Ages in the further history of the trinitarian and christological dogmas. It is an arbitrary delimitation even of the history of dogma in the strict sense to give short shrift to post-Chalcedonian developments in both East and West. Those developments, in turn, make unavoidable a fundamental question about the tenability of a view of historical theology that excludes them.

Taking up a portion of Bach's assignment, but broadening and deepening it, Artur Landgraf has probably added more brand-new data to the material of history of dogma than any scholar, whether Roman Catholic or Protestant, for several generations. His work eventually grew to a size of eight volumes,[180] reprinting many of the individual essays in which Landgraf had staked out new territory for historical theology. He was not content with carrying the account of the ancient dogmas, viz, the doctrine of the Trinity and the doctrine of the person of Christ, through their medieval careers. Instead, he concentrated his attention especially on the doctrine of grace[181] and the doctrine of the Sacraments.[182] Taken together, these two may fairly be called the distinctive dogmatic achievement of Latin Christianity in the Middle Ages, going well beyond the undeveloped state in which they had been left in the dogmatic decrees of the ancient councils and setting the terms within which, to a considerable degree, both the Protestant reinterpretation of the doctrine of the Sacraments and the Jansenist reexamination of the doctrine of grace were carried on.[183] By grounding so much of his research in hitherto unpublished manuscripts rather than in the printed sources with which his predecessors had worked, Landgraf demonstrated, and refuted by demonstrating, the partial nature of the very questions with which historical theology has dealt. And although such problems as 'whether a mouse eats the body of Christ' if it nibbles on a consecrated Host[184] may not be matters of profound interest to later generations of speculative theology,[185] they are precisely the issues whose deeper meaning must be probed by historical theology if it is not to trim its subject matter to suit the tastes of its own time.

More than either Bach or Landgraf, or any other historian of dogma, it was the historians of Scholastic philosophy who compelled a redefinition of the place of medieval doctrine in historical theology. The Thomistic revival during the latter part of the 19th century and the first part of the 20th did not remain with the editing, translating, and annotating of the works of St. Thomas himself; it also compared and contrasted him with his predecessors and successors. Few issues in the history of the Middle Ages have received more scholarly attention from intellectual historians than the question of universals, which runs like a thread through different centuries and different schools of thought.[186] It seemed that one's answer to the question of universals could determine one's stand even on such dogmas as the Trinity, as the controversy between St. Anselm and Roscellinus appeared to prove;[187] theological orthodoxy was dependent upon a rejection of extreme nominalism. The same conclusion could be drawn from the recrudescence of nominalism after St. Thomas.[188] If it could be shown that the theology of Luther was a product of this recrudescence,[189] that only substantiated the conclusion. One could write an account of the history of medieval thought organized around the problem of universals; in such an account, the dichotomy between an Augustinian realism and a rationalistic nominalism would be resolved in the moderate realism of St. Thomas, only to become an issue again in the 14th and 15th centuries.[190] The other issue that engaged scholars was the related one of the influence of Aristotle. Not the nominalists, but the Averroists, became the villains: St. Thomas purged Aristotle of the scepticism imposed upon him by his Arabic commentators and thus made him acceptable for theology.[191]

A preoccupation with these questions led historians of doctrine to concentrate on the prolegomena of theology rather than on its dogmatic content.[192] The 'five ways' of St. Thomas were of greater interest than his doctrine of Baptism. Even in the thought of St. Anselm, the philosophical writings such as the *Proslogion*

The Present Task of the History of Dogma 93

overshadowed theological writings such as the *Cur Deus homo*, both in the anthologies of medieval thought[193] and in the secondary literature.[194] As the excavations of Landgraf have made abundantly clear, there exists a vast amount of dogmatic material whose significance for the history of doctrine has not been examined simply because it does not belong to the line of development in which historians of medieval thought are principally interested. Similarly, Jean Leclercq's introduction to monastic theology[195] places the work of St. Thomas Aquinas in a setting no less important than was the history of medieval Aristotelianism; if, as Leclercq maintains, the Song of Songs 'was most read, and most frequently commented in the medieval cloister,'[196] the implications of this for the history of Christian doctrine, perhaps even for the study of the theology of St. Thomas, deserve to be weighed alongside those of the problem of universals.

Now that several generations of scholars have done their best to revise the traditional definition of scope and subject matter, one must repeat Gustav Krüger's question with some poignancy, if not indeed with genuine bewilderment: 'What is the history of dogma, and why does one study it?'! Kurt Aland is correct in his insistence that a simple rearrangement of the old content of the history of dogma will not do,[197] but even the old concept seems to have been stretched out of recognizable shape. Any distinction between the history of dogma and the history of theology seems to have become untenable; and at least for the Middle Ages and the 19th century, so, presumably, has any distinction between the history of theology and the history of philosophy. Social and ethical teachings belong to the biblical understanding of 'doctrine' at least as much as dogmatic ones do, and they are apparently entitled to consideration in the history of doctrine also. Do the criticisms and amplifications summarized here make the very idea of a history of Christian doctrine impossible?

Toward a Redefinition

While most of these criticisms of Harnack's definition of the scope and subject matter of historical theology have charged it with being too narrow, perhaps a more radical critique is called for. On the basis of the inconsistencies between his statement of the task and his execution of it, one could maintain that, far from being too 'churchly,' it is not churchly enough. Far from paying too little attention to the history of theology as distinguished from the history of dogma, Harnack assigned a disproportionate amount of space to the private ideas of individual theologians, at the expense of dogma in the fullest and most accurate sense of the word. Instead of explaining the various theological parties on the basis of their significance for the formulation of church doctrine, historical theology has often allowed their alignments to determine the categories of the discussion and then has described the formulated dogma as the legitimation of one alternative or as a compromise between alternatives. In a curious way, the radical Protestant theologians of the 18th and 19th centuries have thus repristinated the Eusebian emphasis on the history of doctrine as the history of heresy.[198]

One result of that emphasis in the church histories and catalogues of heresy written by the Church Fathers was a proliferation of party labels.[199] Each shade of theological opinion acquired a title, derived either from a presumed founder (e.g., Ebionites)[200] or from its favorite slogan (e.g., Exoukontians)[201] or from the supposed implications of its doctrine (e.g., Aphthartodoketae).[202] This propensity of Greek polemical theologians to elaborate a taxonomy of heresy[203] was then compounded by the propensity of German historical theologians to invent still more theological schools, on the grounds that a professed doctrinal consensus had in fact glossed over deeper differences, some of them unknown even to their adherents. Thus there has arisen among German historians a distinction between an 'Old Nicene' and a 'Young Nicene' party,[204] as a way of classifying the participants in the half-century of controversy after Nicea. Once coined, these titles seem almost to assume an existence of their own; for example, Friedrich Loofs found that no adherent of the 'Antiochene school' was truly representative of its teachings, and yet the category remained.[205] The study of the history of doctrine could then be thought to consist of learning the nomenclature and, if possible, the pedigree of all these isms, which, together with the dogmas whose promulgation they served to evoke, constituted the principal subject matter of historical theology.

Anyone who has studied the history of dogma at all will be obliged to admit that many dogmas have been formulated in response to theological alternatives as these have been churned up in controversy. No conciliar or confessional promulgation can be properly understood apart from the anathemas it pronounces upon those who teach otherwise.[206] The identification of the antecedents explicitly quoted or implicitly echoed in a dogma does belong to any historical exposition of its meaning, as the *bon mot* quoted earlier from Whitehead suggests.[207] The juridical function of dogma is no less important than its polemical function. It was a requirement of the Code of Theodosius that one profess the orthodox trinitarian faith; to deny it was not only heretical but seditious.[208] Throughout most of its history, therefore, orthodox dogma has depended for its enforcement upon the sanctions of the secular authorities, as well as upon the juridical power of the ecclesiastical establishment itself. 'Confessional development' is inseparable from 'church politics'[209] throughout the history of dogma. But neither the juridical nor even the polemical function of dogma should be emphasized at the expense of all the other keys in which the Church's doctrine may be played.

To find a substitute for Harnack's definition of the history of doctrine as history of dogma, it is necessary to define doctrine in a manner that is simultaneously more comprehensive and more restrictive: more comprehensive in that the polemical and juridical expressions of doctrine in the form of dogmatic decrees and promulgations are not isolated from other expressions of doctrine, such as preaching, instruction, exegesis, liturgy, and spirituality; more restrictive in that the range and content of the doctrines considered are not determined in the first place by the quarrels among theologians but by the development of those doctrines themselves. Christian doctrine, then, may be defined as what the Church believes, teaches, and confesses on the basis of the word of God. This answers one question by begging a great many others, including the question of what the Church is and how it is to be identified. None of these questions can be overlooked, nor can their answers be taken for granted, as the historical theologian makes his decisions about the subject matter to be included in the history of Christian doctrine. Yet a premature resolution of these normative issues could easily cause him to lose sight of sources to which he ought to pay attention as he undertakes a task whose primary function is, we must insist, descriptive rather than normative. On this score, this definition of doctrine endeavors to be more comprehensive. It is more restrictive because it evaluates theologians in relation to their function as spokesmen for what the Church believes, teaches, and confesses, rather than as the miners and minters of theologies issued in their own name.

The definition of Christian doctrine as what the Church believes, teaches, and confesses is based upon the formula in Rom 10.8–10: 'The word is near you, on your lips and in your heart (that is, the word of faith which we preach); because, if you confess with your lips that Jesus is Lord and believe in your heart that God raised him from the dead, you will be saved. For man believes with his heart and so is justified, and he confesses with his lips and so is saved.' It may well be that this formula, or at least the description of the relation between the faith of the heart and the confession of the mouth, is derived from even earlier sources.[210] It certainly is not intended as a technical definition of the connection between 'the word of faith which we preach' and what 'man believes with his heart' and what 'he confesses with his lips.' An important element in the Apostle's argument here is that the preached word creates faith in the heart, for 'faith comes from what is heard, and what is heard comes by the preaching of Christ' (Rom 10.17). This preaching may be said to precede believing; for that matter, confessing is placed before believing in v. 9, while believing is placed before confessing in v. 10. Hence it would be artificial to force these words into a rigid formula. But it does seem warranted to see in them—as, for example, St. Augustine did[211]—a threefold description of how the content of the Christian faith is held, not only by the individual but also by the Christian community. On this basis, and in various combinations, believing, teaching, and confessing are identified as the forms in which Christian doctrine is to be expressed. Thus the Nicene Creed begins with 'We believe';[212] the opening declaration of the Chalcedonian decree has 'We all teach . . . [that one must] confess';[213] the decrees of the Council of Trent employ such formulas as 'ordains, confesses, and declares'[214] or 'teaches and openly and plainly professes';[215] the Lutheran Formula of Concord repeatedly introduces its affirmations of doctrine with the words 'We believe, teach, and confess'[216] or 'our teaching, belief, and confession';[217] and the Reformed Scottish Confession of 1560 employs the formula 'We confess and acknowledge.'[218]

Without drawing absolute lines of distinction between believing, teaching, and confessing—the liturgy, for example, belongs in one way or another to each of them,[219] as does preaching—we may identify certain doctrinal modalities of the Church more closely with one than with the others. Precisely because the Church itself has not divided its formulation of creeds and its promulgation of dogmas from the full range of its doctrinal response to divine revelation, it is a distortion for the historian to do so. The proper context for interpreting any formal statement of Christian doctrine is the spectrum of what has been believed, taught, and confessed. Much of historical theology, therefore, must be concerned with the movement of doctrines between the believing, the teaching, and the confessing of the Church. The movement is not simple, nor does it always go in the same direction. No confession of faith exhausts the full content of what is believed, and therefore the historian must look beyond the bare text of the creed to see the movement of a doctrine from believing through teaching to confessing. But the movement may also be in the opposite direction; for the creed may also exceed the content of what is actually believed or taught at a particular point in history, or it may shape and change that content at another point. In the pregnant formula of Thomas Mann, some doctrines are like deserted houses, still impressive but uninhabited.[220] It may perhaps be stated as a general rule that at any given time the Church believes implicitly more than it teaches explicitly, and that it teaches explicitly more than it confesses officially. Nevertheless, contrary to some simplistic theories of the development of doctrine,[221] the sequence has not always been the same. The narrator of the history of doctrine must be alert to the various possible combinations and connections of believing, teaching, and confessing if he is to do justice to the complexity of that history.

As these three terms are used in this working definition of Christian doctrine, they may be said to embrace several aspects of the life of the Church. The usual scope of historical theology, as already noted, has been determined primarily by polemics and apologetics, by creed and dogma; these are what we shall take to be meant by St. Paul's words '. . . if you confess with your lips that "Jesus is Lord" '; for here he is quoting an early creedal statement,[222] and one that was especially important in the apologetic explanation of the Christian faith to paganism. But that which was confessed with the lips was derived from teaching—from what St. Paul here terms 'the word of faith which we preach.' Under the heading of 'teaching' is included the content of the preached word as the Church, in its teaching office, extracts it by exegesis from the witness of Scripture and communicates it to the faithful through proclamation, instruction, and churchly theology. What the Church confesses and teaches, it presents as a word of faith, 'for man believes with his heart and so is justified'; therefore the history of doctrine is not complete unless it also examines the enigmatic but unavoidable reality of Christian doctrine in the 'believing' that exists in the form of piety, spirituality, and liturgy.

It must be acknowledged that the present state of the source material simply does not permit a fully satisfying account of what was believed, taught, and confessed. In Reuter's rather exaggerated formula, directed against Harnack,

> The history of dogma is in no sense the history of the actual religious faith that animated the community as a matter of authentic experience (perhaps partly in contradiction to the dogma). This, the most glorious aspect of all the ages of Christian history, no scholarly research, however intense, will be able to fathom. For the source upon which one could draw for this purpose, the inner chamber of the hearts of men, is by the nature of things inaccessible.[223]

The earlier stages of the biography of a doctrine are often fragmentary, sometimes ambiguous, and occasionally downright misleading. This realization should temper any claims to finality, but it should not set the terms for the inquiry. There is more to be learned about what was believed and taught than the older history of dogma recognized; and this, in turn, will illumine in meaningful ways the history of what came to be confessed.

CHAPTER FOUR

The Historiography of Doctrine

If it is to be the task of historical theology to study the history of Christian doctrine as what has been believed, taught, and confessed by the Church, the enterprise will be beset by historiographical problems of more than ordinary intricacy. Some of these attend any historical writing; others are produced, or at any rate compounded, by the subject matter. This is not only because the source material has been transmitted in a babel of different languages, at least some of which any historical theologian must acquire, but especially because the cultural heterogeneity symbolized by those languages raises in an acute way all the special questions with which, as previously argued, historical theology is obliged to deal. The intention here is to concentrate only on those historiographical issues that confront the historical theologian with a particular urgency.

Historical and Theological Methods

At least some awareness of the nuances of method is legitimately demanded of a discipline that unites the interests of history and of theology in the manner here found to be characteristic of the history of Christian doctrine. 'Method is mother-wit,' Harnack said,[1] thus voicing a protest against the preoccupation of certain philosophical theologians,[2] then and now, with historical method as a subject of study unto itself. It is, of course, a proper subject for philosophical theology. As Augustine already recognized with great insight,[3] the epistemological analysis developed by classical thought, if pressed to its ultimate implications, required that man's awareness of time and his perception of the past be included in the catalogue of the ways of knowing. The refinement of this inquiry in present-day philosophical literature[4]—and, largely but not completely dependent upon this, in the theological literature[5] of our time—both requires and enables the historical theologian, together with his colleagues in other fields of historical investigation, to develop a greater attention to methodology than has been characteristic of his predecessors. Yet Harnack was making a valid point in his objection to full-length methodological treatises, whose 'paralysis of analysis' could allow theological considerations to intrude, prematurely and unduly, upon what he deemed a technical, largely philological, undertaking.

In so doing, however, Harnack underestimated the degree to which theological considerations unavoidably 'intrude'—and did intrude, moreover, upon his own philological research, not only upon that of men whose interest in the history of dogma was a professedly dogmatic one. Because a dogmatic purpose still is the primary motivation for much of the research in historical theology, probably even for most of it, no examination of the method appropriate to the discipline is valid if it ignores the work of those theologians whose constructive statements of doctrine have emerged from a study of the history of doctrine. To some degree this is true of all contemporary systematic theologians, but three may serve as illustrations, both because of their own intrinsic significance in the theological history of the 20th century and because of the use to which they have put the history of doctrine in their work. The three are Karl Barth, Paul Tillich, and Karl Rahner. Each of them has worked in historical theology as such;[6] both Barth[7] and Tillich[8] took it upon themselves to lecture at length on 19th-century theology, not only as a foil for defining their own thought but also as a means for understanding the peculiar difficulty and the special opportunity of the systematic theologian in the 20th century.

Nevertheless a more important place to look for historical theology in the work of Barth and Tillich, as well as in that of Rahner, is within their systematic theologies. Here they employ variations of what has been earlier termed the dogmatic and the dialectical treatments of the phenomenon of doctrinal change. Rahner's examination of the present state of the christological question,[9] for example, is based on the recognition that the formulation of orthodox Christology was conditioned by the various heresies to which it responded and that it therefore reflects some of their one-sidedness. By thus playing off the dogmas against their antitheses, Rahner makes clear that a full and complete statement of the doctrine of the person of Christ would also have to define itself in relation to other alternatives, less vocally represented in the history of christological heresy, perhaps, but no less crucial for the dialectical understanding of the relation between the divine and the human nature. Such a historical diagnosis makes it possible for Rahner to formulate a more adequate definition of the content of the humanity of Jesus than has been characteristic of dogmatic theology.[10] Tillich is even more explicit in his insistence upon the dialectical character of historical theology:

> Church history is made available to the systematic theologian through a historically critical and ultimately concerned history of Christian thought, formerly called 'history of dogma.' The traditional term 'dogmatics' implies a concern which the more recent term does not express. The 'history of Christian thought' can mean a detached description of the ideas of theological thinkers through the centuries. Some of the critical histories of Christian thought are not far removed from such an attitude. The historical theologian must show that in all periods Christian thought has dealt with matters of ultimate concern and that therefore it is itself a matter of ultimate concern. Systematic theology needs a history of Christian thought written from a point of view which is radically critical and, at the same time, existentially concerned.[11]

Tillich's own lectures on the history of Christian thought were shaped by this insistence, for they were both radically critical[12] and existentially concerned.[13]

Although he differs fundamentally from Tillich's view of systematic theology,[14] Barth seems to have a similar view of the contribution that historical theology can make to systematics, and even uses similar language to express it. For he finds in the doctrine of the Church a ground for taking seriously even those figures and movements in the history of doctrine with whom one disagrees. In the introduction to his history of theology in the 19th century, Barth writes:

> I believe one holy, Catholic, and apostolic Church. And if I seriously intend to listen to a theologian of the past—whether it be Schleiermacher or Ritschl or anyone else—then I must mean this 'I believe' seriously, unless I have been released from this obligation by private inspiration! That is, regardless of my myriad opinions I must include these people in the Christian Church. And in view of the fact that I myself, together with my theological work, belong to the Christian Church solely on the basis of forgiveness, I have no right to deny or even to doubt that they were as fundamentally concerned as I am about the Christian faith.[15]

However, this lack of a 'right to deny or even to doubt' does not imply the lack of a right to criticize and to differ.[16] Even on the dogma of the Trinity, Barth's *Church Dogmatics* explores the history of doctrine to specify how 'person' can mean 'mode of being' and to show that this is not a relapse into Sabellianism.[17]

Perhaps even more common than this continuation of the dialectical and dogmatic methods is the revival of a method repudiated by historians of doctrine since Albrecht Ritschl. As already noted, this method treated the history of individual doctrines, in accordance with the definition and sometimes even the arrangement of these doctrines in Protestant systematic theology.[18] It was later rejected on the grounds that it atomized the total understanding of the Christian faith in a particular individual or group or era, often introducing doctrinal distinctions unknown to the period under study. Those grounds of objection still hold; but in a historical discussion that forms the backdrop to a systematic exposition of Christian doctrine no other approach seems practical. It is not possible to rehearse entire systems of doctrine in order to discover the alternative interpretations of the Eucharist that have been held by theologians of the past. There is no denying that these interpretations are integrally related to other doctrines in the thought of those men. Thus the first major debate in Western theology over the Real Presence, that of St. Paschasius Radbertus and Ratramnus in the 9th century, disclosed an evident congruence between the eucharistic theories of these theologians and their christological and mariological teachings.[19] The supernaturalism of St. Paschasius' idea of sacramental transformation seems to be carried over into his idea of the virginity of Mary *in partu*,[20] while Ratramnus's rejection of the former seems to be consistent with his rejection of the latter.[21] It is historically sound to maintain that the proper method for the interpretation of the eucharistic controversy between these two monastic theologians is a comparison of their two doctrinal systems *in toto*.

At the same time, it is instructive to note that the earlier history of the doctrine of the Eucharist played a prominent part in that controversy. A key phrase in the Radbertian argument is the description of the body present in the Eucharist as 'no other flesh than that which was born of Mary.'[22] The source of this phrase appears to have been St. Ambrose.[23] But the treatise *On the Sacraments* and the treatise *On the Mysteries* of St. Ambrose also figured prominently in the argumentation of Ratramnus against the Capernaitic interpretation of the body present in the Sacrament.[24] It certainly appears proper, therefore, to put one's analysis of this debate on the Real Presence into the context, not of Carolingian theology (legitimate though such a category may be[25]), but of eucharistic theology. Such a method will also be able to trace the fascinating role played by the treatise of Ratramnus in the subsequent history of doctrine. Two centuries after the author's death, it was condemned at the Synod of Vercelli (Sept. 1, 1050), but under the name of Johannes Scotus Erigena.[26] Half a millennium after that, it once more became an issue in the sacramentarian controversies of the Reformation.[27] Nicholas Ridley claimed to have been led by it to reject transubstantiation;[28] at the same time, St. John Fisher drew from it in his attack upon Protestant doctrines of the Lord's Supper.[29] Thus there would appear to be considerable justification for the historical study of discrete doctrines, both as a means of making the subject matter of historical theology available to systematic theology and as a way of emphasizing the very issues of change and continuity in doctrine with whose resolution historical theology as a theological discipline is charged.

Although the adaptability of this method to the purposes of the systematic theologian raises the question of the theological position of the historian with special force, no one writing the history of doctrine can avoid the question. Can the theological a priori be avoided in historical theology, or should it perhaps even be cultivated? Ernest Renan phrases a widely accepted answer to the question with characteristic simplicity:

> To write the history of a religion, it is necessary, firstly, to have believed it (otherwise we should not be able to understand how it has charmed and satisfied the human conscience); in the second place, to believe it no longer in an absolute manner, for absolute faith is incompatible with sincere history. But love is possible without faith. To abstain from attaching one's self to any of the forms which captivate the adoration of men, is not to deprive ourselves of that which is good and beautiful in them.[30]

Neither Renan's statement of the ideal method nor his own application of it[31] makes clear just what combination of objectivity and subjectivity is necessary or permissible. It would seem a safe generalization that the historians of the 19th century, including the historians of religion and of doctrine, tended to be rather naïvely confident about the possibility of approaching their subject matter objectively, while those of the 20th tend to underestimate that possibility unduly.

If one is to judge on the basis of the results, the question of the theological a priori in the historian of doctrine is not really answered in either of these tendencies. What is often dismissed today as positivism[32] was a method of studying and writing history that managed to penetrate deeply into systems of thought not at all congenial to the historian. It is a caricature when Benedetto Croce dismisses Leopold von Ranke's 'boasted impartiality and objectivity, which was based upon a literary device of half-words, of innuendoes, of prudent silences' or when he speaks of Ranke's 'act of resignation before blind contingentism.'[33] Croce himself admitted that he had not done justice to Ranke's work.[34] More subtle, but no less condescending, is Collingwood's estimate of the historical method of positivism, which, he maintains,

> ... led historians to adopt two rules of method in their treatment of facts: (i) Each fact was to be regarded as a thing capable of being ascertained by a separate act of cognition or process of research, and thus the total field of the historically knowable was cut up into an infinity of minute facts each to be separately considered. (ii) Each fact was to be thought of not only as independent of all the rest but as independent of the knower, so that all subjective elements (as they were called) in the historian's point of view had to be eliminated.

> The historian must pass no judgment on the facts: he must only say what they were.[35]

Collingwood finds that 'the legacy of positivism to modern historiography' amounts to 'a combination of unprecedented mastery over small-scale problems with unprecedented weakness in dealing with large-scale problems.' It also prevented historians from dealing with such questions as 'What was the attitude of ordinary people in the Middle Ages toward the Church and its system of creed and doctrine?'[36] If one reads them, however, one finds that 'positivistic' historians such as Ranke did deal with 'large-scale problems,' including some of the very issues Collingwood itemizes. For example, Ranke's observations about the relation between Origenism and Augustinianism[37] or his estimate of the place of Justinian in the history of ideas[38] may still be read and quoted with profit, as they were by Harnack[39]—himself a 'positivist' by this standard, but one who has probably never been accused of combining 'unprecedented mastery over small-scale problems with unprecedented weakness in dealing with large-scale problems.'

It would not be fair to dismiss Collingwood's critique of positivistic historiography so summarily, for Harnack could be cited as evidence in support of Collingwood's theory of historiography rather than in refutation of it. Responding to Dilthey's concept of historical understanding, Collingwood proposed a definition of the historian's knowledge as 'knowledge of the past in the present, the self-knowledge of the historian's own mind as the present revival and reliving of past experiences.'[40] Any such knowledge presupposes the capacity of the historian's mind in the present to 'revive and relive' the experiences of the past with sufficient fidelity to make historical study something more than refined introspection. Applied to the history of Christian doctrine, this presupposition means that the historian's own theological position must enable him to revive what was believed, taught, and confessed in another age of church history. It is not necessary that he believe it himself—nor, for that matter, that he disbelieve it. It is necessary that he be able to understand how, with its assumptions about the word and will of God, the Church did believe, teach, and confess this. Where Harnack's appreciation of the orthodox Christian tradition gave him the capacity to resonate even to a piety he could not share, he was able to interpret it with real empathy as 'the deepest root of dogma;'[41] but where a lack of understanding for the liturgy made such empathy impossible,[42] the result was deficient, not only theologically but above all historically. In this way Harnack's very performance as a historical theologian vindicates Collingwood's diagnosis.

An imposing effort to go beyond both the antithesis between objective and subjective and the contradiction between the theological and the historical method is the 'motif-research' associated with the Lundensian school of theologians and historians.[43] A leading student of the method has defined it as follows:

> In its simplest form, the search for the motif is a search for the meaning behind the terminology or form of expression. It is an attempt to arrive at the affirmation that gave rise to a particular statement of doctrine. The statement itself is determined by the thought-forms of the day and by the positions that it seeks to exclude. The doctrine of the Trinity, for instance, can be understood only if one can discover what the terms 'person' and 'essence' meant to the formulators of the doctrine, the positive content of the faith which they sought to express, and the compromises involved in the various forms of monarchianism against which the Church wished to defend itself.[44]

In his explanation of how the method of motif-research differs both from the investigation of origins and from the formulation of value judgments, Anders Nygren has defined the motif as 'the basic idea or the driving power of the religion concerned, or what it is that gives it its character as a whole and communicates to all its parts their special content and colour.'[45]

The method, he insists, can be applied to any religious tradition, not merely to the Christian, and even to other areas than religion. Specifying in greater detail the distinctiveness of motif-research as a method of historiography, Nygren defends it against the charge that it is subjective or that the identification of the motif is necessarily a matter of intuition rather than of empirical investigation and of scientific verification:

> The question we have to answer here, therefore, is whether it is at all possible by means of scientific analysis to determine the fundamental motif of any given form of religion. The answer can only be an unqualified affirmative. The purpose of the scientific study of religion is not merely to record the actual conceptions, attitudes, and so forth, that are found in a particular religious *milieu*, but more especially to find out

what is characteristic and typical of them all. That is what motif-research deliberately and consistently seeks to do, and is indeed fully capable of doing. What we regard as a fundamental motif need not be a matter of subjective and arbitrary choice, for it is open to objective examination. A religion deprived of its fundamental motif would lose all coherence and meaning; and therefore we cannot rightly regard anything as a fundamental motif unless its removal would have such an effect. This gives us the basic principle on which motif-research must proceed with its analysis.[46]

Because love is generally regarded as the fundamental motif of Christianity, Nygren's investigation concentrates on the development of this theme in Christian history from the beginning until Luther, in whom the understanding of love as *agape*, submerged in the Pseudo-Dionysian and Augustinian distortions,[47] was clearly recovered.

If it is valid as a historical method, motif-research ought to be applicable not only to the development of the single central and fundamental idea of a religion, if such there be, but also to those themes and doctrines in its history that are intimately associated with the fundamental motif. One such theme in Christian thought is the doctrine of the atonement. Taking up the history of this doctrine, Gustaf Aulén's *Christus Victor*[48] has attempted to classify the various theological theories about the saving work of Christ under a number of comprehensive rubrics. The 'subjective' interpretation of the atonement is represented by Peter Abelard's emphasis upon the cross of Christ as a revelation of divine love.[49] The 'satisfaction' theory of redemption through the payment of the debt demanded by divine justice is analyzed on the basis of the *Cur Deus homo?* of St. Anselm.[50] What Aulén identifies as the 'classical' conception of salvation is seen at work in certain Fathers, notably some in the Greek tradition;[51] but its fullest articulation appears in Luther.[52] While both the 'subjective' and the 'objective' theories described the atonement anthropocentrically, the motif of the 'wondrous duel'[53] between Christ and the enemies of man—sin, death, the law, and the devil—made salvation the work of God. Within the structure of these motifs Aulén finds it possible to classify the various metaphors that have appeared in the history of the doctrine of the work of Christ and to relate them to one another both historically and theologically.[54]

As a method for the historiography of Christian doctrine, Lundensian motif-research is liable to various criticisms. Martin C. D'Arcy has acknowledged the positive contribution of Nygren's research to an understanding of the distinctiveness of the Christian view of love, but he has criticized *Agape and Eros* on theological and historical grounds, particularly for its treatment of the Augustinian concept of charity.[55] Even more fundamentally, one can charge it with having perpetuated, or revived, the earlier identification of the Reformation as the *terminus ad quem* of the history of doctrine.[56] Both the idea of love, according to Nygren's reading of its history,[57] and the doctrine of the atonement, according to Aulén's version of its development,[58] have appeared in their fullness and purity first in the New Testament and then in Martin Luther, but seldom if ever during the intervening centuries of church history. It would be an *ad hominem* oversimplification to attribute this historical construction merely to the circumstance that both Anders Nygren and Gustaf Aulén were Lutheran professors of theology at the university of Lund and eventually became Lutheran bishops. Perhaps more pertinent would be the observation that, in its execution rather more than in its definition, the method of motif-research, *pace* Nygren's disclaimers, is not 'entirely indifferent to the question of value'[59] but presupposes a fairly evident philosophical and theological position, e.g., the value of distinction in preference to synthesis;[60] and it would seem to be more than coincidence that many elements of this position bear an affinity to the theology of Luther[61] and to the philosophy of 19th-century Idealism.[62]

In its basic intention, however—or, if one may term it so, in its fundamental motif—motif-research offers important methodological assistance to historical theology. For it recognizes that 'the idea or belief may have exactly the same form without having at all the same meaning, if in one case it is a basic conception, while in the other it is more loosely attached.'[63] Therefore it is not enough simply to trace the career of a dogma from one verbal formulation to the next, as though the absence of such a formulation proved the absence of the dogma or the presence (perhaps indeed prominence) of the formulation were evidence that the dogma is a living force. Instead, the method of historical theology must be aware of the many subtle connections between what is believed, what is taught, and what is confessed at any given point in the history of the Church. Although Lundensian theology has probably been more optimistic than it has a right to be about its capacity to discover 'the meaning behind the terminology or form of expression'[64] of a church doctrine, this 'meaning behind' is to a significant degree accessible—provided that 'behind' is taken concretely in a chronological, not only abstractly in a hermeneutical, sense. Or, to put our modification of motif-research in another way, its viability as a theological method for the systematic statement of doctrine may well be subject to the vigorous demurrers that Gustaf Wingren has raised about it,[65] but as a method for the historiography of doctrine[66] it has provided some indications of a way out of the impasse between Ranke and Collingwood, or between Harnack and Bultmann.[67]

If Christian doctrine is defined as we have defined it here, as what the Church believes, teaches, and confesses, it would appear to be the soundest historical method to begin a posteriori with that which the Church confesses, viz, with dogma. This has been articulated in the formal, creedal, juridical statements of synods, councils, and popes. Yet whenever it has been articulated, it has claimed to rest upon earlier and deeper articulations of Christian doctrine. To a considerable degree—that is, to a greater degree than has been characteristic of the manuals of the history of dogma—one can go from what is confessed to the 'meaning behind it' in what is taught by means of the exposition of Scripture, the proclamation of the gospel, and instruction of the young (all of which are, in turn, shaped by that which has been confessed and is still being confessed in creed and dogma). Moreover, Scripture is expounded after having been read in the liturgy; the gospel is preached in association with a 'pastoral prayer' or other invocation of divine assistance; and the young are instructed in the practice of piety at least as much as in the dogmas of the Church. Hence the historian of doctrine cannot be content even with what is taught as the 'meaning behind' what is confessed; he must also try to reach what is believed as the 'meaning behind' what is taught. He will not always be able to reach it. Much less will he be able to begin with what is believed, but not yet taught or confessed, and to anticipate what will come to be taught and confessed. But it is possible for the historian, after the fact of what was taught and especially of what was confessed, to discern in what was believed how the Church came to teach a doctrine and how it felt obliged eventually to confess it as well.

The evidence for the thesis that 'God' was a widely accepted title for Jesus Christ in the early Church is quite impressive: an ancient homily,[68] an early martyrology,[69] a problematical[70] but incontestable pagan account,[71] a primitive eucharistic prayer.[72] In the face of such evidence about what was believed in the Church, the proper method of historical theology is to ask how Christian doctrine moved from these inchoate affirmations about Christ as God, which were subject to all sorts of distortions and oversimplifications, to the unambiguous statement of the *homoousios* which, a half-century or so after the Council of Nicea, was accepted (and imposed) as the consensus of orthodox Christianity.[73] Beginning with this confession, historical theology must work its way back through the conflict among all the various theories that were taught in the Church, to the Church, and even by the Church, to what was believed in the devotional life of the Church and celebrated in its liturgical life. This latter is, in some basic sense, the 'fundamental motif' of the trinitarian orthodoxy that came to prevail.[74] Whether this orthodoxy was an adequate statement of the meaning of divine revelation is finally a theological issue. But it is a historical issue, susceptible at least partly of solution by historical method, to determine how it expressed in a confession the doctrine present in what the piety and the liturgy of the Church were believing and in what the exegesis, the proclamation, and the instruction of the Church were teaching. This is what historical theology must attempt to do.

The Contexts of Theological History

All of the methods just analyzed depend in part for their procedure upon a recognition of the context of a doctrine. According to Nygren's motif-research, for instance, what a creed or doctrine, 'an idea, belief, or sentiment really means, can only be decided in the light of its own natural context.'[75] As it is articulated in the sources, however, a doctrine may appear in several settings at once, so that deciding which of these is 'its own natural context' requires consideration of the various ways in which doctrine has been related to context in theological history.

The Historiography of Doctrine   111

It is conceivable that Christian doctrines could be classified on the basis of their own natural contexts, with some being labeled as belonging most properly to philosophical theology (e.g., the definition of the deity of God), some to liturgical theology (e.g., the Real Presence in the Eucharist), some to exegetical theology (e.g., the relation of the historical Jesus to the pre-existent Logos according to the New Testament). But as soon as such specific doctrines are named, it becomes clear that any such classification would be arbitrary, artificial, and not very helpful.

More useful perhaps is an analysis of the question of context based on the history of the discipline of historical theology itself. Although it seems impossible to suggest any doctrine whose development is explicable solely in relation to one frame of reference, the development of certain doctrines has been clarified at one or another point in the history of scholarship by a fresh understanding of how a particular frame of reference helped to give shape to the Church's teaching and confession. The methodological discussion here has already shown that the history of theology stands not only between history and theology but also (and sometimes more importantly) between ecclesiastical history and intellectual history. When the balance between the intellectual and the ecclesiastical has been ignored by scholars, the result has been a more or less exclusive concentration on one context at the expense of others. Perhaps the best illustration of this is the history of scholarship in medieval studies. Étienne Gilson has observed:

> Studies on the medieval philosophies are without number. . . . But in the midst of such an abundance of histories of medieval philosophy, how many histories of medieval theology are to be found? As against twenty volumes on the philosophy of St. Thomas Aquinas, how many historical expositions of his theology are there? During the past hundred years the general tendency among historians of medieval thought seems to have been to imagine the middle ages as peopled by philosophers rather than theologians.[76]

And the assumption behind this general tendency was that the principal context of the history of doctrine in the Middle Ages was the philosophical one.[77]

Some chapters of the history of theology have been illumined chiefly by church history, that is, by research into doctrine that has related it to the life and structure of the Church within which it developed. Frequently such research has acted as a corrective upon an interpretation of the history of doctrine that had resolved the tension between ecclesiastical history and intellectual history too easily in favor of the latter. The converse overemphasis has also distorted some histories of doctrine by supposing that the intra-ecclesiastical explanation of a doctrine is automatically the most appropriate one. Yet doctrine *is* what the Church believes, teaches, and confesses, not merely what one systematic thinker, however brilliant and original he may have been, sets forth as his private theological construction. It follows from this that an examination of the churchly setting for a doctrine must always be part of the historical investigation of its origin. This must be an investigation of more than the decrees of prelates and the legislation of synods. The distinction between the 'ordinary' and the 'extraordinary' magisterium of the Church,[78] useful as far as it goes, may still assign undue importance to these legislative actions of the Church's administrators, at the cost of the even more ordinary teaching that goes on between all the members of the Church, ordained or not. This process is never irrelevant for the history of Christian doctrine, and in some cases it is the context on the basis of which historical theology has succeeded in determining what the doctrine may have meant.[79]

The doctrine of the Trinity may serve as an illustration. There can be no denying that it is an important chapter in intellectual history, a more important one than many histories of philosophy have recognized.[80] Charles Norris Cochrane has brilliantly stated the place of this doctrine in the history of classical thought:

> When considered in relation to the philosophic background, Trinitarian Christianity presents itself, not as dogma, but as the rejection of dogma, not as the assertion but rather as the denial of anthropomorphism and myth; and it calls for a final and conclusive expulsion of these elements from the description of ultimate reality as the preliminary to a starkly realistic account of nature and of man. . . . Accordingly, in the Trinity, Christian wisdom discovers that for which Classicism had so long vainly sought, viz. the *logos* or explanation of being and motion, in other words, a metaphysic of ordered process. In so doing, it does justice to the element of truth contained alike in the claims of classical materialism and classical idealism; while, at the same time, it avoids the errors and absurdities of both.[81]

To be established as something more than an insight into the trinitarian speculation of St. Augustine,[82] Cochrane's thesis would have to be checked against the larger development of the dogma, especially in the Greek Fathers of the 4th century. But even on the basis of the theologoumena of St. Augustine alone it is clear that the history of philosophy dare not skip over the Council of Nicea and its aftermath, but must relate Christian trinitarianism both to the pre-Christian career of such ideas as *logos* and *ousia* and to the post-Nicene development of philosophy in Byzantium and in the Latin Middle Ages.

Neglected though it may have been in the histories of philosophy, the relation between the doctrine of the Trinity and Greek philosophy has bulked large in the histories of dogma. As Harnack put it, 'The formula of the Logos legitimized speculation, that is, Neo-Platonic philosophy, within the faith of the Church.'[83] The vicissitudes of this formula in the theological debates before Nicea are then described as virtually tantamount to the entire history of the doctrine of the Trinity, so that 'the acceptance of the Logos-christology in the rule of faith'[84] and 'the victory of the Logos-christology also in the Orient'[85] become the decisive steps leading up to the promulgation of the dogma of the Trinity in 325. And thus Tillich could summarize the background of that dogma in his lapidary fashion: 'When early Christianity calls Jesus of Nazareth the Messiah and identifies him with the divine Logos, the trinitarian problem becomes the central problem of religious existence. The basic motive and the different forms of trinitarian monotheism become effective in the trinitarian dogma of the Christian church.'[86] Although Harnack acknowledged that the Christian exegesis of certain crucial passages of the Old Testament was a major factor in the designation of Christ as God,[87] yet on the basis of the relative amount of space he assigned to these various factors from the life of the Church, it is the Logos doctrine, with its legitimation of Greek philosophical speculation, that seems to be decisive for him.

In the history of patristic scholarship since Harnack, the clarification of the dogma of the Trinity has not been achieved primarily by further investigation of the lineage of the idea of the Logos, even though this investigation has connected Christian speculation with its Greek and Jewish roots in interesting ways.[88] Rather, it has been from the history of the Church that new insights into the origins of trinitarianism have come. Especially fruitful has been the very area whose significance Harnack had dismissed,[89] the history of worship. Georg Kretschmar, for instance, has examined the significance of Baptism and the Eucharist for the doctrine of God as Father, Son, and Holy Spirit.[90] What was believed in the baptismal and eucharistic practice of the Church was taught in its catechetical instruction[91] and eventually confessed in its creeds. Although Kretschmar's researches did not carry him into the period of the Arian controversies,[92] it is clear that the liturgical argument must receive a large share of the credit for the victory of orthodoxy. The Arians and their orthodox opponents had in common the liturgical practice of worshiping Jesus Christ;[93] but if the Logos was created out of nothing, this practice was an idolatrous adoration of 'a creature and a work.'[94] They also had in common the usage of baptizing in the name of the Father and of the Son and of the Holy Spirit;[95] if the Son was a creature, this meant that one was baptized 'into the name of the Unoriginated and the originated.'[96] The question was: Which doctrine of the relation between the Father and the Son is faithful to the way of worship taken for granted by all parties to the controversy? Without denying that the idea of the Logos gave intellectual respectability and speculative expression to this doctrine, research in historical theology has found the origins of the doctrine not primarily in a philosophical context but in a liturgical one.

Other chapters in the history of doctrine have had to depend for their elaboration almost exclusively on historians of ideas, especially on historians of philosophy and historians of literature. As Daniel J. Boorstin has pointed out, speaking specifically about the development of American ideas:

> Of the new specialties which have prospered within the last half century, one of the most prolific has been 'Intellectual History.' . . . From the beginning this specialty was closely allied to the history of literature, a fact which helped the study quickly become respectable abroad. This also tended to make it a discipline for reworking familiar ground, and hence perhaps less useful than other disciplines for discovering what is distinctive about American culture.[97]

Whatever may be its usefulness as an explanation for the history of the American spirit, intellectual history grounded in the history of literature has proved to be an extremely fruitful context for the understanding of certain Christian doctrines at certain times. And no scholar has contributed more to such understanding than Perry Miller,[98] to whose 'monumental *New England Mind*' Boorstin specifically refers.[99] It does not seem an exaggeration to state that the interpretation of the history of Protestant doctrine between the Reformation and the Enlightenment has been fundamentally recast as the result of Miller's recognition of the proper context for the study of Puritan divinity.

Puritanism had long been a puzzle both to historians of politics and to historians of Christianity.[100] Its relation to the great intellectual currents of the 17th century was difficult to chart. Like many other denominational labels, including 'Christian' itself,[101] the name 'Puritan' was originally a term of derision.[102] But it differed from many other labels because the opprobrium connoted by it was, if anything, intensified after the theological controversies had subsided, and the opprobrium affected not only the popular conception of the Puritans but also the historical interpretation. Perry Miller, writing in 1959, described the attitude that was prevalent when, more than a quarter-century earlier, he had undertaken his study: 'My contemporaries and I came of age in a time when the word "Puritan" served as a comprehensive sneer against every tendency in American civilization which we held reprehensible—sexual diffidence, censorship, prohibition, theological fundamentalism, political hypocrisy. . . . I dared not profess, even in a sentence, that I considered the intellect of Puritans worth serious examination.'[103] The prejudices of the popular mind and the conclusions of historical research thus tended to reinforce each other; and they continued to do so until Puritanism came to be reinterpreted, not in the light of the tendencies that 'we now associate with the intellectual history of the century . . . deism, skepticism, or scientific rationalism,'[104] but in the light of what Puritans believed and of how they thought.

This reinterpretation was not achieved primarily by church historians, but by intellectual historians, who put Puritan thought into its philosophical, theological, and ecclesiastical contexts. The philosophical context was provided by the new logic and rhetoric of Peter Ramus,[105] the theological context by the 'federal theology' of the covenant of grace,[106] the ecclesiastical context by Congregationalism.[107] As Miller puts it, 'There were evidently Ramists who were not federalists, and federalists who were not Congregationalists, but the secret of the New England mind is simply that New Englanders were all three at once.'[108] In the interaction between these three contexts, first in England and then in New England, the major themes of both the religious and the political thought of 17th-century Puritanism became visible. Miller freely acknowledged that some of this had been recognized by earlier scholars, notably by George Park Fisher,[109] whose *History of Christian Doctrine* had related Puritan theologians such as William Ames and John Owen to the development of Reformed theology.[110] But, Miller observes, church historians such as Fisher 'wrote in a manner so pontifical, out of a concern which I may venture to call so purely taxonomic, that their works never penetrated the awareness of historians of American civilization.'[111] And by failing to relate his interpretation of Puritan theology to the total context, even so distinguished a historical theologian as Fisher could declare quite unambiguously that 'the settlers of New England were strict Calvinists,'[112] which was an accurate but not an adequate way to describe their theological stance.

What was missing in such a designation of Puritanism was, above all, an understanding of its Ramist orientation. Historians of logic had long been aware of the diffusion of the thought of Ramus during the 17th century, but the extent of its influence was not recognized.[113] Thus the 11th edition of the *Encyclopaedia Britannica* notes that 'Ramus's works appear among the logical textbooks of the Scottish universities, and he was not without his followers in England in the 17th century.'[114] But we now know that the logic and dialectic of Ramus, both through his own books and through textbooks based upon him,[115] were a major component of Puritan education[116] as the Ramist system passed 'from Cambridge, England, to Cambridge, New England, and thence to New Haven.'[117] Here the Ramist method of analysis was applied to the subject matter of Christian theology. For example, the Puritan (and generally Protestant) insistence that the Catholic and universal Church is a reality even if it does not possess a visible structure[118] was justified on the basis of the Ramist theory of ideas, since 'the essence did not need a visible manifestation to have an existence; it was just as real if it remained a concept. . . . We define the Church by deriving the idea from our experience of the churches.'[119] Combined with the federal theology, which systematized the relation between God and man as a series of covenants, this method gave Puritan thought the 'instrument of reason'[120] it needed both for its exposition of Christian theology and for its development of political theory. It is for the latter that Puritanism is usually studied by historians; but the political theory must be viewed in the light of the theology, which must in turn be read in the context of the philosophy. As Perry Miller summarizes:

> The covenant doctrine might, therefore, be held the capital instance of the Puritans' deliberate effort to combine their piety with their intellectual concepts, to preserve the irrational force of revelation and yet to harmonize it with the propositions of reason and logic. . . . Perhaps it would not be amiss to say that though the covenant doctrine was elaborated by orthodox Puritans against Arminianism and Antinomianism, yet in their attempt to fend off these heresies the orthodox took up many ideas not so much for theological as for social and economic reasons.[121]

Miller's concluding observation suggests that another relevant context for the interpretation of history of Christian doctrine is social, political, and economic history. The juridical status of dogma meant that orthodox Christian doctrine was not only what the Church believed, taught, and confessed, but also what the State enforced under sanctions of civil law.[122] Therefore it was impossible for any historian of doctrine to ignore altogether the social and political context of orthodoxy. But during the 19th century, when the history of dogma was developing, the idealistic interpretation of history was subjected to its most severe challenge by the theories of dialectical materialism.[123] Even scholars who were not Marxists at all were compelled to give new attention to the social and economic factors in the history of ideas and to recognize that philosophical and religious doctrines have sometimes been an expression of (or even a rationalization for) positions that were determined by the class struggle.[124] The growing attention being given to Marxist scholarship by Christian theologians will almost certainly bring with it a new awareness of this context of Christian doctrine.[125] But the awareness must be supported by a greater readiness than that of either traditional Marxist theory or traditional Christian theology to consider the subtle relations between all the various factors in doctrinal history, the sort of attitude evident in this judgment by a distinguished Roman Catholic historian:

> There can, I think, be no question but that in the history of Christendom from the patristic period down to modern times, heresy and schism have derived their main impulse from sociological causes, so that a statesman who found a way to satisfy the national aspirations of the Czechs in the fifteenth century, or those of the Egyptians in the fifth, would have done more to reduce the centrifugal force of the Hussite or the monophysite movements than a theologian.... Even if the Egyptians had accepted the doctrine of Chalcedon they would have found some other ground of division so long as the sociological motive for division remained unaltered.[126]

Two works of H. Richard Niebuhr, one published in 1929,[127] and the other in 1937,[128] refined this insight into the 'nontheological factors'[129] of doctrinal history while avoiding a simplistic reduction of all dogma to a mere function of its sociological milieu. Another substantial examination of the social context of a system of doctrine is W. H. C. Frend's monograph on Donatism.[130] Frend's scholarly interest in the social context of Donatist teaching led him to undertake an investigation of the Donatists that extended beyond the literary evidence about the sect (practically all of it hostile)[131] to the archeological remains of Donatist churches and communities.[132] Examining the history of Christianity in Numidia, the principal seat of Donatism, Frend was able to identify a remarkable congruence between the several theological positions represented in the Donatist controversy and the social and political, in fact tribal and national,[133] divisions of North Africa. Compromised by its involvement in the social and economic order, Catholic Christianity was vindicating its own privileges when it defended the sanctity of its bishops and the integrity of its Sacraments; and 'practical issues prevented the Catholics from making any serious move to alleviate the prevalent social misery and oppression.'[134] If Frend's preoccupation with context has sometimes led him to an oversimplification of the relation between religion and environment,[135] he has nevertheless made it impossible for any historical theologian to treat the conflict between St. Augustine and the Donatists as an issue in pure dogmatics.[136] The social context may not explain away any of the doctrinal issues in that conflict, but it is pertinent to all of them.

The pitfalls of accounting for a doctrinal issue by an excessively facile application of the social context are well illustrated by the use of feudalism to explain St. Anselm's theory of the atonement. Here again the pervasive influence of Harnack's scholarship may be seen. John McIntyre has said that 'the most searching criticisms of St. Anselm are submitted by A. Harnack, those of the other commentators being variations of, or deductions from, what Harnack had said.'[137] One of the criticisms cited by Harnack,[138] but rejected by him in a debate with Hermann Cremer,[139] was the claim that the Anselmic idea of the death of Christ as satisfaction was derived from the Germanic concept of *wergild*,[140] the forfeit paid for the death or violation of a person under feudal law. Christ gave His life as a *wergild* in place of the punishment that humanity would otherwise have been obliged to undergo for its violation of the honor of God. Plausible as this contextual explanation of satisfaction may sound, it overlooks the more proximate context of the idea in the penitential system of the Latin Church.[141] As Fairweather has argued, 'The connection of this system with the theology of the atonement began quite early . . . so that the background of Anselm's doctrine is much more complex than the exponents of a simple "feudalist" interpretation recognize.'[142] Yet even here the historical theologian must be sure to consider the possibility that the penitential notion of satisfaction, in whose elaboration Tertullian, a lawyer,[143] played an influential role,[144] may have originally been shaped by the Roman law and then perhaps also by Teutonic law,[145] and that therefore the social and political context may, in a more subtle fashion than that suggested by Cremer, have helped to give content to the description of the death of Christ as a satisfaction offered to the injured justice of God.

But in the literature of the history of dogma the outstanding instance of the context's determining the course of the history of dogma is the idea of the Hellenization of Christianity, to which we have referred several times.[146] Although this idea is usually attributed to the work of Harnack, who was its leading interpreter,[147] it has been a recurring theme of Christian polemics since patristic days.[148] An early heresiography, *The Little Labyrinth*, probably a work of Hippolytus,[149] attributed the adoptionist heresy to the influence of Euclid and Aristotle;[150] and Nestorius charged that his Alexandrian opponents had been 'led astray by the mentality of the Greeks.'[151] But the modern appeal to the Greek context of dogma is more fundamental than these occasional aspersions; it extends not only to heresy but especially to orthodoxy, not only to this or that concept but to dogma itself. In the present discussion it is necessary only to note the immense contributions of this notion to the history of historical theology. Much of the modern debate about the adequacy of the traditional Christian doctrine of God has been provoked by the thesis that this doctrine is heavily freighted with Greek preconceptions, especially in its definition of the absoluteness and impassibility of the divine nature.[152] Another doctrine whose Hellenization and de-Hellenization has been a matter of vigorous controversy among theologians is the idea of the rational, immortal soul; here, too, the historical examination of the involved relations between Christian doctrine and its philosophical context has been instrumental in clarifying the issues as perhaps no other method would have done.[153] Few questions are more fruitful for research in the history of doctrine than the question of context.

Periodization in Historical Theology

Not only is it possible to interpret the same chapter of the history of Christian doctrine within any of several contexts, some of them more illuminating than others; it is also possible to note that in the history of theology the contexts have not always been the same. The selection of the proper context for the study of what the Church was believing, teaching, and confessing at a given point in time is determined also by the historian's presuppositions about how the history of Christian doctrine is to be divided into periods. For instance, the programmatic essay of Ernst Troeltsch on the historic significance of the Reformation, translated into English under the unfortunate title *Protestantism and Progress*,[154] based its argument upon a distinction between the religious questions characteristic of medieval culture and those that are distinctive of modern culture. By determining that Luther's question 'How do I find a God who is gracious to me?' was basically a medieval question, even though his answer to it was quite unmedieval, Troeltsch felt able to assign the beginning of the modern period of history to a later century, moving it from the Reformation to the Enlightenment.[155]

This is only one illustration of the attention given to the issue of periodization in historiography. In another disquisition on the distinctiveness of the modern period, Mandell Creighton, himself a church historian,[156] summarized the difficulties and the necessity of periodization briefly but well:

> Any division of history is doubtless arbitrary. But it is impossible for history to discharge all the obligations which, from a strictly scientific point of view, are incumbent upon it. If we accept the position that history is concerned with tracing the evolution of human affairs, we are continually being driven further back for our starting-point. . . . A pause must be made somewhere. Humanity must be seized at some period of its development, if a beginning is to be made at all. The selection of that point must be determined by some recognisable motive of convenience.[157]

When the field of historical research is the development of a single area of human thought and expression, such as the doctrines of the Christian Church, this 'recognisable motive of convenience' must, of course, be justified on the basis of the development of the field itself. The identification of 'turning points in history' is notoriously difficult. As a recent biographer of Disraeli has suggested, 'If all the historians who have used this expression are right, English history would be as full of turnings as the Hampton Court maze.'[158] The historian tends to choose his turning points on the basis of the tendencies and events that he regards as important or interesting: the division of history into periods is determined by what seem to have been the stages in the evolution of these tendencies.

Thus the question of context and the question of periodization are intimately related. If the institutional history of the Church in its relation to the social and political order is thought to be the context that has determined the growth of Christian doctrine, one may divide the material of doctrinal history on that basis. In some instances, such a criterion of periodization will prove to be quite applicable. It has even been argued by Eduard Schwartz, who is also the author of an outstanding study of Constantine,[159] that the trinitarianism of St. Athanasius must be connected with the political and economic history of the 4th century rather than with the development of dogma.[160] Schwartz contended, against church historians and historians of dogma such as Harnack, that only the total culture of an age provided a proper context for the study of the life and teaching of the Church in that age, and that decisions about such questions as periodization had to be based upon this context. In the period of theological history with which Schwartz was dealing, this thesis can be supported with convincing evidence. The conversion of Constantine and the Council of Nicea do serve as a 'turning point' not only for the history of doctrine and the history of the institutional Church but for the history of the Roman Empire as well. For the empire, this sequence of events meant the end of the principle of 'Roma Aeterna: the apotheosis of power,'[161] if not also 'the triumph of barbarism and of religion.'[162] For the Church as an institution, it meant the formation of an alliance with the government upon which the administration of Christendom was to depend for more than a millennium. And for the development of doctrine, it meant the official adoption of a creed by a council, the establishment of dogma as legislated doctrine, with all the mighty consequences of this step for the future of Christian faith and thought.

The congruence of imperial, ecclesiastical, and dogmatic history is not always so tidy. It is not as easy, for instance, to arrange the history of doctrine in the Middle Ages on the basis of such a congruence. Perhaps one can make a case for this arrangement in the interpretation of the theology of the 9th century, which is sometimes even called 'Carolingian theology.'[163] It is certainly remarkable that around the middle of the 9th century all the following theologians were on the scene in the territories that had been ruled by Charlemagne: Rabanus Maurus, Ratramnus, St. Paschasius Radbertus, Gottschalk, Johannes Scotus Erigena, Hincmar of Reims, Walafrid Strabo, Servatus Lupus, and Prudentius of Troyes.[164] By creating a political and cultural ambience within which such intellectual activity could flourish, Charlemagne may well deserve to have a period in this history of theology named for him. But no other medieval monarch, secular or ecclesiastical, seems worthy of such a distinction. For the designation of the 13th century as a chapter in theological history, scholars would probably turn neither to Innocent III[165] nor to Frederick II,[166] noteworthy though both of them were also for the history of doctrine, but to Aristotle. Whatever may be an adequate definition of the term 'Scholastic,'[167] it has become the label both for a distinctive genre of theology and for the way of philosophizing associated with it. So decisive is the position of Aristotle in the intellectual history of the time, both philosophical and theological, that Étienne Gilson could clarify the thought of both Dante and St. Thomas by comparing their attitudes toward the authority of Aristotle,[168] and even elucidate the puzzling exegesis of *Paradiso* 10:133-138.[169] Not only historians of philosophy and theology but students of Dante as well have found this convincing.[170] Too rigid an application of the category 'Scholastic' to this period could deprive it of such illumination, but the category has proved useful as a major division in the history of theology.

The concentration of historical theology on history of dogma has affected not only the choice of subject matter but also the periodization of the history. The official promulgation of a dogma, as at Nicea or Chalcedon or Trent, provides a convenient fulcrum. With this as a point that is fixed chronologically and perhaps even theologically, one can arrange the earlier and the later history of the doctrine in the categories shaped by the conciliar decree. For all the dangers in this method,[171] it does seem to provide a sensible answer to the question of periodization. If, for example, the christological definition of the Council of Chalcedon is taken as such a watershed, it becomes convenient—in fact, as the literature shows, all too convenient[172]—to read back from it into the theological development of the preceding centuries, relating some formulas to Alexandrian teaching,[173] some formulas to the Antiochene tradition,[174] and the central emphasis of the definition through the *Tome* of Pope St. Leo I to St. Ambrose and the Latins.[175] The subsequent development of the doctrine of the person of Christ can then be viewed also in relation to Chalcedon.

The christological defenses of the icons of St. John of Damascus and by St. Theodore of Studios[176] can be interpreted as the application of a Chalcedonian dialectic to the definition of the image. Much of the christological controversy between Lutheran and Reformed theologians during the 16th and 17th centuries concentrated on the conflicting claims to represent Chalcedonian orthodoxy,[177] while the rise of modern critical research into the life of Jesus has been characterized as an effort to shake off the 'grave-clothes' of Chalcedon.[178]

Determining the periods of the history of doctrine on the

basis of dogmatic decisions becomes less satisfactory if one undertakes to study more than one doctrine. This scheme of periodization could lead back to the method of treating the material doctrine by doctrine, for the 'definitive' formulation of one dogma (if there has been one at all) may bear very little relation to the state of another doctrine in the same period or even in the same system of doctrine. The trinitarian doctrine of St. Augustine must be seen in the light of 'the Catholic faith'[179] confessed by the Council of Nicea and its 'Catholic exponents.'[180] But as he himself learned in the course of the Pelagian controversy, his anthropological doctrine could not so easily establish its legitimate parentage.[181] Even after the Augustinian doctrine had been more or less officially sanctioned, the differences between East and West on the doctrine of original sin remained so fundamental that it would be a gross distortion of the history of this doctrine to use the condemnation of Pelagianism at the Council of Ephesus in 431[182] or the dogmatic formulas of the Synod of Orange in 529[183] as the basis for periodization. And it would, of course, be impossible to apply this criterion to the history of those articles of faith, such as the atonement, whose status as doctrines of the Church has not been fixed by what the Church confessed at a particular date in some synod or controversy but must be traced through the development of what was believed and taught liturgically, homiletically, and catechetically. The periods in the history of the doctrine of the work of Christ are, consequently, less obvious than those in the history of the doctrine of the person of Christ. When Robert S. Franks undertook to write *A History of the Doctrine of the Work of Christ in Its Ecclesiastical Development*,[184] he let the four major parts of his two-volume work be determined by more general categories of period—patristic, medieval, 'old Protestant' (the Reformation and the 17th century), and 'modern Protestant' (since the Enlightenment)—but arranged his chapters and subdivisions according to the theologians and theological schools that had contributed something to the discussion of the atonement.

It has become customary for historians and theologians to cite the handling of the question of periodization as one of the chief inadequacies in the *Magdeburg Centuries*.[185] Employing the subdivisions itemized earlier,[186] the *Centuries* arranged the history of the Church according to units of 100 years each. They have been criticized—for example, by Schleiermacher[187]—for arbitrarily superimposing a meaningless and unnatural unit, the century, upon the historical material. They should instead have examined the data of church history to determine where the natural divisions into periods ought to fall. In a spirited defense of the *Centuries*, Karl Heussi, who had previously devoted a monograph to the historiography of Mosheim,[188] replied to such criticisms that periodization in the modern sense of the word had not been the aim of the Centuriators at all. Their fundamental purpose was a polemical one, and in the service of this they assembled a vast amount of historical detail to prove that the true doctrine had deteriorated under the papacy. Only to the extent that this purpose determined the selection of facts can the *Centuries* be said to possess an overall pattern. But since this pattern is not, in the modern sense of the word, a historical one, but a theological one, there are no historical periods; for 'the whole work is in fact an unusually comprehensive storehouse of polemical material, arranged for greater convenience into fixed chronological and topical schemata.'[189] The presuppositions for periodization simply did not exist.

One of those who criticized the *Centuries* on this score was Baur,[190] who also gave thoughtful consideration to the problem of periodization. His monograph of 1838 on the history of the doctrine of reconciliation divided that history into three periods: from the beginnings to the Reformation, from the Reformation to Kant, since Kant (who had died 30 years earlier, in 1804).[191] The first was the period of 'unmediated objectivity'; the second, the period of 'transition from the standpoint of unmediated objectivity to subjectivity'; the third, the period of 'objectivity mediated through subjectivity.' When he took up the history of the doctrines of the Trinity and the Incarnation in 1841–43, Baur soon recognized the lopsidedness of a distribution of material that could lump 15 centuries of patristic and Scholastic theology into a single period while identifying the thought of one generation of Protestant philosophical theology as a period unto itself. Employing the same principle of division on the basis of the antithesis between objectivity and subjectivity, Baur saw the development from the beginnings to Chalcedon as the first period, that from Chalcedon to the Reformation as the second, and that since the Reformation as the third.[192] And when he went beyond the doctrines of reconciliation, Trinity, and Incarnation to a comprehensive history of dogma (in lectures, not in a book written by himself[193]), he kept this latter division but moved the terminus of the first period from 451 to 590–604, the pontificate of St. Gregory I.[194] This evolution of his outline of the history of dogma suggests that Baur came to his ideas of periodization through the same combination of Hegelian speculation and scholarly research that was, as previously noted, characteristic of his entire work as a historical theologian.

In keeping with the definition of Christian doctrine presented earlier, the following arrangement of the material of the history of doctrine seeks to take account both of the processes of change as these have been discussed and of the several contexts of historical theology. Five major divisions are here proposed:

1. The Emergence of the Catholic Tradition (100-600).
2. The Spirit of Eastern Christendom (600–1700).
3. The Growth of Medieval Theology (600-1300).
4. Reformation of Church and Dogma (1300–1700).
5. Christian Doctrine and Modern Culture (since 1700).

Within each of these periods the institutional history of the Church must be kept in mind, not on its own account, but for its bearing upon the history of doctrine. The dogmatic definitions of doctrine by one or another agency of the institutional Church will naturally be prominent; but because Christian doctrine is defined as what is believed, taught, and confessed, not merely as what is confessed, the definitions cannot automatically be taken as 'turning points.' The outline assumes that the division between the West and the various parts of the East has been as decisive for the doctrinal history of the Church as for its institutional history. Therefore the period during which East and West more or less shared the development is taken as a unit; here the cardinal dogmas of orthodox Christianity were defined, the principal forms of liturgical doctrine were developed, and the dominant methods of biblical exegesis were established. The second part carries the history of doctrine in Eastern Christianity through its Byzantine and Syriac expressions to its domestication in Russian culture and its codification in the 17th century (even though such a term as codification is only loosely applicable to Eastern Orthodoxy). The Western development during the same period seems to demand a major line of demarcation at the point of the Reformation, but treating the Reformation as the beginning of modern Christian doctrine seems less and less justified in the light of recent research both into the Reformation and into the period since the Enlightenment. Hence the age of the Reformation is taken to include the late medieval developments that shaped it and the 17th-century history, both Protestant and Roman Catholic, that was shaped by it. Finally, the period from 1700 to the present may be interpreted as the time when both East and West defended or interpreted or reinterpreted Christian doctrine in relation to a new culture.

Each of these judgments involves a host of assumptions both about Christian doctrine and about its history. Some of these assumptions have been developed in this study, but others can be articulated only in the detailed exposition of the history of doctrine itself. One assumption about the historiography of doctrine does require to be made explicit now: that the interrelations between one Christian doctrine and another, as well as the interrelations between one period of doctrinal history and another, make the attempt to encompass the history of doctrine in what must probably be called a 'panoramic' view as imperative as it is audacious.

This assumption is supported by a distinguished Byzantinist and medievalist whose contributions to ecclesiastical and doctrinal history have been notable:

> A single author cannot speak with the high authority of a panel of experts, but he may succeed in giving to his work an integrated and even an epical quality that no composite volume can achieve. Homer as well as Herodotus was a Father of History, as Gibbon, the greatest of our historians, was aware; and it is difficult, in spite of certain critics, to believe that Homer was a panel. History-writing to-day has passed into an Alexandrian age, where criticism has overpowered creation. Faced by the mountainous heap of the minutiae of knowledge and awed by the watchful severity of his colleagues, the modern historian too often takes refuge in learned articles or narrowly specialized dissertations, small fortresses that are easy to defend from attack. His work can be of the highest value; but it is not an end in itself. I believe that the supreme duty of the historian is to write history, that is to say, to attempt to record in one sweeping sequence the greater events and movements that have swayed the destinies of man. The writer rash enough to make the attempt should not be

criticized for his ambition, however much he may deserve censure for the inadequacy of his equipment or the inanity of his results.[195]

Although these sage comments were intended as a defense for undertaking a history of the Crusades, they are equally applicable to the history of Christian doctrine.

CHAPTER FIVE

Historical Theology as a Theological Discipline

The primary requirement of historical theology is that it be good history. For too long a time, historical research associated with 'sacred' matters was able to claim a privileged status as a way of avoiding the harsh demands of critical scholarship. In Harnack's words, 'The historian above all else has to deal with the establishing of the facts. It is his sacred duty to ascertain the truth of the facts. Pity the historian who takes this problem lightly, or who falsifies it! There is in his case no excuse: he is a traitor to his sacred call.'[1] From Harnack's biography it is clear that, although he felt deeply every snub administered by the official bodies of the church, which excluded him from the sort of responsible involvement in church and ministry to which he aspired,[2] the unkindest cuts of all were those that came from some of his fellow historians, who accused him of allowing his theological preconceptions to affect his historical judgments.[3] In his preface to the English translation of his *History of Dogma*, dated May 1, 1894, he therefore declared:

> In taking up a theological book we are in the habit of enquiring first of all as to the 'stand-point' of the Author. In a historical work there is no room for such enquiry. The question here is, whether the Author is in sympathy with the subject about which he writes, whether he can distinguish original elements from those that are derived, whether he has a thorough acquaintance with his material, whether he is con-

scious of the limits of historical knowledge, and whether he is truthful. These requirements constitute the categorical imperative for the historian.[4]

From what has been said already it will be evident that, with some severe modifications, the definition here given of the task of historical theology as chiefly a historical discipline is in agreement with Harnack's.

This does not mean, however, that it cannot also be a theological discipline; in fact, the more faithful it is to its historical vocation, the more useful it will be in its theological function. Although the method of historical theology and the criteria for judging its results are fundamentally historical, its usual locus is within the theological enterprise. Here it was that historical theology arose as a field of inquiry and instruction;[5] and despite the interest in the subject among 'secular' historians[6] and the contributions being made to it by the researches of intellectual historians,[7] it is in the course of the study of theology that scholars usually become acquainted with the history of Christian doctrine, and it is to other theologians that they usually address the results of their work. Surveys of theological education indicate that historical theology has established itself as a standard course in the seminary curriculum of widely divergent denominational traditions.[8] Its relation to church history varies considerably; sometimes it is taught as part of church history, while at other times church history is made prerequisite to it. Historical theology does not occupy an equally well-established place in Roman Catholic theological education, but the enrichment of offerings in this field is part of many proposals for the revision of the seminary curriculum.[9]

Even in Protestant theological education, however, historical theology is a recent arrival. By the time it had become an accepted partner in the community of theological scholarship, the other partners had long since been assigned their roles. Although church history was a later addition to the curriculum than Scripture and dogmatic theology, it tended to include the history of doctrine as part of its responsibility. The older fields were even less open to influence from historical theology. The resistance of systematic theologians to the work of men like Semler[10] was based on the recognition that the task of a dogmatics, whether orthodox or rationalistic, would be gravely complicated by the adoption of a historical approach to the meaning of dogma. Proponents of a more radically biblical theology, on the other hand, frequently seemed reluctant to assign any positive function to historical theology, for they were aiming their program at the elimination of those elements of the authority of dogmatic tradition that had been retained by the Reformation. The history of dogma, then, could have only a negative role. As Elert has put it, 'The principle of scriptural authority of biblicism does indeed draw a final boundary against phenomenalism and relativism, but in its evaluation of ecclesiastical dogma it is in agreement with them.'[11] Where does the history of doctrine fit into theological scholarship?

The usual answer has been to designate it an 'auxiliary science.'[12] This designation need not be quite as patronizing as it appears. The study of the Bible and the summary of Christian doctrine (which has included moral teaching during most of its history) would appear to be indispensable components of any Christian theology, regardless of its cultural setting. Elements of both may be discerned already in the New Testament. The Christian adaptation of the Old Testament to the purposes of the gospel is attributed to the teachings of Jesus Himself: 'Today this scripture has been fulfilled in your hearing' (Luke 4.21). The risen Christ is identified in the Emmaus pericope as the source for a messianic interpretation of 'Moses and all the prophets' (Luke 24.27). It may be an anachronism to speak of a 'catechism of primitive Christianity,' as Alfred Seeberg did already in 1903.[13] But New Testament research since that time has confirmed the presence, behind the New Testament, of forms of Christian instruction directed both at potential converts and at believers. By the time the Pastoral Epistles were written—their date and authorship are a subject of controversy, at least partly for this reason[14]—the content of Christian teaching had been standardized in sufficient detail to warrant speaking of it as a 'deposit' (1 Tim 6.20; 2 Tim 1.12,14), perhaps in the legal sense of that word.[15] It does not seem to be an anachronism, therefore, to find a continuity for both exegetical and dogmatic theology somewhere in the New Testament. However, there is no similar continuity between the historiography of the Acts of the Apostles and later church histories.[16] As Hugh Jackson Lawlor says, 'Eusebius of Caesarea was the first writer to conceive the idea of presenting to the world a history of the Christian Church as a unit standing by itself.'[17] Even the *Ecclesiastical History* of Eusebius could be called an 'auxiliary discipline' in relation to his dogmatic writings and especially his vast exegetical output, for its primary purpose was apologetic.[18] Perhaps it could be said that the history of doctrine does not belong to the *esse*, but to the *bene esse*, of theology.

Historical Research and Biblical Study

The relation between historical theology and biblical study would, at first glance, appear to be relatively easy to determine for both Roman Catholic and Protestant thought. If the sources of divine revelation are to be sought simultaneously in Scripture and in tradition or 'traditions,'[19] it would seem to be the task of historical theology to show how postbiblical traditions gradually make clear what is unclear in the Bible. The norm for this assignment will then be set by the teachings that the development of doctrine and, eventually, its official voice declare to be binding upon all believers. Ultimately, of course, the criteria for such research are not determined by historical scholarship, but by theological commitment. Thus the post-Tridentine view of the relation between the Bible and postbiblical development went beyond purely historical judgments, as has been pointed out in the case of St. Robert Bellarmine:

> The positive theologian . . . is not an historian in the proper sense of the word. He has little interest in the individual historical manifestations of Christian teaching. He strives after something which is above all that is merely temporal and contingent in the historical development of Christian doctrine. He seeks to arrive at the eternally true content of the formulae of faith. There is then a decided difference between a proof from tradition and a purely historical proof.[20]

With so clear-cut a theological a priori in hand, the historical theology determined by the theory that both the Bible and the traditions of the Church are bearers of revelation seems prepared to decide quite easily what is authentic in the history of those traditions and what is not.

The Protestant alternative to this theory of history was, however, no less dominated by a theological a priori. In principle, it might seem that the idea of *sola Scriptura*, when applied to the relation between historical theology and biblical study, would liberate each of these disciplines from the obligation to conform itself to the other. Historical theology could then trace the fluctuations of church doctrine as it vacillated in its fidelity to the biblical message, while the study of that message could proceed in accordance with its own canons, untrammeled by what had happened after the close of the New Testament. In fact, no such liberation took place either for biblical study or for historical theology. The achievements of the *Magdeburg Centuries* in uncovering long-neglected chapters of historical theology are substantial.[21] Yet the fundamental aim and ultimate outcome of their research was not historical, and the description of St. Bellarmine's historical scholarship just quoted from E. A. Ryan could as well have been spoken of the *Centuries* or of his redoubtable opponent, Martin Chemnitz.[22] Acknowledging that there were several senses in which the word 'tradition' could be used legitimately in theology, Chemnitz nevertheless rejected the notion of an independent source of revelation apart from Scripture.[23] To cite the most delicate point, Chemnitz was therefore obliged, in his critique of the Council of Trent[24] but even more in his dogmatic lectures based upon Melanchthon[25] and in his treatise on christology,[26] to expound the dogma of the Trinity as an explicitly biblical doctrine rather than as the result of controversy and of the reflection of the Church upon the data of the biblical message. Either the history of Christian doctrine after the New Testament faithfully reflected what was already explicit in that message or it represented an apostasy from it.

If the relations between historical theology and biblical study are themselves examined historically, the patterns that emerge differ from both these theories. When the authoritative role of tradition as the interpreter of Scripture has been articulated without critical historical scholarship, the 'decided difference between a proof from tradition and a purely historical proof'[27] may easily become a pretext for determining the answer to 'purely historical' questions on other than historical grounds. Among such questions most critical scholars would include the authorship of books of the Bible.[28] The Mosaic authorship of the Pentateuch is defended by conservative Protestant theologians on the basis of such sayings of Jesus as Luke 16.31, the contention being that, as the incarnate Son of God, He could not have erred in ascribing the Pentateuch to Moses.[29] It was defended by the Pontifical Biblical Commission, under the date of June 27, 1906, on the basis of 'many testimonies taken together from both Testaments, the perpetual consensus of the Jewish people, also the constant tradition of the Church,' to which was added 'internal evidence that is drawn from the text itself.'[30] Where the consensus of tradition was by no means so unanimous, as in the question of the Pauline authorship of the Epistle to the Hebrews,[31] there it was the canon of the New Testament, defined at the fourth session of the Council of Trent,[32] that nevertheless provided the Commission with the authorization to dismiss objections that had been raised on literary and historical grounds.[33] These isagogical matters were not to be decided by the methods and canons of historical study. By distinguishing between those 'few things [in Sacred Scripture] whose meaning has been declared by the Church' and all the 'many things [that] remain' to be dealt with by means of literary, archeological, and historical research, the encyclical *Divino afflante Spiritu* of Sept. 30, 1943, attempted to clarify the respective roles of authority and scholarship in biblical study.[34]

More directly relevant to the work of the history of doctrine was another controversy in the area of biblical study, the dispute over the authenticity of the 'Johannine comma,' the words interpolated in 1 Jn 5.7.[35] On purely textual grounds the added words are indefensible.[36] Finding no evidence for them in his Greek manuscripts, Erasmus eliminated them from his edition of the Greek New Testament in 1516;[37] but the interpolation had been printed in the Complutensian Polyglot of 1514,[38] and Erasmus inserted it into his edition of 1522 when one Greek manuscript (apparently written at Oxford about 1520)[39] was produced containing the passage. Because the Vulgate was thought to contain the dubious passage,[40] defense of the authenticity of the Vulgate, based upon the decree at Trent,[41] was taken to imply a vindication of the Johannine comma. But it was also the unambiguous affirmation of orthodox trinitarianism in it that made the interpolation important for theological reasons. One of the most widely accepted conclusions of 19th-century history of dogma was the thesis that the dogma of the Trinity was not an explicit doctrine of the New Testament, still less of the Old Testament,[42] but had evolved from New Testament times to the 4th century. This conclusion reinforced the textual evidence that the Johannine comma was spurious, for the words 'and these three are one' seem anachronistic when viewed in the light of the development of the doctrine of the Trinity. Yet conservative Protestant theologians simultaneously affirmed its authenticity and denied that the dogma of the Trinity had evolved at all;[43] and the Holy Office, on Jan. 13, 1897, forbade Roman Catholics to question the passage.[44] Within both Protestantism[45] and Roman Catholicism,[46] this defense of the Johannine comma has since yielded to the evidence of the manuscripts, with which there has really been no arguing all along; but it seems likely that this evidence has finally been permitted to speak for itself because there has also come a gradual acceptance of the results of the history of doctrine. The interpolation may now be recognized as probably an allegorical trinitarian expansion upon the text, one that suggested itself to a reader contemporary with the controversies over the dogma of the Trinity. Thus a textual variant such as the Johannine comma becomes a datum for historical theology.[47]

Another function that historical research can perform for biblical study is to subject the traditional exegetical foundation for certain dogmas to critical examination. When the demand is voiced that biblical scholarship conform itself to a dogma that itself claims to rest upon biblical study,[48] this is either an argument in a circle or an acceptance of the principle that even a hallowed conclusion of interpretation is reformable in the light of new knowledge about the meaning of the biblical text. Such reconsideration does not automatically annul the dogma, which almost never depended for its validity upon a single exegesis of a single passage.[49] It could even be argued that—in theory, if not always in practice—the Roman Catholic concept of an authoritative ecclesiastical magisterium with the power to promulgate dogma sets the biblical scholar free to determine the meaning of any particular text on the basis of sound scholarship, while the Protestant view of *sola Scriptura* makes the consequences of such scholarship dogmatically far more devastating.[50] When the study of the Bible no longer has the responsibility of proving that the dogmas of the Church are simply tantamount to the message of Scripture, historical theology can examine the scriptural proof of the Church Fathers with a view toward determining which were the principal passages upon which they hung their argument. If the exegesis at work in such a proof requires further study, this is a task for the biblical scholar; but his historical colleague does his job by pointing this out.

There are many illustrations of this in the history of the relations between dogma and exegesis. One case, involving both the problem of exegesis and the problem of translation, is the traditional Western interpretation of the closing words of Rom. 5.12, which the Latin Bible took to mean: '. . . in whom all have sinned.'[51] Not only is this the translation given in the Vulgate, but it seems to have been the translation familiar to St. Augustine.[52] In the context of the whole verse, 'in whom' could then be taken to refer to the opening words: 'Therefore as sin came into the world through one man and death through sin. . . .' And so the verse would mean that sin had come into the world through one man, Adam, in whom all men had sinned. So, it seems, St. Augustine read the verse, and he counted it of sufficient importance for his doctrine of original sin to make its omission from the argument of his opponent a key point in his rebuttal: 'In quoting these words of mine, he took care to omit the testimony of the Apostle which I adduced, by the weighty significance of which he felt himself too hard pressed. For, after saying that men at their birth contract original sin, I at once introduced the Apostle's words: "By one man sin entered into the world, and death by sin; and so death passed upon all men, *for in him all men sinned.*" '[53] He even sought to use his knowledge of Greek[54] to prove that the phrase 'in whom' could only refer to Adam and that 'all men are understood to have sinned in the first "man," because all men were in him when he sinned.'[55]

In support of this exegesis St. Augustine cited the authority of 'the sainted Hilary,' who took this verse to mean that 'all have sinned in Adam, as it were in the mass; for he himself was corrupted by sin, and all whom he begot were born under sin.'[56] St. Cyprian, who was his proof that the doctrine of original sin was not an innovation,[57] does not seem, at least in his extant writings, to have interpreted the 'in whom' of Rom 5.12 this way.[58] Nor, for that matter, do many other Church Fathers seem to have done so. St. Ambrose can be quoted in favor of such an interpretation, as his words 'In Adam I fell, in Adam I was cast out of Paradise, in Adam I died' seem to suggest.[59] When one turns from the Latin Fathers to the Greek, the patristic consensus that St. Augustine was so eager to obtain does not substantiate his interpretation; for 'in whom' is a mistranslation of a Greek phrase that simply means 'because' (RSV) or more archaically 'for that' (AV). It was the teaching of the Greek Fathers no less than of the Latin that sin had entered the world through Adam, as the first part of Rom 5.12 states; but men made this sin of Adam their own by voluntarily identifying themselves with him in their sin, 'because all have sinned,' as the second part of Rom 5.12 states.[60] It would therefore be a misreading not only of the words of the Apostle but also of the writings of the Fathers if tradition were invoked as an authority to require of the exegete that he take these words to refer to the Augustinian theory that all men have sinned in Adam. This would certainly have implications for the theological reconsideration of the dogma of original sin,[62] but by discovering the heterogencity of the patristic exegesis of this verse—not to mention the inaccuracy of the Latin translation of it—historical theology contributes also to the work of the biblical scholar.

That contribution is not, however, merely the negative one of clearing the way for the biblical scholar to do his own work. Historical theology has no less a responsibility to investigate the history of exegesis in such a way that contemporary study of the Bible may be enlightened by it. The record of tradition's having been used as an obstacle to biblical scholarship should not be permitted to obscure this positive role. As historical research, by showing that the exegetical tradition is by no means as homogeneous as it may seem, refutes the claims of hegemony for any one interpretation, so it may also liberate the biblical scholar from the exegetical fashions of the moment by giving him a perspective on the text that seems new because it is very old. Premature commitment to one method of interpretation—for example, to word study[62] or to the prebiblical and nonbiblical analogies for biblical ideas[63]—may easily cause him to exclude from consideration other hermeneutical systems that are more congenial to the text than his own. The insistence of the Protestant Reformers on the literal interpretation of the stories of creation and the fall, although it was defended both as the requirement of the best scholarship of their time and as the only way to be faithful to the meaning of the biblical narratives, actually helped to alienate Protestant theology from the development of modern science and also did an injustice to the literary form of the Book of Genesis.[64] Similarly, Luther's polemical rejection of the eucharistic interpretation of chapter 6 of the Gospel of John[65] deprived him and those who followed him of the illumination that the exegetical tradition could have brought to this profound and difficult chapter. There is still much value, not only for the historian of theology but also for the modern exegete, in those biblical commentaries—outstanding among such are the works of Joseph Lightfoot on *Galatians* (1865), *Philippians* (1868), and *Colossians with Philemon* (1875)[66]—in which close study of the text is combined with detailed attention to its patristic interpreters.

Even the exegesis of the most familiar and the most carefully analyzed passages of the Bible can sometimes be deepened by a study of the exegetical tradition. One such passage is the prologue to the Gospel of John. As noted earlier, its doctrine of the pre-existent Christ as Logos has been a prominent element in the historiography of the dogma of the Trinity.[67] Two chapters in the earlier history of the Logos doctrine have aroused special interest for their possible bearing on the development of the trinitarian formulas of the Church.[68] As apparently the most explicit warrant in the New Testament for cosmological speculation about the pre-existent Christ, the Johannine idea has been compared with the Greek conceptions of the Logos, going back at least to Heraclitus.[69] Another line of inquiry, not necessarily opposed to the first, has concentrated on the affinities and differences between St. John and Philo of Alexandria in their views of the nature of the Logos.[70] Although some advocates of one or another theory of derivation have made exclusive claims, most scholars have been willing to acknowledge that in the New Testament's use of the title Logos—and even more in the subsequent development of the term—there are echoes of many different religious and philosophical traditions.

One tradition had received less consideration in the debates of the 19th century than it deserved: the personification of Wisdom in the Old Testament and in postbiblical Jewish literature.[71] Bringing this tradition into prominence as a possible source for the Logos doctrine was an achievement of J. Rendel Harris, a New Testament scholar of 'unconventional and speculative mind, and immense, if at times somewhat unbalanced, erudition.'[72] In 1917 Harris published his study of Jn 1.1–14.[73] Here he contended that Logos in the prologue represented a substitution for the earlier Sophia, which, as a feminine noun, did not seem an appropriate title to attach to Jesus. In chapter 8 of the Book of Proverbs a personified Wisdom had spoken as the consort of the Creator in the formation of the world and as the revealer of His will to men.[74] These are the works assigned in the prologue of St. John to the Logos, who enlightens every man that comes into the world and who was the agent through whom all things were made. In the beginning was Wisdom, and Wisdom was with God. By attaching his doctrine of the Incarnation to this personification, the Evangelist was writing a Christian gloss[75] upon chapter 8 of Proverbs, which was, in turn, a gloss of sorts upon chapter 1 of Genesis.[76] Harris did not win universal acceptance for all the details of his thesis,[77] but it has become a commonplace of New Testament scholarship that 'the title Logos does not come from the Greek philosophical (specifically Stoic) tradition, which is supposed to have been transmitted to the Evangelist through Philo of Alexandria. . . . In the Old Testament and Jewish literature there appears the figure of "Wisdom," which is a parallel to the "Word." '[78]

This parallel between the Wisdom of the Book of Proverbs and the Logos of the Gospel of John was, in turn, a commonplace of patristic exegesis. Many, perhaps most,[79] of Harnack's references to Christ as Wisdom in his *History of Dogma* are citations of heretical literature;[80] and such a Gnostic text as the Pistis Sophia, on which Harnack wrote a monograph in 1891,[81] illustrates the prominence of speculations about a personified Sophia in Gnostic thought. But Harnack does not give similar attention to the importance of this personified Sophia[82] in the development of orthodox trinitarianism. According to him, the eighth chapter of Proverbs is one of 'the passages quoted so often by the Arians,'[83] but he gives the impression that it did not figure as prominently in St. Athanasius. Yet an examination of the *Orations against the Arians* would show not only that this chapter occupied more space in Athanasius' discussion than any other from either the Old Testament or the New,[84] but also that St. Athanasius used the passage chiefly as a positive source for orthodox doctrine and not merely as an issue with heretical doctrine.[85] As Georg Kretschmar has put it:

> From the very outset Wisdom was a cosmic reality; and when the ecclesiological significance of Sophia receded, its application to the creation remained and even received a new emphasis. Thus the co-ordination of creation and redemption finds an echo now in the co-ordination of Wisdom and Logos. . . . In this way Sophia ultimately becomes the heavenly archetype not of the Church, but of Christ. This is the sense in which Justin and the Alexandrians employ Proverbs 8 as scriptural proof. Word and Wisdom apply to Jesus of Nazareth in equal measure.[86]

Except perhaps for St. Justin[87] and Origen,[88] few of the Church Fathers were acquainted at first hand with the rabbinic interpretations of Proverbs 8, but modern study of these interpretations has at this point reinforced the patristic use of this chapter to help explain the prologue to the Gospel of John.

The history of exegesis has also developed into a field (or subfield), and it deserves to be studied for its own sake.[89] The interrelations between the four senses of Scripture[90] belong not only to the development of Christian hermeneutics but also to the general history of literature.[91] But it is no less essential that the history of doctrine be attentive to the history of biblical interpretation. It was as interpreters of the Bible that most great theologians wanted to be known,[92] and therefore it is in relation to their exegesis that their theology must be studied. Both Roman Catholics and Protestants have commented on the hiatus between modern biblical scholarship and modern systematic theology: Protestant systematicians seem to be operating with a different conception of authority and with a canon within the canon, so that the elements of primitive Catholicism discerned within the New Testament by Protestant biblical scholars do not become part of Protestant dogmatics.[93] The hiatus within Roman Catholic scholarship may be less obvious, but it is no less significant.[94] In part, this loss of connection has been brought on by the failure of historians of doctrine to give attention to the history of exegesis. If it were accurate to say that even the orthodox dogmas of the Trinity and the person of Christ developed primarily as a result of philosophical speculation within a context determined by the secular thought of the ancient world, then modern theology would seem to be justified when it proceeds on the same basis. To occupy a responsible place as a proper theological discipline, historical theology must build bridges to biblical theology by studying the history of the theological interpretation of Scripture.

History—Doctrinal and Ecclesiastical

In a letter quoted earlier[95] Adolf Harnack asserted that scholars like himself had the obligation to prepare commentaries on books of the New Testament. But as that very quotation indicates, Harnack thought of himself first of all as a church historian. The chairs he occupied at Giessen, Marburg, and Berlin were all designated as professorships of church history. It was with other historians, rather than with biblical scholars or systematic theologians, that Harnack found himself communicating—with other church historians, but also with 'secular' historians, such as Theodor Mommsen.[96] Mommsen and Harnack found a common bond both in their investigations of late antiquity[97] and, even more, in their devotion to historical scholarship; for, as Harnack's daughter and biographer puts it, 'In Harnack Mommsen experienced theology as a science—a combination, as he himself confessed in drastic language, that he had never experienced before.'[98] During the quarter-century after Mommsen's death in 1903, Harnack was in many ways alienated even further from the theologians—above all, of course, from his former student Karl Barth—and he came to identify his work as a historical theologian increasingly with that of other historians.

Whatever may have been the personal reasons that were responsible for this identification in Harnack's case, the connections between history of doctrine and ecclesiastical history are such that even those historians of dogma whose main interest has been dogmatic have been obliged to justify the enterprise on historical rather than theological grounds.[99] At the same time, church historians (and even scholars in church history whose own field has been broader in its context than the history of the Church) have nevertheless found in the history of doctrine an unavoidable subject for investigation.[100] There is no clear and simple formula for the division of labor between the church historian and the historical theologian.[101] Here again the achievements and failures of scholarship may serve as the basis for a more general discussion of the contribution that the history of doctrine may make to the study of the history of the Church. The following discussion concentrates on the work of 20th-century scholars, even though earlier generations of historical theologians have been no less productive in their influence upon those colleagues who have dealt 'merely' with church history.

One of the most effective results of the scholarship of certain historical theologians has been the restoration of justice to certain figures in the history of the Church who have been slandered both by their own contemporaries and by later generations of Christians, including later generations of theologians and church historians. The slogan of Philipp Konrad Marheineke, that over the doctrinal controversies of the past there should rest 'the peace of history,'[102] has thus been fulfilled, although not in the sense he had in mind. At least since Gottfried Arnold,[103] the radical revisionists in church history have been questioning the justice of the the conventional verdicts upon the teachers and teachings of the past. The valid correctives that they have provided are, however, vitiated by a relativism for which there is finally no genuine heresy. As Walter Nigg has suggested, this quick and easy way of disposing of the problem of heresy has many affinities to the very orthodoxy it spurns;[104] but the mystery of heresy is far too profound to bear such summary treatment. Neither the automatic repetition of the anathemas nor the automatic nullification of the anathemas, but the careful reexamination of the documents is what is called for. The historian must be aware of the disadvantages imposed upon him by his separation from the controversy, and he must not suppose that his historical method will automatically enable him to overcome that disadvantage.[105] Nevertheless, he can sometimes succeed in setting the record straight.

The fundamental reconsideration of the theology and spirituality of Origen that has taken place in the scholarship of the 20th century[106] has affected the interpretation not only of the history of doctrine in the ante-Nicene period but of other aspects of church history as well. Now that the ascetic thought of Origen has been explored in depth through the work of scholars such as Völker,[107] the roots of Christian monasticism can be traced with somewhat greater confidence. The controverted issue of the relation between mysticism and the gospel, which includes the definition or redefinition of mysticism in a Christian setting,[108] has been placed in a new light by the realization that it is 'to Origen that we must ascribe at least the remote beginnings of St. John of the Cross's spirituality of the desert, St. Bernard's analogy between mysticism and marriage, St. Bonaventure's devotion to the humanity of Christ and Tauler's devotion to the eternal Word.'[109] Above all, however, the new research into Origen has lifted from him much of the stigma that his name has carried for centuries.[110] It has shown him to be 'a man of the Church,'[111] who, even in his *On First Principles* sought first to define the boundaries of ecclesiastical doctrine[112] and only then went on to put forth suggestions about the doctrinal questions that had not yet been determined by the Church. He did teach doctrines that the Church eventually condemned, but he was not a heretic in the precise sense of the word. Other such heretics of past centuries whose cases have been reopened by historical scholars of the 20th include Pelagius[113] and William of Ockham.[114]

Perhaps the most dramatic appeal from the verdict of the past to the judicial review of history has been in the case of Nestorius. It had been suspected for a long time that he may have been the victim of deliberate slander and distortion. Even Luther, whose own christological theories inclined in the opposite direction from those of Nestorianism,[115] revised the conventional estimate of Nestorius that he had received from the polemical literature and came to the conclusion that Nestorius had 'meant it seriously' when he claimed to agree with orthodoxy about the two natures in Christ.[116] Nevertheless, the older histories of dogma went on attributing to Nestorius the views that are recited by St. Cyril of Alexandria and his other opponents. Because of his special theological interest in the reconstruction of traditional christological doctrine, Thomasius saw in Nestorius the 'extreme'[117] left wing of the Antiochene school; 'all the implications that Cyril finds in his doctrine are there: it is a destructive attack upon the facts of Christian consciousness.'[118] But during and shortly after the time of Thomasius two seemingly unrelated theological forces were at work to compel a reassessment both of 'the Antiochene school' and of Nestorius's relation to it. The interaction between these two forces is an example of how historical research and theological discussion may affect each other.[119]

During the debates of the 19th century over biblical interpretation, the hermeneutics of Antioch acquired a special significance as an ancestor of the historical-critical method, by contrast with the allegorical or spiritual exegesis of Alexandria and its modern counterpart, the dogmatic exegesis of Protestant orthodoxy.[120] The Antiochenes had been occupied with the events of the life of Jesus and with His moral development;[121] they had limited the messianic interpretation of the Old Testament to a relatively few passages, instead of allegorizing a christological meaning everywhere;[122] they had looked critically at the received opinions about the authorship of biblical books.[123] In these and other ways they endeared themselves to the very scholars who, in addition to their interest in the critical study of the Bible, were writing the histories of dogma. The Antiochenes were, Harnack says, 'outstanding because of their methodical study of Scripture, their sober thinking under the influence of Aristotle, and their strict asceticism. For several decades they were the only ones who dealt with the christological dogma scientifically.'[124] Seeberg, who had followed Thomasius's interpretation in the first edition of his own *History of Dogma*,[125] came to revise his estimate of Antioch sharply, repudiating his earlier 'mistake'[126] and describing Antiochene Christology as 'without question superior, in scientific clarity and in precision of systematic exposition, to all the Christologies of Greek antiquity.'[127]

Nestorius was a beneficiary of this favorable attitude toward the theology of Antioch, but by itself it could not have brought about the radical change in the interpretation both of Antioch and of Nestorius that has taken place among almost all historians regardless of their denominational or theological positions; among the few exceptions are Martin Jugie[128] and Christian Pesch.[129] What has precipitated this widespread interest in the theology of the Antiochene school and in the teaching of Nestorius is the new availability of their own writings. Only in 1880–82 did the commentaries of Theodore of Mopsuestia on the Pauline epistles appear in print,[130] although portions had been published earlier. Theodore's other works, his commentaries[131] and his catechetical lectures,[132] were published between 1932 and 1940. Scholars now have access to his writings, albeit in Syriac or Latin translation (except for some Greek fragments), and have produced a succession of monographs on his theology and his exegetical method.[133] Nestorius, too, has become able to speak for himself. Friedrich Loofs, with great care and wide-ranging erudition, collected all the bits and pieces available of Nestorius's writings both from the polemical works of his opponents and from manuscripts; this collection appeared in 1905.[134] As he himself acknowledged,[135] Loofs was aware at the time that another and potentially more explosive discovery of Nestoriana had been made, and a few years later it appeared: *The Book of Heraclides* was published in 1910, both in a Syriac translation of the lost Greek original and in a French translation of the Syriac.[136] Thus we have access to the very words of Theodore and of Nestorius as no previous generation of Western Christians has had since perhaps the 5th century. The result has been a vigorous scholarly debate, whose final results are not yet in.[137] Whatever those results may prove to be, however, it is obvious that the conventional estimate of the place of Nestorius in the church history of the 5th century must be revised. And it is noteworthy that, although the ecclesiastical historians and political historians had been urging such a reconsideration of the case of Nestorius, it was the doctrinal historians who, for all their theological preconceptions, brought about the reconsideration and thus compelled a reconstruction not only of the theological history of the 5th century but of its church history as well.

As the interaction of doctrinal and ecclesiastical history in the interpretation of Nestorius suggests, however, the connection between the two is not a simple matter. For while historical theology has sometimes corrected the work of church history by identifying the hidden theological issues in historical or biographical narratives, it has also managed, perhaps no less often, to degrade such narratives into something presumed to be less worthy of serious intellectual attention than the history of Christian thought. In the first instance, it has amplified and corrected an account of the history that was less complete because it had not given adequate attention to the implicit understanding of doctrine at work in the event. In the second, it has distorted an account by assuming that no other factors in the event—be they biographical or social or political or economic—can have mattered as much as the doctrinal, so that all other fields of study may be depressed into 'auxiliary sciences' in relation to the history of doctrine. The relation of doctrinal and ecclesiastical history may be clarified by an examination of one instance of each of these oversimplifications.

When the doctrinal issues at work in a complex chapter of church history are overlooked, its full dimensions can be seriously distorted. An entire series of such chapters could be cited from standard accounts of the history of Eastern Christendom after the 5th or 6th century. Recent investigations have shown how pervasive was the notion among Western scholars, especially among German Lutheran historians of dogma, that the dogmatic development of Eastern Orthodoxy had atrophied after St. John of Damascus.[138] Therefore even the dogmatic debate over the permissibility of the worship of icons, with its vast implications for the whole range of doctrinal questions from the transcendence of God to ecclesiology and eschatology, was handled without a grasp of the fundamental problems at stake in it.[139] Similarly, it proved possible to dismiss the bitter controversy about the Filioque—which revealed diametrically opposed views of authority in the Church,[140] of the relation between the immanent and the economic in God,[141] perhaps even of the unity of the Godhead as such[142]—as an exercise in metaphysical futility or as the pretext for a quarrel whose real origins lay anywhere except in the area of doctrine.[143] Yet both of these questions at least had the advantage of having engaged Western theologians, either as allies (in the case of the Iconoclastic controversy[144]) or as opponents (in the case of the Filioque), and therefore of having some place within the Occidental scheme of what constitutes Christian doctrine.

Although it also had implications for East-West relations, because of the possibility of Thomistic overtones in the debate,[145] the controversy set off by the devotional practices of the Hesychasts has been a source of bewilderment to Western scholars, both Roman Catholic and Protestant. At best, they have sought to relate it to the earlier history of the monastic communities on Mount Athos and to the distinctive forms of prayer and meditation developed there.[146] More usually perhaps, they have concentrated on the bizarre aspects of the case, such as the regulation of breathing by the mystic or the quasi-hypnotic state induced in him.[147] It was almost inevitable that attention to these aspects of Hesychasm should raise the question of extra-Christian influences; and there was some debate among the scholars about this.[148] Meanwhile, the doctrinal issues raised during the controversy itself either were ignored or were treated as one of its more exotic features: a distinction between the being of God and His 'energies' involved dogmatic considerations for which very few Western scholars were prepared. Thanks to the exigencies of history, émigré Orthodox theologians have been compelled to carry on their scholarly work in the West, especially in France and in America; and out of their researches has come an interpretation of the Hesychast controversy that moves the issues of doctrine to the center and the issues of syncretism and of mystagogic techniques to the periphery.[149] By tracing the origins of these doctrinal questions back to the earliest stages of monastic theology, these scholars have shown that the debate between Gregory Palamas and Barlaam involved the very core of Christian teaching and Christian faith. Not only the history of doctrine but the history of Christianity during the 14th century has been set straight as a result of their work—work that might never have been undertaken except for an interest in historical theology.

At the same time, it must be acknowledged that historical theology may easily become so heady a wine that the other questions of church history are forgotten. Perhaps the outstanding example of such theologism in the scholarship of the 20th century has been Luther research. As noted earlier,[150] the investigation of Luther's teaching has frequently served as a vehicle for a scholar's own constructive theological proposals, so that the various sides in a debate over Luther's doctrine often correspond to the various theological parties in Lutheran or Protestant thought; a good example is the question of Luther's doctrine of inspiration.[151] Even the moot question of the date of Luther's 'discovery of the gospel' soon becomes the occasion for a dispute about that discovery and thus about the meaning of the gospel in past and present.[152] Out of this scholarship have come monographs of the highest order, dealing with most of the major doctrines in Luther's thought. Many of his theological formulas, such as 'righteous and a sinner at the same time,'[153] have become part of the theological vocabulary, and his *Lectures on Galatians* of 1535[154] provide the theologian with a key to the central message of the Reformation.

Yet it should be mentioned that, despite the preponderance

of German and Scandinavian scholarship in the study of the theology of Luther, it remained for an American scholar who was not a Lutheran, Roland H. Bainton, to write the only fresh biography of Luther in two or three generations.[155] As Heinrich Bornkamm has pointed out,[156] German research on Luther has not produced a full-length biography since that of Julius Köstlin, which first appeared in 1875.[157] When another American scholar, Erik Erikson, who is neither a theologian nor a church historian but a psychoanalyst, applied to the biography of Luther some of the methods that have come from the study of human personality,[158] Luther scholars who had studied or written essays only about his doctrine found it difficult to respond.[159] Opinions vary, also among students of literary biography, about the validity of these methods when applied to the dead.[160] The presidential address of William L. Langer at the American Historical Association in 1957 described psychological study as the most neglected resource in the equipment of the historian.[161] Various biographies—to name two of the most successful, Ernest Jones's life of Sigmund Freud[162] and Leon Edel's account of Henry James[163]—have sought to exploit it. But when it was employed to penetrate the mind of one of the most fascinating and candid personalities in the history of Western culture, the reaction among the professionals expressed either defensiveness or bafflement. Generations of historical theology without biography had poorly prepared them for such an approach. They have proved to be no better prepared for the approach of the Marxists to the history of the Reformation. As long as economic determinism concentrated on vilifying Luther for his stand in the Peasants' War of 1525, it could perhaps be countered by careful analyses of the deeper theological motives behind that stand.[164] But when Marxist scholarship turned to the economic origins and implications of the Reformation in various European lands, historical theology had to yield to church history; and church history, in turn, had to learn to pay more attention to social and economic factors than it had tended to do.[165]

The scholarship of the 19th and 20th centuries has assured to doctrinal history a permanent place in the field of ecclesiastical history. Standing as it does between church history and systematic theology, the history of doctrine is caught in a probably unavoidable cross fire, from which no pat formula provides relief. It is clear that when historical theology has neglected its ties with church history—and, for that matter, with intellectual history, the history of philosophy, or the history of literature—its integrity as a scholarly discipline has suffered and so has its potential contribution to theology. If the definition of the field set forth in the preceding discussion is a valid one, it would seem to require that the procedures, the assignments, and the training of the historical theologian be determined by his vocation as a historian. This would also seem to imply, as previously noted,[166] that the early centuries of the history of dogma occupy a prominent place in the scholarly equipment of every historical theologian, regardless of the period on which he concentrates in his own research and writing. From all of this it would follow in turn that a significant share of the reinterpretation of the history of doctrine will continue to come from church historians, rather than from theologians or historians of theology, because it is only in the context of church history that certain questions will be raised.

Dogmatics and History of Dogma

In spite of all that has been said thus far about the place of historical theology among the theological disciplines, most theologians, regardless of their own special field, would probably justify it primarily on the basis of the contribution it can make to systematic theology. As already noted, an examination of the history of any doctrine is often the best possible preliminary to a constructive statement of it. The careers of theologians such as Albrecht Ritschl show, moreover, that not only the study of individual doctrines but scholarly work in the total history of dogma has frequently served as a training for the future dogmatician.[167] It is an indication of this special relation between historical theology and systematic theology that in programs of study leading to the doctorate the student may often concentrate on the history of Christian doctrine under the aegis of either church history or theology, and that the field of theology often draws most of the students in this area. Even where these academic arrangements do not apply, however, historical theology has become a basic element in the work of the systematic theologian. Perhaps even more than the exegete, the systematic theologian needs the history of doctrine to provide him with both freedom and insight.

The origins of historical theology in the Enlightenment's critique of the Christian tradition have helped to determine its role as a liberator from the authority of a monolithically defined orthodoxy. An explicit presupposition of the Vincentian canon was the existence of a dogmatic consensus in the tradition that was, if not quite unanimous on every issue, nevertheless clearly discernible in the documents of church history.[168] It is the special calling of the history of doctrine to show that this presupposition is a simplistic reduction of a heterogeneous body of material to a single theological position, whether it be one of the several positions represented in that material or a later synthesis superimposed upon it. Harnack formulated this calling of the history of doctrine in his memorandum of 1888: 'Cardinal Manning made the frivolous statement: "One must overcome history by dogma"; but we say the opposite: one must refine dogma by history, and we as Protestants have the complete certainty that we do not thereby destroy, but build.'[169] Especially in church bodies such as Roman Catholicism and Lutheranism, where a traditional dogmatics has dominated the work of systematic theology, this refinement of dogma by history has been one of the distinctive features of the 19th and 20th centuries. The study of history has helped to bring about a liberation from the dead hand of the past.

No less dramatic, and in some instances more important, has been the liberation from control by the immediate present. Lord Acton described this achievement in his well-wrought Victorian prose: 'History must be our deliverer not only from the undue influence of other times, but from the undue influence of our own, from the tyranny of environment and the pressure of the air we breathe. It requires all historic forces to produce their record and submit to judgment, and it promotes the faculty of resistance to contemporary surroundings by familiarity with other ages and other orbits of thought.'[170]

This humanizing and civilizing force of historical study can give the systematic theologian a healthy detachment from the transiency of dogmatic fashion. Some of the same tentativeness that history has taught him to maintain about the notion of a simple dogmatic consensus from the past carries over into an unwillingness to embrace any new system as a resolution of all theological difficulties. For no such system is proof against the doctrinal change that has affected all its predecessors. If this tentativeness is not accompanied by the readiness, also born in part of the study of history, to accept the confessional responsibility of the theologian, it can lead to doctrinal scepticism and theological relativism. But so many of the warnings about these perils turn out to be appeals in support of a particular dogmatic panacea that the theologian will do well not to be intimidated by them prematurely, but to consider them only after he has permitted the force of the historical study of doctrine to do what it is intended to do for him and for his theological reflection. Then there will be the opportunity and the obligation to raise the question of continuity in doctrine and to look for alternatives to historicism.

By its investigations into all the major doctrines of Christian theology, the scholarship of the past 100 years in the history of dogma has to a considerable degree shaped the dogmatics of the present in all the churches. Nor has it done so only negatively, by uncovering the pluralism of doctrinal development; its contributions are positive as well. During those 100 years ecclesiology has become, for Protestants no less than for Roman Catholics, the object of a lively theological interest. Undoubtedly, the sources of this interest must be sought in a variety of historical forces, some of which have been mentioned earlier.[171] But interacting with such forces as these has been the discovery by historians of doctrine that, even though the Scholastics did not usually include a fully articulated ecclesiology in their systems and the Reformers often spoke as though they were subordinating the Church to the individual, the doctrine of the Church has been central to the content of what Christians believed, taught, and confessed. This has led, in turn, to a new emphasis upon the doctrine of the Church in constructive theological discussion. Some 19th-century theologians went so far as to hail the period they were inaugurating as 'the age of ecclesiology.'[172]

The Protestant theologian who so dominated this period as to earn the sobriquet 'the church father of the nineteenth century,'[173] Friedrich Schleiermacher, does not, at first examination, seem to have fostered this restoration of ecclesiology. For in *The Christian Faith* he had proposed the 'preliminary thesis' that the difference between Protestantism and Roman Catholicism could be defined in this way: 'The former makes the relation of the individual to the Church dependent upon his relation to Christ, but the latter on the contrary makes the relation of the individual to Christ dependent upon his relation to the Church.'[174] Yet he himself went on to qualify this 'preliminary' judgment by assigning to the Church a decisive place in his own dogmatics.[175] Thinkers who learned their theology from Schleiermacher, moreover, were the very generation that saw, perhaps more clearly than any since the Reformation, that the relation to Christ and the relation to the Church could not be placed in any such disjunction.[176] Both their own contemporaries and present-day historians have therefore claimed to discern 'Romanizing tendencies' in the thought of men like August Vilmar, Wilhelm Loehe, and Theodor Kliefoth.[177] Nor was the new emphasis upon ecclesiology confined to this right wing among Schleiermacher's pupils. Ritschl saw his own position in relation to Schleiermacher at least partly as one of having recovered the importance of the Church.[178] This he did primarily through his historical work, in which he dealt both with the rise of Catholicism in the early Church and with the emergence of Lutheranism after the Reformation.[179] Ritschl's sense not only for the 'idea' of the Church but for its forms and institutions[180] was rooted in his study of its history, but it contributed to a new ecclesiology that went far beyond anything that either Schleiermacher or Ritschl had supposed.

A striking instance of how far this new ecclesiology could go on the basis of its historical research has been supplied by the form-critical method of studying the New Testament.[181] When scholars like Rudolf Bultmann and Martin Dibelius applied this method of analysis to the stories and sayings of the New Testament, their primary intent was anything but the aggrandizement of the Church. Doctrinally speaking, their concern was more with Christology than with ecclesiology; they sought to make the message of the Christian gospel clearer, not to make the Christian community more important, and the impact of their work on Christology has been great. Their conclusions mean, however, as the work of the New Testament scholar John Knox has made clear,[182] that Christology and ecclesiology are inseparable—one is almost tempted to say indistinguishable—not only in the interpretation of the Gospels but also in the constructive statement of Christian theology today. The historical study of the New Testament has thus led to a profound restatement of ecclesiology.

No less profound has been the outcome of the historical research into the doctrine of the Church among the Protestant Reformers. In direct refutation of Schleiermacher's thesis, this research has concluded that the Church was central to the theology of both Luther and Calvin. Luther's doctrine of the Church has become a major issue for both historical investigation and theological discussion,[183] while students of Calvin have come to such conclusions as these:

> Calvin has no tolerance for any solitary piety that detaches itself from this active interchange of spiritual values. The Church is an indispensable agent in the divine plan of salvation. As Cyprian says, she is Mother to all to whom God is Father; and she remains the nurse of the Christian life in her children: 'Since there is no way of entrance into life unless she conceive us in her womb, give us birth, unless, moreover, she keep us under her protection and guidance. . . . For our weakness is such that we may not leave her school until we have spent the course of our life as her pupils.'[184]

Thanks to such historical insights, Protestant theologians have reopened the ecclesiological question.

This change came just at a time when other lines of historical research were compelling Roman Catholic theology to reconsider some of the ecclesiological emphases that it had developed in opposition to Protestantism. The 'primacy text' of St. Cyprian's *On the Unity of the Catholic Church*, an important though highly controverted proof that the authority of the papacy could claim great antiquity, has been placed in its historical context as a statement that St. Cyprian revised when Rome made too much of it.[185] The confusing formulation on the relation between Scripture and 'tradition' or 'traditions' at the Council of Trent has been closely scrutinized in the light of contemporary documents, and extreme views of its implications have been modified.[186] A similar reconstruction of history has taken place in the interpretation of the schism between East and West. The recriminations that used to fill not only the controversial treatises but also the historical accounts have gradually been replaced. Cardinal Hergenröther's study of Photius,[187] which was written just before the First Vatican Council, demonstrated that the responsibility for the mutual excommunication had to be laid at Western as well as Eastern doors, and that even dogmatically the terms 'heretical' and 'orthodox' were not so easy to assign. These studies in the history of the doctrine of the Church, which could be supplemented by many other titles, have liberated Roman Catholic theology from the need to repeat the simplistic formulas of earlier controversies, and have replaced these formulas with descriptions of the Church that, if less neat, are more faithful to historical reality and therefore, ultimately, also to dogmatic truth.

It would not be fair, however, to ignore the perils in the influence of historical studies on dogmatics. One peril, evident in the study especially of St. Thomas and of Luther,[188] is that of concentrating historical study upon one figure or period of the history of doctrine and ignoring the larger picture. The result is a distortion of the historical record, for the theological hero under consideration tends to be portrayed as the fountainhead for ideas and insights that he received from his predecessors and contemporaries.[189] It is also a theological distortion. The correctives that the patristic tradition supplies to Thomism in such areas as the Christian understanding of history do not receive due consideration.[190] At the same time, the long discussions in both the *Summa Theologiae* and the *Summa contra gentiles* of natural theology set the pattern for the 'fundamental theology' of the textbooks. Similarly, such statements from Luther as the one quoted earlier in criticism of the term *homoousion*[191] have passed from one secondary account to another as proof that he really was not trinitarian in his theology, providing even sympathetic interpreters of his thought with justification for ignoring the place of this dogma in his view of God.[192] Harnack's critique of a Luther research isolated from Luther's sources applies not only to historical theology but also (because of the place of Luther study in Continental Lutheran dogmatics) to systematic theology. A slight variant on these distortions is what is usually termed a 'theology of repristination.' This term has been applied especially to those forms of Protestant dogmatics whose golden age is not the Reformation but the confessional orthodoxy that followed it. Here the Reformers tend to be interpreted in the light of the confessional documents, and these in turn in the light of the Protestant scholastics who elaborated them into a theological system.[193] Some of the advocates of this theology have been men of impressive historical erudition, but their history is trimmed to suit a given set of dogmatic conclusions.

Often the reaction to this use of history for dogmatic purposes is the kind of 'historicism' condemned in *Humani generis* of Aug. 12, 1950: 'Concentrating its attention only on the events of human life, it subverts the foundations of any absolute truth or law, as regards both philosophical matters and Christian dogmas.'[194] What the encyclical condemns in historicism is both its historical immanentism, which rules out the role of supernatural intervention and divine revelation in human affairs, and the consequent relativism, which treats all statements of either philosophical or theological doctrine as historically conditioned and therefore incapable of having binding force for all time. From the history of modern theology it is obvious that this is no creature of a critic's imagination, but a clear and present danger. Ernst Troeltsch expressed the conclusion of many students of history when he wrote:

> 'The task of damming and controlling [the stream of historical life] is therefore essentially incapable of completion and essentially unending; and yet it is always soluble and practicable in each new case. A radical and absolute solution does not exist.... History within itself cannot be transcended.... In history itself there are only relative victories.'[195]

The question of how to construct a dogmatics that meets and transcends the challenge of such historicism is probably the most fundamental issue raised for systematic theology by historical theology. And although the task here does not include finding an answer to that question, it does oblige us to raise the corresponding question, which is addressed specifically to historical theology: Where and how, if at all, does historical theology locate the continuity of what the Church has believed, taught, and confessed? The question of truth and the question of continuity are, to be sure, not identical; but for a truly Catholic understanding of the history of Christian doctrine they are finally inseparable.

Conclusion

Historical theology takes its rise from the question of doctrinal change, but it issues in a quest for doctrinal continuity.[1] A proper consideration of that quest would far exceed the confines of the subject matter here discussed, for defining the nature of the truth of revelation and identifying the locus of dogmatic authority are not problems that yield their resolutions to the research of the historian. They are, in their implication, issues of the faith and teaching of the Church, in fulfillment of its charter and in obedience to its Lord. These concluding remarks, therefore, are not presented as 'a theology of historical theology,' nor as a theory of doctrinal continuity. Their intent is perforce much more modest: to itemize some of the considerations that, in the light of historical theology, seem fundamental to any quest for continuity.

The conclusion seems unavoidable—although it would certainly be controverted by many theologians—that the fact of change somehow belongs to the very definition of Christian truth. Theologians who find the Incarnation paradigmatic for all other doctrines attempt to come to terms with this fact by means of various kenotic theories about the limitations of the human nature of Christ[2] and, a fortiori, of the human nature of the Church in its history. As the 'fullness of Him who fills all in all' (Eph 1.23), the Church participates in His unity with the Father and the Holy Spirit; as the Body of Christ, however, it also shares the 'form of a slave' (Phil 2.7).³ Therefore, to quote two encyclicals issued by Pius XII in 1943, one may say simultaneously that 'the most loving knowledge' with which Christ knows His own applies to His Mystical Body and to all its members;⁴ and that in the writers of Sacred Scripture there were 'certain kinds of exposition and narration' that they shared with their own times, so that the very history of the revelation in the Bible must be seen in the light of the differences between the world views of different historical periods.⁵ Although the metaphor 'Body of Christ' has sometimes been pressed far beyond its proper scope,⁶ especially as a principle of theological epistemology, the valid point of such formulations is the recognition that the Church, which participates in the historical process, can 'know the truth' only within the confines of that process.

Another way of stating this thesis is to assert that the historical process needs to be seen by Christian theology as a medium of growth, not as a source of embarrassment. That it has been a source of acute embarrassment is evident from the preceding discussion. As it defined itself in the classical period of the formative councils, Christian orthodoxy was bound up with the claim not only that there had not been change but that there could not be change in the doctrine of the Church. Heresy could change; dogma could not. There is much reason to believe that, in addition to the arguments usually adduced in support of this claim, as these arguments have been summarized in the early discussion above, there was also at work an assumption about the relation between time and eternity, between being and becoming, by which history was assigned a lesser reality than the superhistorical realm, from which the truth of revelation was thought to have come.⁷ If the life and the structures of the Church were involved in the historical process, as no one could deny that they were, one needed nevertheless to insist that the Church as such belonged to the transcendent order of reality, despite its participation in the immanent order. So also, the doctrines of the Church had to be grounded in the 'really real' beyond history, even though they were regrettably historical, all too historical, in their genesis and development.

By invoking the christological analogy, despite its ambiguity, the position implied in this study would seem to demand a reversal of this polarity. To Christian faith, the teaching about the pre-existence and eternal lordship of the Son of God is an inescapable corollary of what it believes about Jesus of Nazareth, whom it confesses to be the Christ of God.[8] His historical immanence is therefore no mere episode in His cosmic and timeless career but the constitutive fact about Him, from which the doctrine of the Church is entitled, on the basis of revelation, to predicate of Him a relation to God the Father and to the Holy Spirit in the Holy Trinity. It would seem to be axiomatic that any theology—such as, perhaps, that of Clement of Alexandria[9] —for which it is easier to speak about the pre-existence of the Logos or the glorification of the ascended Lord than about the life and teaching, the suffering and death, of Jesus of Nazareth has subtly transformed the central affirmations of the gospel from confessions about happenings to speculations about essences. But if it is the character of the gospel to be a narrative of the events that bring salvation, it would have to follow that Christian doctrine, as *doctrina evangelii*, must share in this relation between the evangelical and the historical, and that therefore the historical nature of doctrine and of its development ought to be a kind of presumptive evidence that, in this respect at any rate, it has been faithful to its fundamental charter.

Because historical theology implies that history must become a category for the formulation of Christian doctrine, it is unacceptable to retort, with Jacques Maritain, that the idea of development 'is not a metaphysical instrument and it does not concern itself with the analytical explanation of being; it is an historic instrument and concerns the historical explanation of becoming.'[10] At the same time, the historical treatment of doctrine does need to be warned against the paralysis of a historicism that foreshortens the very meaning of dogma by treating it exclusively as a function of the time in which it arose. As Maritain observes in the discussion just cited, 'To enclose a metaphysic in a compartment of history is not a way to give evidence of a sense of history; and it is no proof of philosophic sense to think that there is nothing more in a metaphysic than the scientific imagery which, in a given era, permitted it to exemplify itself in the plane of phenomena.'[11] As the earlier discussion here attempted to show, it is a trivialization of the documents of the history of doctrine to ignore their professed status as witnesses to what the Church believes, teaches, and confesses about something that is true and ultimate.

In the present context, the key word in this formula is 'confesses.' The imperative to 'speak of what we have seen and heard' (Acts 4.20) follows directly from the indicative of the gospel. But as the seeing and the hearing take place only under the conditions of historical existence, so the speaking must also. An interpretation of doctrinal truth which, with H. Richard Niebuhr[12] and others, we would call 'confessional' is an attempt to go beyond the antithesis between historical relativism and the claim to absolute truth. With the former it shares the recognition that it is not given to any mortal, be he Christian believer or not, to apprehend and to articulate timeless truth in a timeless way; with the latter it shares the conviction that one must affirm the truth of the faith as though his life depended on it, for it does. This same combination of perspectives, which the theologian applies to himself and to his own time, he must apply as well to the fathers and brethren who have gone before. The natural inclination seems to be to acknowledge with alacrity that previous generations were conditioned by their history, but to suppose that, even in that acknowledgment, one has himself been spared such conditionedness. What Gordon S. Haight has said of Herbert Spencer would apply to many other thinkers: 'He believed in the evolution of everything except his own theories.'[13] Historical relativism and dogmatic absolutism may be contradictory in principle, but they are often combined in fact. The traditionalism sketched above in the treatment of the problem of doctrinal change resolves the contradiction by claiming absoluteness not only for its own formulas but also and especially for those of the history of dogma. A 'confessional' position recognizes the relativity both of past and of present formulas, but it confesses with no less force and conviction. Winston Churchill, whose insights into the nature of change illumined this discussion earlier, was also aware of the danger of paralysis from historical relativism. 'In war, as in life,' he observed, 'it is often necessary, when some cherished scheme has failed, to take up the best alternative open, and if so, it is folly not to work for it with all your might. I therefore turned my guns round too.'[14] And a little later he added: 'The veils of the future are lifted one by one, and mortals must act from day to day.'[15] The theologian believes that 'day to day pours forth speech' (Ps 19.2), and the *Te Deum* sings, 'Day by day we magnify Thee.' Acting responsibly and confessing faithfully from day to day is, therefore, in accordance with sound theology.

It is no less in accord with sound theology to insist that the Church's past be included as a full participant in this act of confession. The Chalcedonian definition attached its christological formulation to the symbols of Nicea and Constantinople with the words 'Following, then, the holy Fathers.'[16] Such 'following' was no mere parroting of patristic or even conciliar theology, but a statement of what the confessors at Chalcedon intended as a faithful witness—*in* their own time but *for* all time—to the continuity of the Christian and Catholic faith. Far from acting as a damper on theological creativity, this inclusion of the dead in the circle of doctrinal discussion acts as a stimulus to it. As already noted several times,[17] one of the principal uses to which the history of doctrine is put is to be a resource for defining doctrinal options and for finding some options that might otherwise be overlooked because of the currents of theological opinion. Relativism, by contrast, is hard pressed to show that dogmatic statements determined by a world view now past must still be taken seriously. Thus the doctrine of the Trinity was dethroned from its position as 'the central dogma of Christian theology,'[18] becoming, in the dogmatics of Schleiermacher, an appendix to the main body of systematic theology.[19] Schleiermacher's familiar bon mot that certain doctrines may be 'entrusted to history for safekeeping'[20] became an axiom by means of which thinkers such as Ernst Troeltsch could consign much of the orthodox tradition to irrelevance.[21]

The inclusion of fathers as well as brethren in the circle of theological discussion means that the proper doctrinal rubric for the theological evaluation of historical theology is the doctrine of the Church. As the study of historical theology compels one to ask how such a variety of doctrines could have developed within the Christian community, so a truly Catholic ecclesiology enables one to begin to come to terms with this variety. This is the implication of Albert C. Outler's argument that unity in the Christian community precedes and produces unity in Christian doctrine, not vice versa.[22] Historically, we are able to include in our catalogue of believers and saints men who diverged from one another in their theology. What held St. Thomas Aquinas and

St. Bonaventure together was eminently more important than what divided them; nevertheless, they disagreed on basic questions and on fundamental doctrines.[23] These things divided them from each other, but it was within the one Church that they carried on their disagreement. The continuity of Christians with one another both within a period of history and between periods is neither identical with doctrinal agreement nor separable from it, but it is a function of that unity which the Church finds not in its members but in its Lord. As the preface to the Augsburg Confession put it, speaking about the controversy between Roman Catholicism and Lutheranism, 'We all have our existence and carry on our conflicts under one Christ.[24] There is an ecumenicity in time as well as an ecumenicity in space, and this calls for a doctrine of the unity of the Church that will take up into itself both the fact of theological variety and the fact of doctrinal change. Historical theology does not have the vocation of producing such a doctrine, but it does raise the issues to which it must be addressed. It also draws from the history of Christian doctrine many of the resources out of which such a doctrine can emerge.

Abbreviations Used in the Notes

AncChrWr	Ancient Christian Writers. Westminster, Md., and London, 1946–.
Denz	H. Denzinger, *Enchiridion symbolorum*, ed. A. Schönmetzer. 32d ed. Freiburg i.Br, 1963.
Grill-Bacht Konz	A. Grillmeier and H. Bacht, *Das Konzil von Chalkedon: Geschichte und Gegenwart*. 3 v. Würzburg, 1951–54.
NicPNicChFath	A Select Library of the Nicene and Post-Nicene Fathers, ed. P. Schaff. 14 v. New York, 1886–1900; 2d series, ed. P. Schaff and H. Wace, 1890–1900.
PG	Patrologia Graeca, ed. J. P. Migne. 161v. Paris, 1857–66.
PL	Patrologia Latina, ed. J. P. Migne. 217v.; indexes 4v. Paris, 1878–90.
PRE[1]	J. J. Herzog, ed., *Realencyklopädie für protestantische Theologie und Kirche*. 1st ed. 22v. Hamburg, 1854–68.
PRE[2]	J. J. Herzog, G. L. Plitt, and A. Hauck, eds., *Realencyklopädie für protestantische Theologie und Kirche*. 2d ed. 18v. Leipzig, 1877–88.
PRE[3]	J. J. Herzog and A. Hauck, ed., *Realencyklopädie für protestantische Theologie und Kirche*. 3d ed. 24v. Leipzig, 1896–1913.

Schroeder Trent	H. J. Schroeder, trans., *Council of Trent: Canons and Decrees, 1545-63*. St. Louis, 1941.
SourcesChr	Sources chrétiennes, ed. H. de Lubac et al. Paris, 1941–.
TU	Texte und Untersuchungen zur Geschichte der altchristlichen Literatur. Berlin, 1882–.
WA	D. Martin Luther, *Werke*. Kritische Gesammtausgabe, Weimar, 1883–.

Notes

Notes to the Introduction

1. Aquinas *Summa Theologiae* 1, 1.6 *ad* 1.
2. J. A. Möhler, *Symbolik oder Darstellung der dogmatischen Gegensätze der Katholiken und Protestanten nach ihren öffentlichen Bekenntnisschriften*, ed. J. R. Geiselmann (2v.; Darmstadt, 1958–61), 2:726.
3. W. Elert, *Die Kirche und ihre Dogmengeschichte* (Munich, 1950), p. 3; *Der Ausgang der altkirchlichen Christologie: Eine Untersuchung über Theodor von Pharan und seine Zeit als Einführung in die alte Dogmengeschichte* (Berlin, 1957), p. 313.
4. A. von Harnack, *Lehrbuch der Dogmengeschichte* (3v.; 5th ed.; Tübingen, 1931), 1:15–25. Hereafter cited *Lehrbuch*.
5. J. Gottschick, 'Theologie, Begriff und Gliederung,' PRE² 15:419–432.
6. K. R. Hagenbach, *Encyklopädie und Methodologie der theologischen Wissenschaften* (1st ed., Leipzig 1833; 12th ed., Leipzig 1889).
7. K. R. Hagenbach, 'Encyklopädie, theologische,' PRE¹ 4:9–16.
8. K. R. Hagenbach, 'Kirchengeschichte,' PRE¹ 7:622–634.
9. Hagenbach, 'Kirchengeschichte,' PRE¹ 7:622.
10. Cf. G. Heinrici, 'Encyklopädie, theologische,' PRE³ 5:351–364.
11. Thus most of the articles in the *Zeitschrift für historische Theologie* (1832–75) dealt with church history, not merely with the history of Christian doctrine.

12. Cf. P. C. Hodgson, *The Formation of Historical Theology: A Study of Ferdinand Christian Baur* (New York, 1966); W. Pauck, *Harnack and Troeltsch: Two Historical Theologians* (New York, 1968).
13. In the following sentences I have adapted portions of my article, 'Dogma,' in M. Halverson and A. A. Cohen, eds., *A Handbook of Christian Theology: Definition Essays on Concepts and Movements of Thought in Contemporary Protestantism* (New York, 1958), pp. 80–82.
14. Lk 2.1, Acts 16.4, Acts 17.7, Eph 2.15, Col 2.14; Heb 11.23 is dubious, since the word appears only in the Codex Alexandrinus and a few other manuscripts.
15. Ignatius *Magnesians* 13; cf. J. B. Lightfoot, *The Apostolic Fathers* 2–II (2d ed.; London, 1889), pp. 137 n.
16. Cf. Origen *Contra Celsum* 3.76, tr. H. Chadwick (Cambridge, 1953), p. 179.
17. See G. W. H. Lampe, *A Patristic Greek Lexicon* (Oxford, 1961), pp. 377–378.
18. See p. 61 below.
19. There is a long and useful note on patristic use of the term *ad* Basil *De Spiritu Sancto* 27.66 in NicPNicChFath, 2d series, 8:41, n. 1.
20. See pp. 20–21 below.
21. See p. 89 below.
22. See, for example, W. H. Principe, *Alexander of Hales' Theology of the Hypostatic Union*, v.2 of *The Theology of the Hypostatic Union in the Early Thirteenth Century* (Toronto, 1967), pp. 73–81.
23. Harnack, *Lehrbuch*, 3:311.
24. Denz 802.
25. Schroeder Trent 75.
26. See pp. 88–89 below.
27. J. E. Sandys, *A History of Classical Scholarship* (3v.; Cambridge, 1908–21).
28. Cf. O. W. Heick, *A History of Christian Thought* (2v.; Philadelphia, 1965–66), 1:3–16.
29. A Library of Protestant Thought (New York, 1964–). The general introduction to the series states: 'A Library of Protestant Thought is a collection of writings intended to illumine and interpret the history of the Christian faith in its Protestant expression. It is as variegated in its literary forms and theological positions as is the movement it mirrors. Tracts, letters, sermons, monographs, and other types of literature comprising the heritage of Protestant thought find a place in this series.'
30. Cf. Seeberg, *Lehrbuch der Dogmengeschichte* (4v.; 5th ed.; Basel, 1953–54), 3:148. Hereafter cited *Lehrbuch*.

31. See pp. 115–117 below.
32. G. P. Fisher, *History of Christian Doctrine* (2d. ed.; Edinburgh, 1897).
33. R. Seeberg, *Text-Book of the History of Doctrines*, tr. C. E. Hay (2v.; Grand Rapids, Mich., 1952).
34. Fisher, *History of Christian Doctrine*, p. 3.
35. Cf. G. Kittel, *Theologisches Wörterbuch zum Neuen Testament* (Stuttgart, 1935–), 2:165, n. 7.
36. Gregory of Nyssa *Epistle 24*, PG 46:1089A.
37. *Theodori episcopi Mopsuesteni in epistolas B. Pauli commentarii*, ed. H. B. Swete (2v.; Cambridge, 1880–82), 1:114, 2:153, 2:260.
38. Cyril of Jerusalem *Catecheses illuminandorum*, IV:2, PG 33:456.
39. N. Bonwetsch, *Grundriss der Dogmengeschichte* (2. ed.; Gütersloh, 1919); R. Seeberg, *Grundriss der Dogmengeschichte* (2d ed.; Leipzig, 1905); A. Harnack, *[Grundriss der] Dogmengeschichte* (4th ed.; Tübingen, 1905).
40. E. Fueter, *Geschichte der neueren Historiographie* (Munich and Berlin, 1911); J. W. Thompson and B. J. Holm, *A History of Historical Writing* (2v.; New York, 1942); H. E. Barnes, *A History of Historical Writing* (2d ed.; New York, 1962); G. P. Gooch, *History and Historians in the Nineteenth Century* (2d ed.; Boston, 1959).
41. Seeberg, *Lehrbuch*, 1:20–26; Harnack, *Lehrbuch*, 1:25–47; F. Loofs, *Leitfaden zum Studium der Dogmengeschichte*, ed. K. Aland (6th ed.; Tübingen, 1959), pp. 1–8.
42. R. G. Collingwood, *The Idea of History* (New York, 1956).
43. Cf. V. A. Harvey, *The Historian and the Believer: The Morality of Historical Knowledge and Christian Belief* (New York, 1966); R. L. Hart, *Unfinished Man and the Imagination: Toward an Ontology and a Rhetoric of Revelation* (New York, 1968), pp. 191ff.
44. See p. 61 below.
45. See the comment quoted on p. 99 below.
46. Cf. pp. 219–223.

Notes to Chapter One

1. A. N. Whitehead, *Adventures of Ideas* (Harmondsworth, Eng., 1948), p. 45.
2. Whitehead, *Adventures of Ideas*, p. 114.
3. 'I write about the things in our past that appear significant to me and I do so as one not without some experience of historical and violent events in our own time.' W. S. Churchill, *A History of the English-Speaking Peoples* (4v.;

New York, 1963), 1:x; cf. J. H. Plump, 'The Historian,' A. J. P. Taylor et al, *Churchill Revised: A Critical Assessment* (New York, 1969), pp. 133–169.
4. W. S. Churchill, *The Second World War* (6v.; New York, 1961), 2:469.
5. 'No one can understand history without continually relating the long periods which are constantly mentioned to the experiences of our own short lives. Five years is a lot. Twenty years is the horizon to most people. Fifty years is antiquity. To understand how the impact of destiny fell upon any generation of men one must first imagine their position and then apply the time-scale of our own lives. Thus nearly all changes were far less perceptible to those who lived through them from day to day than appears when the salient features of an epoch are extracted by the chronicler' (*History of the English-Speaking Peoples,* 1:34).
6. W. S. Churchill, *Marlborough: His Life and Times* (4v.; London, 1967), 2:342.
7. Churchill, *History of the English-Speaking Peoples,* 2:231; *Marlborough,* 3:180.
8. Churchill, *Marlborough,* 1:286.
9. Aristotle *Metaphysics,* 983–990; cf., for example, *Physics* 207–208.
10. Cf. H. Diels, *Die Fragmente der Vorsokratiker,* ed. W. Kranz (5th ed.; Berlin, 1934–35).
11. W. Jaeger, *Aristotle: Fundamentals of the History of His Development,* tr. R. Robinson (2d ed.; Oxford, 1948), p. 3.
12. H. F. Cherniss, *Aristotle's Criticism of Presocratic Philosophy* (Baltimore, 1935).
13. 'Eudemos von Rhodos,' *Paulys Realencyklopädie der klassischen Altertumswissenschaft,* ed. G. Wissowa et al (Stuttgart, 1893–), 6:898–899.
14. W. Jaeger, *The Theology of the Early Greek Philosophers* (Oxford, 1947), p. 5.
15. Cf. F. Schwenn, *Die Theogonie des Hesiodos* (Heidelberg, 1934).
16. Sich in den Geist der Zeiten zu versetzen,
    Zu schauen wie vor uns ein weiser Mann gedacht,
    Und wie wir's dann zuletzt so herrlich weit gebracht.
Goethe, *Faust,* ll. 571–573. Cf. A. Bergstraesser, *Goethe's Image of Man and Society* (Chicago, 1949), pp. 205–231 for Goethe's own view.
17. Heb 1.1–2; cf. L. Goppelt, *Christentum und Judentum im ersten und zweiten Jahrhundert: Ein Aufrisz der Urgeschichte der Kirche* (Gütersloh, 1954), p. 257 on this idea.

18. A. von Harnack, *Lehrbuch der Dogmengeschichte* (3v.; 5th ed.; Tübingen, 1931), 2:107. Hereafter cited *Lehrbuch*.
19. Cf. J. Madoz, *El concepto de la tradición en S. Vincente de Lérins: estudio historico-critico del 'Commonitorio'*, Analecta Gregoriana, 5 (Rome, 1933).
20. Vincent of Lérins *Commonitorium* 2, PL 50:640.
21. Cf. W. Elert, *The Structure of Lutheranism*, tr. W. A. Hansen (Saint Louis, 1962), pp. 287–288.
22. J. A. Möhler, *Symbolik oder Darstellung der dogmatischen Gegensätze der Katholiken und Protestanten nach ihren öffentlichen Bekenntnisschriften*, ed. J. R. Geiselmann (2v.; Darmstadt, 1958–61), 1:414–415; J. H. Newman, *An Essay on the Development of Christian Doctrine*, int. G. Weigel (New York, 1960), 36–41.
23. This interpretation of Vincent is, however, rendered questionable by the recent discovery and publication of his compilation of passages from Augustine, *Excerpta Vincentii Lirinensis según el Códice de Ripoll, No.151*, ed. J. Madoz (Madrid, 1940).
24. Cf. G. Bonner, *St. Augustine of Hippo: Life and Controversies* (London, 1963), pp. 319–320.
25. On the entire question the essay of H. Reuter, 'Augustin und der katholische Orient,' *Augustinische Studien* (Gotha, 1887), pp. 153–228, still bears careful study.
26. Vincent of Lérins *Commonitorium* 2, PL 50:640.
27. John Keble quoted it as '*Quod semper, quod ubique, quod ab omnibus*—Antiquity, Universality, Catholicity' in his sermon on 'Primitive Tradition,' September 27, 1836, reprinted in E. R. Fairweather, ed., *The Oxford Movement*, A Library of Protestant Thought (New York, 1964), p. 77; John Henry Newman likewise quoted it as 'always, everywhere, and by all' in Lecture II of his *Lectures on the Prophetical Office of the Church*, reprinted in Fairweather, *Oxford Movement*, p. 129.
28. Vincent of Lérins *Commonitorium* 2, PL 50:640.
29. Vincent of Lérins *Commonitorium* 4, PL 50:642.
30. '. . . ut prope cunctis Latini sermonis episcopis,' Vincent of Lérins *Commonitorium* 4, PL 50:642.
31. See Harnack, *Lehrbuch*, 2:109–110.
32. J. H. Newman, *The Arians of the Fourth Century* (3d ed.; London, 1871), p. 454. This note on 'The Orthodoxy of the Body of the Faithful during the Supremacy of Arianism' had originally appeared as an article in July, 1859.
33. Vincent of Lérins *Commonitorium* 4, PL 50:642.
34. Vincent of Lérins *Commonitorium* 17, PL 50:660–662.
35. Vincent of Lérins *Commonitorium* 17, PL 50:663.
36. Vincent of Lérins *Commonitorium* 24, PL 50:670.

37. Vincent of Lérins *Commonitorium* 23, PL 50:667.
38. Vincent of Lérins *Commonitorium* 23, PL 50:668: '*in suo genere.*'
39. Vincent of Lérins *Commonitorium* 23, PL 50:667–670.
40. Vincent of Lérins *Commonitorium* 23, PL 50:668.
41. F. C. Baur, *The Epochs of Church Historiography*, ed. and tr. P. C. Hodgson, *Ferdinand Christian Baur on the Writing of Church History*, A Library of Protestant Thought (New York, 1968), pp. 59–60.
42. Theodore of Mopsuestia *Theodori episcopi Mopsuestini in epistolas beati Pauli commentarii*, ed. H. B. Swete (2v.; Cambridge, England, 1880–82), 1:13.
43. Cyril of Alexandria *Quod unus sit Christus*, SourcesChr 97:308.
44. Eusebius of Caesarea *Historia ecclesiastica* 1.1, Sources Chr 31:3.
45. On innovation as an issue in Eusebius, cf. J. Pelikan, *The Finality of Jesus Christ in an Age of Universal History: A Dilemma of the Third Century* (London, 1965), pp. 48–57.
46. Eusebius of Caesarea *Historia ecclesiastica* 2.13, Sources Chr 31:66–68.
47. Eusebius of Caesarea *Historia ecclesiastica* 5.16, Sources Chr 32:46–52.
48. 'But for him,' writes Philip Carrington, 'we would know little about all this,' *The Early Christian Church* (2v.; Cambridge, Eng., 1957), 2:475.
49. Socrates Scholasticus *Historia ecclesiastica* 1.8, PG 67:68.
50. Cf. E. Schwartz, 'Eusebius,' *Paulys Realencyklopädie der klassischen Altertumswissenschaft*, ed. G. Wissowa et al, 6:1370–1439.
51. W. Bauer, *Rechtgläubigkeit und Ketzerei im ältesten Christentum* (2d ed.; Tübingen, 1964), pp. 134–197, is a brilliant interpretation.
52. J. Quasten, *Patrology* (3v.; Westminster, Md., 1950–), 1:278–313, catalogues the earliest examples of this literature, most of it no longer extant.
53. Cf. R. M. Grant, ed., *Gnosticism* (New York, 1961), for a convenient and authoritative collection.
54. For an early but thorough examination of this issue, see F. Sagnard, *La gnose valentinienne et la témoignage de saint Irénée* (Paris, 1947).
55. Whitehead, *Adventures of Ideas*, p. 68.
56. See pp. 102–103 below.
57. Cf. Newman, *Essay on Development*, pp. 50–51.

58. Irenaeus *Adversus haereses* 4.17.5. *Sancti Irenaei episcopi Lugdunensis Libros quinque adversus Haereses*, ed. W. W. Harvey (2v.; Cambridge, 1857), 2:197–199.
59. See the notes from various writers collected by Harvey.
60. Irenaeus *Adversus haereses* 4.18.5, Harvey 2:205–208, translating the Greek fragment.
61. 'Formula Concordiae,' *Corpus Reformatorum* (Halle, 1834–), 3:75; cf. W. Köhler, *Zwingli und Luther: Ihr Streit über das Abendmahl nach seinen politischen und religiösen Beziehungen* (2v.; Leipzig and Gütersloh, 1924–53), 2:432–455.
62. See G. Wingren, *Man and the Incarnation: A Study in the Biblical Theology of Irenaeus*, tr. R. Mackenzie (Philadelphia, 1959), pp. 165–166; and D. van den Eynde, 'Eucharistia ex duabus rebus constans,' *Antonianum* 15 (1940):17–19.
63. R. E. Weingart, 'The Atonement in the Writings of Peter Abailard' (unpublished Ph.D. dissertation, Yale University, 1964) is a recent examination of many of these issues.
64. P. Abelard *Sic et non*, preface, PL 178:1339.
65. Cf. M. Grabmann, *Geschichte der scholastischen Methode* 2v.; Graz, 1957), 1:236–243, on some of Abelard's predecessors.
66. Abelard *Sic et non*, preface, PL 178:1341.
67. Abelard refers specifically to Mt 27.9, where the words of Zechariah are attributed to Jeremiah.
68. Abelard *Sic et non*, preface, PL 178:1341.
69. Abelard *Sic et non*, preface, PL 178:1341–1342.
70. Abelard *Sic et non*, preface, PL 178:1344.
71. Grabmann, *Scholastische Methode*, 2:212.
72. Abelard *Sic et non*, preface, PL 178:1344.
73. Abelard *Sic et non*, preface, PL 178:1345.
74. A. O. Lovejoy, *The Great Chain of Being: A Study of the History of an Idea* (New York, 1960), p. 6.
75. Lovejoy, *Great Chain of Being*, pp. 67–98.
76. A. O. Lovejoy, ' "Nature" as Norm in Tertullian,' *Essays in the History of Ideas* (New York, 1955), pp. 308–338.
77. Augustine *De Trinitate* 1.7, PL 42:824.
78. Augustine *De Trinitate* 1.31, PL 42:844.
79. Augustine *Contra epistulam Parmeniani* 3.24, PL 43:101.
80. J. H. Newman, *Apologia pro vita sua*, ed. M. J. Svaglic (Oxford, 1967), p. 110.
81. W. H. C. Frend, *The Donatist Church: A Movement of Protest in Roman North Africa* (Oxford, 1952), pp. 125–140.
82. See p. 153 below.

83. M. Bévenot, *St. Cyprian's De Unitate Chap. 4 in the Light of the Manuscripts* (London, 1938), p. 61.
84. Cyprian Epistle 73:21, *Corpus scriptorum ecclesiasticorum latinorum* (Vienna, 1866–), 3–2:795.
85. G. G. Willis, *Saint Augustine and the Donatist Controversy* (London, 1950), p. 103.
86. Augustine *Contra Iulianum* 2.10.34, PL 44:697.
87. Augustine *Contra Cresconium grammaticum donatistam* 3.3.3, PL 43:497.
88. Augustine *De gestis Pelagii* 12.27, PL 44:336.
89. On the implications of this, cf. J. Pelikan, *Development of Christian Doctrine: Some Historical Prolegomena* (New Haven, 1969), pp. 79–94.
90. Augustine *De nuptiis et concupiscentia ad Valerianum comitem* 2.51, *Corpus scriptorum ecclesiasticorum latinorum* 42:308.
91. G. Ferretti, *L'influsso di S. Ambrogio in S. Agostino* (Faenza, 1951) is a brief but useful study.
92. Much of the pertinent material has been collected by G. Mártil, *La tradición en San Agustin a través de la controversia Pelagiana* (Madrid, 1943), pp. 67–89.
93. Augustine *De praedestinatione sanctorum* 14.27, PL 44:980.
94. Augustine *Contra duas epistulas pelagianorum ad Bonifatium* 4.12.32, PL 44:636–637.
95. See pp. 4–5 above.
96. J. H. Newman, *Sermons, Chiefly on the Theory of Religious Belief, Preached before the University of Oxford* (London, 1843), p. 324.
97. E. A. Wuenschel, 'The Definability of the Assumption,' *Catholic Theological Society of America, Proceedings,* 2 (New York, 1947), pp. 72–102, summarized most of the arguments just before the actual promulgation of the dogma.
98. Pelikan, *Development of Christian Doctrine,* pp. 9–39.
99. J. C. Murray, *The Problem of God: Yesterday and Today* (New Haven, 1964), p. 53.
100. A. Hahn, *Bibliothek der Symbole und Glaubensregeln der Alten Kirche* (3d ed.; Hildensheim, 1962), p. 161.
101. Denz 723.
102. E. Hirsch, *Geschichte der neuern evangelischen Theologie* (5v.; Gütersloh, 1949–54), 4:105; but even here Luther's doctrine of the atonement did not fit the pattern (see p. 107 below).
103. See pp. 109–110 below.
104. Quasten, *Patrology,* 2:124–125.

105. Gregorius Thaumaturgus *In Origenem oratio panegyrica*, PG 10:1061.
106. Athanasius *De decretis Nicaenae synodi* 6.27, PG 25:465.
107. Athanasius *De sententia Dionysii*, PG 25:480–521, is his attempt to claim the Origenist tradition as support for the Nicene doctrine.
108. Eusebius *Historia ecclesiastica* 6.2.10, SourcesChr 41:85.
109. A. Harnack, [*Grundriss der*] *Dogmengeschichte* (4th ed., Tübingen, 1905), p. 136.
110. Harnack, *Lehrbuch*, 2:236.
111. Epiphanius *Panarion* 76.3, *Die griechischen christlichen Schriftsteller der ersten drei Jahrhunderte* (Leipzig, 1897–), 37:343–344.
112. Epiphanius *Panarion* 64, *Die griechischen christlichen Schriftsteller der ersten drei Jahrhunderte*, 31:403–523.
113. Cf. K. Holl, 'Die Zeitfolge des ersten origenistischen Streites' and the comments of Adolf Jülicher in K. Holl, *Gesammelte Aufsätze zur Kirchengeschichte* 2 (Tübingen, 1928), pp. 310–350.
114. Cf. G. Bardy, 'St. Jerome and Greek Thought' in F. X. Murphy, ed., *A Monument to Saint Jerome* (New York, 1952), pp. 85–112, esp. 102ff.
115. Cf. F. X. Murphy, *Rufinus of Aquileia* (Washington, 1945), pp. 59–81.
116. Rufinus *Apologia in Sanctum Hieronymum* 1.44, PL 21:684.
117. Jerome *Apologia adversus libros Rufini* 1.20, PL 23:413–414.
118. Denz 209.
119. Socrates *Historia ecclesiastica* 6.7, PG 67:684–688.
120. Theophilus of Alexandria, tr. Jerome, Epistle 98.9, PL 22:799.
121. Denz 403–411.
122. Denz 421–438.
123. Cf. Diekamp, *Die origenistischen Streitigkeiten im sechsten Jahrhundert und das fünfte allgemeine Konzil* (Münster, 1899), pp. 77–98.
124. Cf. J. Pelikan, *From Luther to Kierkegaard: A Study in the History of Theology* (St. Louis, 1950), pp. 24–48.
125. See the chapter on 'Modernism and History' in J. Ratté, *Three Modernists: Alfred Loisy, George Tyrrell, William L. Sullivan* (New York, 1967), pp. 5–42.
126. Denz 3401–66, 3475–3500.
127. See Ratté, *Three Modernists*, pp. 339–352.
128. See 1 Cor 4.2.
129. Hahn, *Bibliothek*, p. 161.

130. H.-W. Gensichen, *We Condemn: How Luther and 16th Century Lutheranism Condemned False Doctrine*, tr. H. J. A. Bouman (St. Louis, 1967).
131. F. Schleiermacher, *Der christliche Glaube nach den Grundsätzen der evangelischen Kirche im Zusammenhange dargestellt* (7th ed.; Berlin, 1960), 1:129–134.
132. Cf. L. Hödl, 'Sentenzen,' *Lexikon für Theologie und Kirche*, ed. J. Höfer and K. Rahner (2d ed., Freiburg, 1957–67), 9:670–674.
133. See, for example, M. Richard, 'Les florilèges diphysites du V⁰ e du VI⁰ siècle,' Grill-Bacht Konz 1:721–748.
134. H. G. Beck, *Kirche und theologische Literatur im byzantinischen Reich* (Munich, 1959), p. 446.
135. K. Holl, *Die Sacra Parallela des Johannes Damascenus*, TU 16–1 (1896).
136. Aristotle *Topica* 101b.
137. Cf. R. McKeon, 'Truth and the History of Ideas,' *Thought, Action and Passion* (Chicago, 1954), 54–88.
138. H. O. Taylor, *The Mediaeval Mind: A History of the Development of Thought and Emotion in the Middle Ages* (4th ed.; London, 1938), 2:333.
139. See pp. 13–14 above.
140. Grabmann, *Scholastische Methode*, 2:212.
141. On this problem in canon law, see S. G. Kuttner, *Harmony from Dissonance: An Interpretation of Medieval Canon Law* (Latrobe, Pa., 1960).
142. For a critique of this notion, cf. Harnack, *Lehrbuch*, 3:368–369, n. 1.
143. 'Ist Abälard Rationalist?' Grabmann, *Scholastische Methode*, 2:177–199.
144. Grabmann, *Scholastische Methode*, pp. 210ff.
145. As David Knowles has put it, 'His ideas lingered in the minds of his disciples, and many of them came to the surface, unacknowledged, in the golden age of scholasticism. It would be difficult to instance any other theologian, accused so often and justifiably of error, who has given so much of method and matter to orthodox thought.' *The Evolution of Medieval Thought* (London, 1962), p. 130.
146. M. Grabmann, *Die theol. Erkenntnis- und Einleitungslehre des hl. Thomas von Aquin auf Grund seiner Schrift 'In Boethium de Trinitate' im Zusammenhang der Scholastik des 13. und beginnenden 14. Jahrhunderts dargestellt* (Fribourg, 1948), p. 151.
147. Cf. J. Hofmeier, *Die Trinitätslehre des Hugo von St. Viktor dargestellt im Zusammenhang mit den trinitarischen Strömungen seiner Zeit* (Munich, 1963), pp. 282–296.

Notes 175

148. M. de Wulf, *An Introduction to Scholastic Philosophy Medieval and Modern*, tr. P. Coffey (New York, 1956), p. 64.
149. Aquinas *Summa theologiae* 1, 29. 3.
150. Pseudo-Dionysius *De divinis nominibus* 1.1, PG 3:588.
151. Pseudo-Dionysius *De mystica theologia* 3, PG 3:1032.
152. B. Dekker, 'Prolegomena' to *Sancti Thomae de Aquino Expositio super librum Boethii de Trinitate* (Leiden, 1965), p. 44.
153. Cf. Grabmann, *Erkenntnis und Einleitungslehre*, pp. 13-32.
154. E. K. Rand, *Founders of the Middle Ages* (New York, 1957), pp. 142-149.
155. Boethius, *The Theological Tractates*, tr. H. F. Stewart and E. K. Rand, Loeb Classical Library (Cambridge, Mass., 1968), pp. 2-127.
156. Boethius *Contra Eutychen* 3, Loeb Classical Library, pp. 84-85.
157. Boethius *Contra Eutychen* 3, 84-85.
158. G. L. Prestige, *God in Patristic Thought* (London, 1956), p. 163.
159. On the date, cf. the note of T. C. Lawler to an earlier letter, AncChrWr 33:195-196.
160. Jerome Epistle 15.5, PL 22:357 (AncChrWr 33:73).
161. Aquinas *Summa Theologiae* 1, 29.3 *ad* 1.
162. É. Gilson, 'Pourquoi saint Thomas a critiqué saint Augustin?' *Archives d'histoire doctrinale et littéraire du moyen-âge* (Paris, 1926-), 1:5-127.

Notes to Chapter Two

1. G. P. Gooch, *English Democratic Ideas in the Seventeenth Century* (2d ed.; New York, 1954), p. 7.
2. Cf. R. H. Bainton, *The Travail of Religious Liberty* (New York, 1958), pp. 33-176.
3. G. P. Gooch, 'The Growth of Historical Science,' *Cambridge Modern History* (London, New York, 1902-12), 12:816.
4. J. Burckhardt, *The Civilization of the Renaissance in Italy*, tr. S. G. C. Middlemore (New York, 1958), p. 324.
5. H. E. Barnes, *A History of Historical Writing* (2d ed.; New York, 1962), p. 105.
6. For a critical evaluation of Blondus, see E. Fueter, *Geschichte der neueren Historiographie* (Munich and Berlin, 1911), pp. 106-110.
7. Cf. G. Gordon, *Medium Aevum and the Middle Age* (Lon-

don, 1925), on the origins of the concept of 'medieval' in the work of Flavius Blondus.
8. J. A. Symonds, *Renaissance in Italy* (7v.; new ed.; London, 1904), 1 : 239ff.
9. Cf. F. Schevill, *Medieval and Renaissance Florence* (New York, 1963), pp. 500–502, comparing Machiavelli and Guicciardini as historians.
10. See the comments of Fueter, *Historiographie*, p. 62, on Machiavelli.
11. Fueter, *Historiographie*, pp. 65–69.
12. Cf. F. Gaeta, *Lorenzo Valla: Filologia e storia nell' umanesimo italiano* (Naples, 1955), for a recent study.
13. *The Treatise of Lorenzo Valla on the Donation of Constantine*, ed. and tr. C. B. Coleman (New Haven, 1922).
14. See, for example, Valla, *Donation*, pp. 152–155.
15. See the brief but incisive comments of L. W. Spitz, *The Religious Renaissance of the German Humanists* (Cambridge, Mass., 1963), pp. 274–277.
16. *The Doctrine of Addai, the Apostle, Now First Edited in a Complete Form in the Original Syriac with an English Translation and Notes*, ed. G. Phillips (London, 1876), compares Addai's version of the story with that transmitted by Eusebius.
17. Eusebius, *Historia ecclesiastica* 1.13, SourcesChr 31 : 40–45; see G. Bardy's note 4, p. 41.
18. Cf. A. von Harnack, *The Mission and Expansion of Christianity in the First Three Centuries*, tr. J. Moffatt (New York, 1961), p. 102, n. 1; and the critical examination of the evidence by W. Bauer, *Rechtgläubigkeit und Ketzerei im ältesten Christentum*, pp. 6–48.
19. See E. von Dobschütz, *Christusbilder: Untersuchungen zur christlichen Legende*, TU 18 : 102–196.
20. Dobschütz, *Christusbilder*, pp. 197–263.
21. J. N. D. Kelly, *Early Christian Creeds* (London, 1952), pp. 368–397.
22. On the backgrounds of the tradition cited by Rufinus, see J. N. D. Kelly, AncChrWr 20 : 100–101, n. 7.
23. Rufinus *Commentarius in symbolum apostolorum*, 2, PL 21 : 337, AncChrWr 20 : 29–30.
24. See, for example, Pseudo-Augustine Sermo CCXLI, *De symbolo*, 1, PL 39 : 2189.
25. J. Hardouin, *Acta conciliorum et epistolae decretales ac constitutiones summorum pontificum (34–1714)* (11v. in 12; Paris, 1715), 9 : 842–843.
26. D. G. Monrad, *Die erste Kontroverse über den Ursprung des apostolischen Glaubensbekenntnisses* (Gotha, 1881),

dealing not only with Valla, but also with the Council of Florence.
27. *Laurentii Vallensis, pro se, et contra calumniatores, ad Eugenium IIII. Pont. Max. Apologia* (Strasbourg, 1522), 21v.–22v. (in the Beinecke Library, Yale University).
28. There is a good summary of Valla's theological thought in C. E. Trinkaus, Jr., 'Introduction' to Valla, *Dialogue on Free Will*, in *The Renaissance Philosophy of Man*, E. Cassirer, P. O. Kristeller, and J. H. Randall, Jr., eds. (Chicago, 1948), pp. 147–154.
29. R. H. Bainton, 'Man, God, and the Church in the Age of the Renaissance,' W. K. Ferguson et al, *The Renaissance* (New York, 1962), p. 93.
30. On Valla's relation to the Church, cf. H. J. Grimm, 'Lorenzo Valla's Christianity,' *Church History*, 18 (1949): 75–88.
31. Cf. J. Pelikan, *Obedient Rebels: Catholic Substance and Protestant Principle in Luther's Reformation* (New York and London, 1964), pp. 109–112.
32. 'Disputatio I. Eccii et M. Lutheri Lipsiae habita,' WA 2:262.
33. J. Eck, *Theses 405* (1530), thesis 30, *Quellen und Forschungen zur Geschichte des augsburgischen Glaubensbekenntnisses*, ed. W. Gussman (Kassel, 1930), 2:107.
34. Luther, 'Disputatio ... Lipsiae habita,' WA 2: 288.
35. Luther, 'Disputatio ... Lipsiae habita,' WA 2:283.
36. Cf. H. Jedin, *Geschichte des Konzils von Trient*, 1 (2d ed.; Freiburg, 1951), pp. 472–473.
37. S. Runciman, *The Medieval Manichee: A Study of the Christian Dualist Heresy* (new ed.; New York, 1961), p. 17.
38. Cf. H. Lämmer, *Die vortridentinisch-katholische Theologie* (Berlin, 1858), p. 161.
39. W. Preger, *Matthias Flacius Illyricus und seine Zeit* (2v.; Erlangen, 1859–61), 2:310–412.
40. Apology of the Augsburg Confession, XVIII, 2, *The Book of Concord* (Philadelphia, 1959), p. 225.
41. Ambrosius Catharinus Politus, *Apologia pro veritate catholicae et apostolicae fidei ac doctrinae adversus impia ac valde pestifera Martini Lutheri dogmata* (1520), Book V, ed. J. Schweizer, Corpus Catholicorum 27 (Münster, 1956), p. 339.
42. Cf. R. Seeberg, *Lehrbuch der Dogmengeschichte* (4v.; 5th ed.; Basel, 1953–54), 4:426–429.
43. *Rationis Latominianae pro incendariis Lovaniensis scholae sophistis redditae, Lutheriana confutatio*, Luther, WA 8:117–118; tr. G. H. Lindbeck, *Luther's Works*, (St. Louis and Philadelphia, 1955–), 32:244.

44. See, for example, the materials collected in G. L. Prestige, *God in Patristic Thought* (London, 1956), pp. 200–209. St. Augustine's misgivings about trinitarian terminology are also pertinent here; cf. A. Schindler, *Wort und Analogie in Augustins Trinitätslehre* (Tübingen, 1965), pp. 166–168.
45. As a recent study of the Reformation in England and Scotland has put it, the Reformation 'had weakened all the traditional beliefs without engendering any revolutionary enthusiasm among the people for some new ideal. Respect for the old order had broken down.' J. Ridley, *John Knox* (New York, 1968), p. 98.
46. J. M. Headley, *Luther's View of Church History* (New Haven, 1963), pp. 164–170.
47. M. Luther, *Von den Konziliis und Kirchen*, WA 50:509–653.
48. Cf. Pelikan, *Obedient Rebels*, pp. 54–76.
49. The Franciscan theologian Peter Crabbe had published his *Concilia omnia* in 1538. There is a copy of this book in the Library of Congress; cf. J. T. McNeill, ed., J. Calvin, *Institutes of the Christian Religion*, Library of Christian Classics (Philadelphia, 1960), 1172, n. 9.
50. Luther, *Von den Konziliis und Kirchen*, WA 50:580–585; see pp. 143–145 below.
51. Cf. Headley, *Luther's View*, p. 45.
52. On this element in his thought, especially as it emerged in controversy, cf. E. Staehelin, *Das theologische Lebenswerk Johannes Oekolampads* (Leipzig, 1939), pp. 598ff.
53. J. J. Herzog, 'Oekolampad,' PRE² 10:721.
54. *De genuina verborum Domini, Hoc est corpus meum, juxta veterissimo auctores expositione liber* 'Basel, 1525).
55. See O. Ritschl, *Dogmengeschichte des Protestantismus* (4v.; Leipzig and Göttingen, 1908–27), 3:90–91, for an interpretation of this in its historical context.
56. Cf. J. Pelikan, *Luther the Expositor* (St. Louis, 1959), pp. 120ff.
57. Philipp Melanchthon, 'Epistola Phil. Melanchthonis ad Ioa. Oecolampadium de coena domini,' *Melanchthons Werke*, ed. R. Stupperich, 1 (Gütersloh, 1951–):296–300.
58. See F. H. R. Frank, *Die Theologie der Konkordienformel historisch-dogmatisch entwickelt und beleuchtet* (4v.; Erlangen, 1858–64), 3:397ff.
59. Most of all, of course, historical research was invoked in the eucharistic and christological debates; cf. Ritschl, *Dogmengeschichte des Protestantismus* 4:70–106.
60. Mijo Mirković, 'Predgovor' to Matija Vlačić Illirik, *Katalog svjedoka istine* (Zagreb, 1960), pp. xi–xlix.

61. Cf. note 39 above.
62. The *Clavis scripturae sacrae* first appeared in 1567; I have used an edition dated 'Basel, 1628.'
63. H. Scheible, *Die Entstehung der Magdeburger Zenturien: Ein Beitrag zur Geschichte der historiographischen Methode* (Gütersloh, 1966), has presented the first full-length treatment of this often mentioned but rarely studied work.
64. On the polemical intent of the *Centuries*, cf. Fueter, *Historiographie*, pp. 251–252.
65. F. C. Baur, *The Epochs of Church Historiography*, ed. and tr. P. C. Hodgson, *Ferdinand Christian Baur on the Writing of Church History*, A Library of Protestant Thought (New York, 1968), pp. 82–84.
66. Baur, *Epochs*, p. 97.
67. *Centuriae*, I. Praefatio, quoted in Baur, *Epochs*, p. 97.
68. On these two principles and the controversy over them, cf. P. Hefner, *Faith and the Vitalities of History: A Theological Study Based on the Work of Albrecht Ritschl* (New York, 1966), pp. 54–55.
69. Preger, *Flacius*, 2:449–450.
70. Gustave Bardy, 'Introduction,' SourcesChr 73:79.
71. Preger, *Flacius*, 2:450.
72. K. Heussi, 'Centuriae,' *Harnack-Ehrung* (Leipzig, 1921), pp. 328–334.
73. P. Polman, 'Flacius Illyricus, historien de l'Église,' *Revue d'histoire ecclésiastique*, 27 (1926): 27–73.
74. For a bibliography, cf. *A. Cesare Baronio: Scritti vari* (Sora, Italy, 1963).
75. *Annales ecclesiastici Caes. Baronii S. R. E. Presb. Cardinalis* (12v.; Antwerp, 1602–58), 1:525–529.
76. Baronius *Annales* 1:480–484.
77. Cf. C. J. Hefele, *Histoire des conciles d'après les documents originaux*, tr. H. Leclercq (9v.; Paris, 1907–), 3–1:377–538.
78. Baronius *Annales*, 8:318–325.
79. Honorius I, Epistle 4, PL 80:472: 'Unde et unam voluntatem fatemur Domini nostri Jesu Christi.'
80. Baronius *Annales*, 8:552–556.
81. Cf. Baur, *Epochs*, pp. 106–114; Fueter, *Historiographie*, pp. 263–265.
82. Cf. Baur, *Epochs*, pp. 91–96.
83. See pp. 126–127 below.
84. P. Gay, *The Enlightenment: An Interpretation. The Rise of Modern Paganism* (New York, 1966), p. 156.
85. E. Gibbon, *The History of the Decline and Fall of the Roman Empire*, ed. J. B. Bury (7v.; London, 1896–1900), 2:2.

180 *Notes*

86. The 'obvious but satisfactory answer' that he dismissed was to ascribe the success of Christianity 'to the convincing evidence of the doctrine itself, and to the ruling providence of its great Author.'
87. Gibbon, *Decline and Fall*, 2:23.
88. He seems to speak of the resurrection of the dead only in connection with primitive miracles, Gibbon, *Decline and Fall*, 2:29.
89. Gibbon, *Decline and Fall*, 2:23.
90. Gibbon, *Decline and Fall*, 2:25 and note 68, including Bury's addendum.
91. Gibbon, *Decline and Fall*, 2:28–32.
92. The book was published in London in 1749. The subtitle is instructive: 'By which it is shewn, that we have no sufficient reason to believe, upon the authority of the primitive fathers, that any such powers were continued to the church, after the days of the apostles.'
93. Cf. E. E. Reynolds, *Bossuet* (New York, 1963), pp. 150–163, including the brief discussion of Gibbon, pp. 162–163.
94. E. Gibbon, *Autobiography* [original title, *Memoirs of My Life and Writings*], ed. D. A. Saunders (New York, 1961), p. 84.
95. O. Chadwick, *From Bossuet to Newman: The Idea of Doctrinal Development* (Cambridge, Eng., 1957), p. 75.
96. Gibbon, *Decline and Fall*, 2:29.
97. Gibbon, *Decline and Fall*, 2:30; see also 4:90–91, on miracles in the fifth century.
98. Gibbon, *Decline and Fall*, 2:30.
99. Gibbon, *Decline and Fall*, 2:69.
100. Gibbon, *Decline and Fall*, 2:31.
101. Gibbon seems to be thinking especially of Clement of Alexandria *Paedagogus* 2.8, SourcesChr 108:124–153.
102. Tertullian *De spectaculis* 23, Corpus Christianorum, Series Latina (Turnhout, Belg., 1953–), 1:247.
103. Gibbon, *Decline and Fall*, 2:35.
104. Gibbon, *Decline and Fall*, 2:36–37.
105. Gibbon, *Decline and Fall*, 2:47.
106. Gibbon, *Decline and Fall*, 2:38, n. 101.
107. Gibbon, *Decline and Fall*, 2:39.
108. Gibbon, *Decline and Fall*, 7:308.
109. Gibbon, *Decline and Fall*, 2:40.
110. Gay, *The Enlightenment*, p. 368.
111. Cf. G. Bardy, 'Tillemont,' *Dictionnaire de théologie catholique*, ed. A. Vacant et al (15v.; Paris, 1903–50), 15-1:1029–33.
112. D. Knowles, 'The Maurists,' *Great Historical Enterprises: Problems in Monastic History* (London, 1963), pp. 33–62.

113. Cf. the recent study of S. Körsgen, *Das Bild der Reformation in der Kirchengeschichtschreibung Johann Lorenz von Mosheims* (Tübingen, 1966), esp. pp. 16–38, 153–159.
114. Gibbon, *Decline and Fall*, 2:14.
115. Gibbon, *Decline and Fall*, 2:40, n. 106.
116. Gibbon, *Decline and Fall*, 5:97.
117. E. Hirsch, *Geschichte der neuern evangelischen Theologie* (5v.; Gütersloh, 1949–54), 2:355.
118. Cf. the comments on various biases cited in K. Heussi, *Die Kirchengeschichtschreibung Johann Lorenz von Mosheims* (Gotha, 1904), p. 11, n. 5.
119. *Versuch einer unparteiischen und gründlichen Ketzergeschichte* (Helmstedt, 1746), pp. 36–37, cited in Heussi, *Kirchengeschichtschreibung*, p. 52.
120. *Institutiones historiae ecclesiasticae antiquae et recentioris* (Helmstedt, 1755), pp. 948–949, quoted in Heussi, *Kirchengeschichtschreibung*, p. 52, n. 6.
121. *Institutiones*, p. 554r, quoted in Heussi, *Kirchengeschichtschreibung*, p. 66.
122. The translation, which came to seven volumes, was published at Yverdun in 1776.
123. Cf. E. Exman, *The Brothers Harper* (New York, 1965), pp. 110–111.
124. E. Seeberg, *Gottfried Arnold: Die Wissenschaft und die Mystik seiner Zeit* (Meerane i. Sa. 1923).
125. F. H. Littell, *The Origins of Sectarian Protestantism* (New York, 1964), pp. 46–78.
126. E. Seeberg, *Gottfried Arnold*, p. 67.
127. E. Seeberg, *Gottfried Arnold*, pp. 70–71.
128. E. Seeberg, *Gottfried Arnold*, pp. 193–194.
129. E. Seeberg, *Gottfried Arnold*, p. 224.
130. Thus J. H. Kurtz, *Lehrbuch der Kirchengeschichte für Studierende* (2v.; 13th ed.; Leipzig, 1899), 1:13, speaks of it as 'colossally partisan.'
131. E. Seeberg, *Gottfried Arnold*, pp. 598–611.
132. Cf. P. Hornig, *Die Anfänge der historisch-kritischen Theologie: Johann Salomo Semlers Schriftverständnis und seine Stellung zu Luther* (Göttingen, 1961).
133. Cf. Hirsch, *Geschichte der neuern evangelischen Theologie*, 4:48–89.
134. J. S. Semler, 'Einleitung in die dogmatische Gottesgelersamkeit,' S. J. Baumgarten, *Evangelische Glaubenslehre* (3v.; Halle, 1760), 2:19–20.
135. Semler, 'Einleitung,' 3:126.
136. E. Seeberg, *Gottfried Arnold*, p. 610.
137. Cf. Hirsch, *Geschichte der neuern evangelischen Theologie*, 5:58–59.

138. See A. Hauck, 'Münscher, Wilhelm,' PRE³ 13:537–538.
139. A. von Harnack, *Lehrbuch der Dogmengeschichte* (3v.; 5th ed.; Tübingen, 1931), 1:33.
140. F. Loofs, *Leitfaden zum Studium der Dogmengeschichte*, ed. K. Aland (6th ed.; Tübingen, 1959), p. 1.
141. W. Münscher, *Lehrbuch der christlichen Dogmengeschichte*, ed. D. von Coelln (2v.; 3d ed.; Cassel, 1832–34), 1:2.
142. Münscher, *Lehrbuch*, 1:41–76 on the kingdom of Christ, 76–98 on the angels.
143. Münscher, *Lehrbuch*, 2:109–116 on Filioque, 185–308 on the Sacraments.
144. See Coelln's foreword, Münscher, *Lehrbuch*, 1:x xiii.
145. A. Ritschl, 'Ueber die Methode der älteren Dogmengeschichte,' *Jahrbücher für Deutsche Theologie*, 17 (1871): 191–214; see p. 84 below.
146. Münscher, *Lehrbuch*, 1:4–7.
147. D. Knowles, *Great Historical Enterprises*, p. 38.
148. It was just at the end of this period that J. G. Walch launched his monumental edition of Luther (1740–52); cf. W. Moeller and G. Kawerau, 'Walch, Johann Georg,' PRE³ 20:792–797.
149. Cf. H. Quentin, *Jean-Dominique Mansi et les grandes collections conciliaires* (Paris, 1900).
150. See J. de Ghellinck, 'Une édition patristique célèbre,' *Patristique et moyen-âge: Etudes d'histoire littéraire et doctrinale* (Brussels, 1948), 3:339–484.
151. On the relation between this method and intellectual history, cf. H. Thieme, 'Ideengeschichte und Rechtsgeschichte,' *Festschrift für J. v. Gierke* (Berlin, 1950), pp. 266–289.
152. Cf. E. Wolf, *Grosse Rechtsdenker der deutschen Geistesgeschichte* (4th ed.; Tübingen, 1963), pp. 467–542.
153. E. L. Fackenheim, *The Religious Dimension in Hegel's Thought* (Bloomington, Ind., 1967), pp. 165–184.
154. W. Windelband, *A History of Philosophy*, trans. J. W. Tufts (2v.; New York, 1958), 1:10.
155. Cf. J. Pelikan, 'Josef Miloslav Hurban: A Study in Historicism,' *The Impact of the Church upon Its Culture*, ed. J. C. Brauer (Chicago, 1968), pp. 333–352; also F. Kutnar, 'Palackého pojetí společnosti, národa a státu,' *Tři studie o Františku Palackém* (Olomouc, Czech., 1949), pp. 7–42.
156. K. Barth, *Die protestantische Theologie im 19. Jahrhundert* (Zürich, 1952), p. 156. The translation is my own, but the passage does appear in the English version, *Protestant Thought from Rousseau to Ritschl* (New York, 1959), pp. 311–312.

157. W. Geiger, *Spekulation und Kritik: Die Geschichtstheologie Ferdinand Christian Baurs* (Munich, 1964); P. C. Hodgson, *The Formation of Historical Theology: A Study of Ferdinand Christian Baur* (New York, 1966).
158. In the following paragraphs I have adapted some of what I have written about Baur in my 'Editor's Preface' to Hodgson, *Formation of Historical Theology*, pp. ix–x, and in my article, 'Baur, Ferdinand Christian,' *Encyclopaedia Britannica* (1968), 3:298–299.
159. F. C. Baur, *Die sogenannten Pastoralbriefe des Apostels Paulus aufs neue kritisch untersucht* (Stuttgart and Tübingen, 1835).
160. *Die christliche Lehre von der Versöhnung in ihrer geschichtlichen Entwicklung von der ältesten Zeit bis auf die neueste* (Tübingen, 1838).
161. *Die christliche Lehre von der Dreieinigkeit und Menschwerdung Gottes in ihrer geschichtlichen Entwicklung* (Tübingen, 1841–43).
162. *Vorlesungen über die christliche Dogmengeschichte*, ed. F. F. Baur (3v.; Leipzig, 1865–67).
163. Cf. Hefner, *Faith and the Vitalities of History*, 14–26: 'The Baurian Background.'
164. Hodgson, *Formation of Historical Theology*, p. 238.
165. Hodgson, *Formation of Historical Theology*, p. 241.
166. See the monographs cited in notes 160 and 161 above.
167. On Baur and the problem of periodization, cf. pp. 125–126 below.
168. E. Troeltsch, 'Adolf von Harnack and Ferdinand Christian von Baur 1921,' tr. in W. Pauck, *Harnack and Troeltsch: Two Historical Theologians* (New York, 1968), pp. 97, 99.
169. Cf. Hodgson, *Formation of Historical Theology*, p. 156.
170. Baur, *Epochs*, pp. 241–245.
171. See the bibliography appended to this monograph.
172. Although the English literature on Möhler is sparse, there is a useful summary in S. Bolshakoff, *The Doctrine of the Unity of the Church in the Works of Khomyakov and Moehler* (London, 1946), pp. 217–262.
173. It is now available in a new edition by J. R. Geiselmann (2v.; Darmstadt, 1958–1961); see p. 165, n. 2 above.
174. F. C. Baur, *Der Gegensatz des Katholizismus und des Protestantismus* (Tübingen, 1834); cf. Hodgson, *The Formation of Historical Theology*, pp. 22–23.
175. J. A. Möhler, *Symbolik oder Darstellung der dogmatischen Gegensätze der Katholiken und Protestanten nach ihren öffentlichen Bekenntnisschriften*, ed. J. R. Geiselmann (2v.; Darmstadt, 1958–61), 1:415–416.

176. J. A. Möhler, *Die Einheit in der Kirche oder das Prinzip des Katholizismus, dargestellt im Geist der Kirchenväter der drei ersten Jahrhunderte,* ed. J. R. Geiselmann (Cologne, 1957).
177. Cf. Geiselmann's comments in Möhler, *Symbolik,* 2:743.
178. Quoted from the manuscripts, Möhler, *Symbolik,* 2:705.
179. Möhler, *Symbolik,* 2:717.
180. J. R. Geiselmann, 'Der Einflusz der Christologie des Konzils von Chalkedon auf die Theologie Johann Adam Möhlers,' Grill-Bacht Konz 3:341–420.
181. J. A. Möhler, *Athanasius der Grosse und die Kirche seiner Zeit* (2v.; Mainz, 1827), 1:305–333, cited Grill-Bacht Konz, 3:388–390.
182. See H. Fries, 'Die Dogmengeschichte des fünften Jahrhunderts im theologischen Werdegang von John Henry Newman,' Grill-Bacht Konz, 3:421–454.
183. J. H. Newman, *An Essay on the Development of Christian Doctrine,* int. G. Weigel (New York, 1960), p. 53.
184. Chadwick, *From Bossuet to Newman,* pp. 102–119.
185. Hodgson, *Formation of Historical Theology,* p. 157, n. 44.
186. A. O. Lovejoy, 'On the Discrimination of Romanticisms,' *Essays in the History of Ideas* (New York, 1955), pp. 228–253.
187. See Bolshakoff, *Doctrine of the Unity of the Church.*
188. J. H. Nichols, *Romanticism in American Theology: Nevin and Schaff at Mercersburg* (Chicago, 1961), pp. 107–139.
189. Ernest D. Nielsen, *N. F. S. Grundtvig: An American Study* (Rock Island, Ill., 1955), pp. 63–125.
190. Cf. Chadwick, *From Bossuet to Newman,* p. 99.
191. *The Church of the Fathers* (1833), *Essays and Sketches,* ed. C. F. Harrold (3v.; New York, 1948), 3:1–154.
192. See Newman, *Apologia,* ed. Svaglic, 'Note E,' p. 298.
193. *Select Treatises of S. Athanasius, Archbishop of Alexandria, in Controversy with the Arians,* Library of the Fathers (43v.; Oxford, 1838–74), vols. 8 and 19.
194. 'The Nicene Tests of Orthodoxy,' *Select Treatises of St. Athanasius in Controversy with the Arians Freely Translated by John Henry Cardinal Newman* (2v.; London, 1900), 2:226–234.
195. Newman, 'Heresies,' *Select Treatises of Athanasius,* 2:143–149; 'Tradition,' 1:311–314.
196. We have used here the edition cited p. 169, n. 22; see also C. F. Harrold, ed., *An Essay on the Development of Christian Doctrine* (New York, 1949), collating the first and the revised edition.
197. See pp. 20–21 above and the literature cited there.
198. One such is William Archer Butler, *Letters on Romanism*

in Reply to Mr. Newman's Essay on Development (2d. ed.; Cambridge, 1858).

199. See the comments of F. Kattenbusch, 'Newman, John Henry,' PRE³ 14:1–8.
200. Harnack, *Lehrbuch*, 1:46–47.
201. For a recent full-length study, cf. G. W. Glick, *The Reality of Christianity: A Study of Adolf von Harnack as Historian and Theologian* (New York, 1967); also Pauck, *Harnack and Troeltsch*.
202. A. von Harnack, *Zur Quellenkritik der Geschichte des Gnostizismus* (Leipzig, 1873). Unless it is indicated otherwise, all works cited in the balance of this chapter are by Harnack.
203. *De Apellis gnosi monarchica* (Leipzig, 1874).
204. *Patrum apostolicorum opera*, ed. O. v. Gebhardt, T. Zahn, and A. Harnack (Leipzig, 1875).
205. *Die Zeit des Ignatius und die Chronologie der Antiochenischen Bischöfe bis Tyrannus nach Julius Africanus und den späteren Historikern* (Leipzig, 1878).
206. Cf. his review of 'Bishop Lightfoot's *Ignatius and Polycarp*,' *The Expositor*, Series 3, 2 (1885):401–414; 3 (1886):175–192.
207. G. Uhlhorn, 'Ignatius,' PRE² 6:694.
208. M. Christlieb, *Harnack-Bibliographie: Zum sechzigsten Geburtstage Adolf Harnacks zusammengestellt* (Leipzig, 1912).
209. F. Smend, *Adolf von Harnack: Verzeichnis seiner Schriften* (Leipzig, 1927).
210. F. Smend, *Adolf von Harnack: Verzeichnis seiner Schriften 1927–1930*, and Axel von Harnack, *Verzeichnis der ihm gewidmeten Schriften* (Leipzig, 1931).
211. Quoted in A. von Zahn-Harnack, *Adolf von Harnack* (2d ed.; Berlin, 1951), p. 409.
212. The most notable exceptions were several of his public writings during World War I; these were collected in *Aus der Friedens- und Kriegsarbeit* (Giessen, 1916), pp. 279–350. See also H. W. Gatzke, *Germany's Drive to the West (Drang nach Westen): A Study of Germany's Western War Aims during the First World War* (Baltimore, 1966), pp. 132–137.
213. *Die Mission und Ausbreitung des Christentums in den ersten drei Jahrhunderten* (Leipzig, 1902). In the second edition (Leipzig, 1906) the work grew to two volumes. The third edition appeared in 1915, the fourth in 1923.
214. Translated in J. Pelikan, 'Introduction to the Torchbook Edition' of *The Mission and Expansion of Christianity in the First Three Centuries* (New York, 1961), p. vii.

215. 'Das Mönchtum, seine Ideale und seine Geschichte' (1881), *Reden und Aufsätze* (2v.; 2d ed.; Giessen, 1906), 1:81–140. There were translations into Danish, English, Hungarian, Italian, Russian, and Swedish.
216. The most noteworthy of these was *Entstehung und Entwicklung der Kirchenverfassung und des Kirchenrechts in den zwei ersten Jahrhunderten* (Leipzig, 1910), a thoroughgoing critique of the theories of R. Sohm.
217. Cf. *Aus der Friedens- und Kriegsarbeit*, pp. 163–172.
218. A. Harnack and O. v. Gebhardt, eds., *Texte und Untersuchungen zur Geschichte der altchristlichen Literatur* (Leipzig, 1882–).
219. *Geschichte der altchristlichen Literatur bis Eusebius* (3v.; Leipzig, 1893–1904).
220. *Marcion: Das Evangelium vom fremden Gott. Eine Monographie zur Geschichte der Grundlegung der katholischen Kirche* (Leipzig, 1921).
221. *Marcion*, p. iii.
222. Cf. Glick, *Reality of Christianity*, pp. 112–121.
223. R. M. Grant, *Gnosticism and Early Christianity* (New York, 1959), pp. 120–150.
224. See the quotation in Zahn-Harnack, *Harnack*, p. 401.
225. Pauck, *Harnack and Troeltsch*, p. 22.
226. The titles of the three volumes of the *Lehrbuch der Dogmengeschichte* were: I. *Die Entstehung des kirchlichen Dogmas*; II–III. *Die Entwicklung des kirchlichen Dogmas*.
227. On the dates of the various editions and translations, see Smend, *Verzeichnis* (1927), p. 21.
228. Harnack to Loofs, Dec. 20, 1885, Zahn-Harnack, *Harnack*, p. 101.
229. Loofs, *Leitfaden zum Studium der Dogmengeschichte* (6th ed.). In the preface to the third edition (Halle, 1893), p. iv, Loofs had called himself a 'common laborer [*Kärrner*]' in relation to Harnack.
230. *Leitfaden* (Aland ed.), p. 6.
231. *Lehrbuch der Dogmengeschichte* (3v.; 5th ed.; Tübingen, 1931), 3:661–908.
232. See p. 87 below.
233. Cf. Hodgson, *Formation of Historical Theology*, pp. 241–242.
234. Zahn-Harnack, *Harnack*, p. 129.
235. On the significance of this movement for subsequent scholarship, see the comments of W. von Loewenich, 'Lutherforschung in Deutschland' in V. Vajta, ed., *Lutherforschung heute: Referate und Berichte des 1. Inter-*

Notes

nationalen *Lutherforschungskongresses* (Berlin, 1958), pp. 150–171.

236. 'Karl Holl: Rede bei der Gedächtnisfeier der Universität Berlin am 12. Juni 1926,' *Adolf von Harnack: Aus der Werkstatt des Vollendeten,* ed. Axel von Harnack (Giessen, 1930), pp. 275–288.
237. J. Pelikan, 'Adolf von Harnack on Luther' in *Interpreters of Luther: Essays in Honor of Wilhelm Pauck,* ed. J. Pelikan (Philadelphia, 1968), pp. 253–274.
238. *Lehrbuch,* 3:861–863.
239. *Lehrbuch,* 1:21–22.
240. *Lehrbuch,* 3:814 (italics his).
241. Cf. Pelikan, 'Adolf von Harnack on Luther,' pp. 261–262.
242. He spoke of an 'antenna,' Zahn-Harnack, *Harnack,* p. 416.
243. See pp. 119–120 below.
244. *Lehrbuch,* 1:20.
245. Cf. Glick, *Reality of Christianity,* pp. 181–215.
246. Pauck, *Harnack and Troeltsch,* pp. 32–33.
247. Glick, *Reality of Christianity,* pp. 263–317.
248. Smend, *Verzeichnis* (1927), 'Anhang I,' pp. 137–138.
249. The English translation was done by T. B. Saunders and published as *What Is Christianity?* in London in 1901; a new edition, with a foreword by R. Bultmann, appeared in New York in 1957.
250. Zahn-Harnack, *Harnack,* pp. 185–188; Glick, *Reality of Christianity,* pp. 280–302.
251. *What Is Christianity?,* pp. 5–6.
252. Cf. Glick, *Reality of Christianity,* pp. 264–266.
253. Pelikan, 'Introduction' to *Mission and Expansion,* pp. v–vii.
254. Glick, *Reality of Christianity,* p. 88.
255. Harnack to W. Stintzing, quoted in Zahn-Harnack, *Harnack,* p. 23.
256. To the non-specialist, he is perhaps best known for his *Handbuch der alttestamentlichen Theologie,* ed. R. Kittel (Leipzig, 1895).
257. Zahn-Harnack, *Harnack,* p. 191–193.
258. See, for example, J. Moltmann, 'Exegese und Eschatologie der Geschichte,' *Perspektiven der Theologie: Gesammelte Aufsätze* (Munich, 1968), p. 63, n. 18.
259. See pp. 113–114 below.
260. K. Barth, 'The Revelation of God as the Abolition of Religion,' *Church Dogmatics* (New York, 1936–), I/2:280–361.
261. It is interesting that in the evaluation both of St. Bernard, *Lehrbuch,* 3:343–344, and of the *unio mystica* in Protes-

tantism, *Lehrbuch*, 3:873. Harnack explicitly refers to Ritschl.
262. See the discussion in Barth, *Church Dogmatics*, I/2:318–320.
263. K. Barth, *The Epistle to the Romans*, tr. E. C. Hoskyns (Oxford, 1933), p. 13.
264. F. Flückiger, *Der Ursprung des christlichen Dogmas: Eine Auseinandersetzung mit Albert Schweitzer und Martin Werner* (Zürich, 1955).
265. W. Pauck, 'A Brief Criticism of Barth's *Dogmatics*,' *The Heritage of the Reformation* (2d ed.; Glencoe, Ill., 1961), pp. 353–359.
266. Notably *Sources chrétiennes* (Paris, 1941–) and *Corpus Christianorum* (Turnhout, 1953–).
267. Barth, *Church Dogmatics*, I/1:361, 443.
268. The *Lehrbuch der Dogmengeschichte* and the English translations both of the *Lehrbuch* and of the *Grundriss* have all been reprinted photomechanically; only the last has any new material, i.e., an introduction by P. Rieff, *Outlines of the History of Dogma* (Boston, 1957).
269. Despite a fundamental difference of theological perspective, this is evident even in A. Adam, *Lehrbuch der Dogmengeschichte* (Gütersloh, 1965–), 1:20–24.
270. See p. 82 below.
271. Zahn-Harnack, *Harnack*, pp. 144–160: 'Der Kampf um das Apostolikum.'

Notes to Chapter Three

1. See pp. 129–155 below.
2. For a general introduction to the problem, cf. J. Higham, ed., *The Reconstruction of American History* (New York, 1962), where various periods and problems of American secular history are reinterpreted.
3. See C. V. Woodward, 'The Hidden Sources of Negro History,' *Saturday Review* (January 18, 1969), pp. 18–22, reviewing various monographs in the field.
4. Cf. H. S. Smith in H. S. Smith, R. T. Handy, and L. A. Loetscher, *American Christianity: An Historical Interpretation with Representative Documents* (2v.; New York, 1960–63), 2:167–212.
5. A. von Zahn-Harnack, *Adolf von Harnack* (2d ed.; Berlin, 1951), p. 416.
6. F. C. Baur, *Das Markusevangelium nach seinem Ursprung und Charakter: Nebst einem Anhang über das Evangelium Marcions* (Tübingen, 1851).

7. P. C. Hodgson, *Formation of Historical Theology: A Study of Ferdinand Christian Baur* (New York, 1966), pp. 214–217.
8. A. von Harnack, *Luke the Physician, the Author of the Third Gospel and the Acts of the Apostles*, tr. J. R. Wilkinson (New York, 1907); *The Acts of the Apostles*, tr. J. R. Wilkinson (New York, 1909).
9. Harnack to Holl, 1905, Zahn-Harnack, *Harnack*, p. 279.
10. See the brief but moving testimonial of H. Bornkamm, 'Hans Lietzmann,' and the accompanying bibliography of K. Aland *Zeitschrift für die neutestamentliche Wissenschaft und die Kunde der älteren Kirche* (Giessen-Berlin, 1900–), 41 (1940): 1–33
11. For a brilliant summary, see R. Bultmann, 'The Gospels,' *Twentieth-Century Theology in the Making*, ed. J. Pelikan (3v.; London, 1969–70), 1:86–92.
12. Cf. E. C. Colwell, *Jesus and the Gospel* (New York, 1963), 21–41, commenting on recent trends in the historiography of the Gospels.
13. See R. M. Grant, *A Historical Introduction to the New Testament* (New York, 1963), pp. 13–17, 396–423.
14. Luther, for example, paraphrases 1 Cor 15.3–11: 'I did not receive it from others, who were Apostles before me and saw and heard Christ. . . . But I myself have seen Him, just as all the others have and was made an Apostle by Him.' *Das 15. Capitel der 1. Epistel S. Pauli an die Corinther*, WA 36:508.
15. See H. Sasse, *This Is My Body: Luther's Contention for the Real Presence in the Sacrament of the Altar* (Minneapolis, 1959), pp. 352–355.
16. See pp. 35–36 above.
17. Cf., for example, Luther's sermon of May 23, 1535, WA 41:275.
18. Cf. Kelly, *Early Christian Creeds* (London, 1952), pp. 1–29.
19. See E. Stauffer, *New Testament Theology*, tr. J. Marsh (New York, 1955), 235–257, 320–328.
20. Thus James Orr felt able to say, *The Progress of Dogma* (Grand Rapids, Mich., 1952), 33: 'I am warranted in passing over preliminary stages, and in coming at once to the second century.'
21. *Didache*, pp. 9–10, *The Apostolic Fathers*, ed. J. B. Lightfoot (London, 1893), pp. 221–222.
22. J. Muilenburg, *The Literary Relations of the Epistle of Barnabas and the Teaching of the Twelve Apostles* (Marburg, 1929).
23. Many New Testament scholars would assign at least some

of the following books to the second century: Luke–Acts in its present recension; the Gospel of John; the Pastoral Epistles; 2 Peter; Jude.
24. See, for example, A. C. McGiffert, *A History of Christian Thought* (2v.; New York, 1947), 1:1–15, 25–28.
25. E. Lohmeyer, *Kyrios Jesus: Eine Untersuchung zu Phil. 2, 5–11* (Heidelberg, 1928); also O. Cullmann, *The Christology of the New Testament*, tr. S. C. Guthrie and C. A. M. Hall (Philadelphia, 1959), pp. 174–181.
26. F. Hahn, *Christologische Hoheitstitel: Ihre Geschichte im frühen Christentum* (Göttingen, 1963).
27. On the christological testimony of the demons in Mark, cf. J. Bieneck, *Sohn Gottes als Christusbezeichnung der Synoptiker* (Zürich, 1951), pp. 37–38, 51–52.
28. Cf. P. Althaus et al, 'Eschatology' in Pelikan, *Twentieth-Century Theology in the Making*, 1:215–293.
29. See p. 186, n. 215 above.
30. Cf. E. Massaux, *Influence de l'Evangile de Saint Matthieu sur la littérature chrétienne avant Saint Irénée* (Louvain, 1950), pp. 7–17.
31. Cf. A. N. Wilder, *Eschatology and Ethics in the Teaching of Jesus* (2d ed.; New York, 1950).
32. See p. 186, n. 216 above; also A. von Harnack, *The Mission and Expansion of Christianity in the First Three Centuries*, tr. J. Moffatt (New York, 1961), pp. 36–43.
33. W. D. Davies, *The Setting of the Sermon on the Mount* (Cambridge, Eng., 1964), pp. 94–99, 415–435.
34. M. Werner, *Die Entstehung des christlichen Dogmas problemgeschichtlich dargestellt* (Bern-Leipzig, 1941), abridged and tr. S. G. F. Brandon as *The Formation of Christian Dogma* (London, 1957). We shall cite the German edition.
35. Werner, *Entstehung*, pp. 3–15.
36. Werner, *Entstehung*, pp. 78–79.
37. Werner, *Entstehung*, pp. 88–98.
38. Werner, *Entstehung*, pp. 371–388.
39. So, for example, Werner's interpretation of Apollinaris, *Entstehung*, pp. 631–635.
40. G. L. Prestige, *God in Patristic Thought* (London, 1956), pp. 97–101; E. Evans, ed., *Tertullian's Treatise Against Praxeas* (London, 1948), pp. 38–75.
41. Tertullian *Apologeticum, 39.2, Corpus Christianorum*, Series latina (Turnhout, Belg., 1953–), 1:150.
42. Werner, *Entstehung*, pp. 111–113.
43. Cf. J. Pelikan, *The Finality of Jesus Christ in an Age of Universal History: A Dilemma of the Third Century* (London, 1965), pp. 7–18.

44. See the many passages from Tertullian quoted in Pelikan, *Finality*, pp. 9–12.
45. Cf. Pelikan, *Finality*, pp. 38–47 on Montanism.
46. See pp. 63–64 above.
47. Werner, *Entstehung*, pp. 28–34.
48. For a critique of the method, see J. Barr, *The Semantics of Biblical Language* (Oxford, 1961), pp. 206–262.
49. An interesting example, drawn from the Kittel *Wörterbuch*, is W. Zimmerli and J. Jeremias, *The Servant of God* (Naperville, Ill., 1957).
50. H. A. Wolfson, *Philo: Foundations of Religious Philosophy in Judaism, Christianity and Islam* (2v.; Cambridge, Mass., 1947), 1:226–240, 253–261, 287–289.
51. See pp. 138–140 below.
52. R. Bultmann, *Theologie des Neuen Testaments* (Tübingen, 1953), p. 123.
53. A. von Harnack, 'Judentum und Judenchristentum in Justins Dialog mit Trypho,' TU 39–1:47–96.
54. R. L. Wilken, 'Judaism in Roman and Christian Society,' *Journal of Religion*, 47 (1967):313–330.
55. R. L. Wilken, 'Exegesis and the History of Theology: Reflections on the Adam-Christ Typology in Cyril of Alexandria,' *Church History*, 35 (1966):139–156.
56. B. Blumenkranz, *Die Judenpredigt Augustins* (Basel, 1946), and the brief summary in F. Van der Meer, *Augustine the Bishop*, tr. Brian Battershaw and G. R. Lamb (London and New York, 1961), pp. 76–78.
57. PG 48:843–942.
58. C. H. Kraeling, 'The Jewish Community at Antioch,' *Journal of Biblical Literature*, 51 (1932):130–160; G. Downey, *A History of Antioch in Syria from Seleucus to the Arab Conquest* (Princeton, 1961), pp. 447–449.
59. On its origins, see the literature cited p. 176, n. 16–19 above.
60. For example, St. James of Nisibis took part in the Council of Nicea; see the note on Theodoret *Historia ecclesiastica* 2:26, NicPNicChFath 3:91.
61. Cf. A. Vööbus, *History of the School of Nisibis* (Louvain, 1965) for an account of the present state of the material, both published and unpublished.
62. I. Ortiz de Urbina, *Die Gottheit Christi bei Afrahat*, *Oriens Christianus*, 87 (1933).
63. The most authoritative recent summary is that of A. Vööbus, 'Syriac Literature,' *Encyclopaedia Britannica* (1968), 21:586–590.
64. Cf. A. Vööbus, *The Statutes of the School of Nisibis*

(Stockholm, 1962), for a collection of texts previously unknown.
65. For example, the earliest of available Syriac manuscripts, which is in the British Museum, contains the treatise of Titus of Bostra against the Manicheans (available only in Syriac), the *Theophania* of Eusebius of Caesarea (also available only in Syriac), the *Recognitions* of Pseudo-Clement (present also in a Latin version), and the *Martyrs of Palestine* of Eusebius (partially preserved in the original Greek).
66. This was the title of the Hibbert Lectures delivered in 1888 by E. Hatch, *The Influence of Greek Ideas and Usages upon the Christian Church* (4th ed.; London, 1892).
67. Cf. J. Pelikan, *Development of Christian Doctrine: Some Historical Prolegomena* (New Haven, 1969), pp. 25–28.
68. See H. R. Niebuhr, *The Social Sources of Denominationalism* (New York, 1929), esp. pp. 264–284.
69. S. Runciman, *The Eastern Schism: A Study of the Papacy and the Eastern Churches during the XIth and XIIth Centuries* (Oxford, 1956), pp. 159–170.
70. S. Runciman, *A History of the Crusades* (3v.; New York, 1964–67), 3:107–131.
71. E. Hirsch, *Geschichte der neuern evangelischen Theologie* (5v.; Gütersloh, 1949–59), 2:133–138, on how the Pietism of Spener gradually made confessional distinctions unimportant.
72. Cf. R. Seeberg, *Lehrbuch der Dogmengeschichte* (4v.; 5th ed.; Basel, 1953–54), 4:607–608.
73. Cf. C. J. Curtis, *Nathan Söderblom: Theologian of Revelation* (Chicago, 1966), pp. 45–127, on the outstanding example of this relation.
74. This is, at least in part, a consequence of the nature of the sources themselves; thus, for example, the acts of the ecumenical councils are shaped by the confessional and theological partisanship of the post-conciliar debates.
75. For an interesting exception, see R. P. Scharlemann, *Thomas Aquinas and John Gerhard* (New Haven, 1964).
76. Cf. pp. 147–148 below.
77. See, for example, O. H. Pesch, *Theologie der Rechtfertigung bei Martin Luther und Thomas von Aquin* (Mainz, 1967).
78. See p. 37 above.
79. W. Preger, *Matthias Flacius Illyricus und seine Zeit* (2v.; Erlangen, 1859–61), 2:209–210.
80. G. J. Hoenderdaal, ed., *Verklaring van Jacobus Arminius* (Lochem, 1960), pp. 26–27.

Notes 193

81. For a summary of recent scholarship, cf. R. F. Evans, *Pelagius: Inquiries and Reappraisals* (New York, 1968).
82. R. A. Norris, *Manhood and Christ: A Study in the Christology of Theodore of Mopsuestia* (Oxford, 1963), p. 186.
83. G. Florovsky, 'The Quest for Christian Unity and the Orthodox Church,' *Theology and Life,* 4 (1961): 201.
84. Cf. P. Tillich, *Systematic Theology* (3v.; Chicago, 1951-63), 2: 138-150.
85. A. Grillmeier, 'Die theologische und sprachliche Vorbereitung der christologischen Formel von Chalkedon,' Grill-Bacht Konz, 1: 67-102.
86. J. F. Bethune-Baker, *The Meaning of Homoousios in the Constantinopolitan Creed* (Cambridge, Eng., 1901).
87. Prestige, *God in Patristic Thought,* pp. 233-241.
88. C. N. Cochrane, *Christianity and Classical Culture: A Study of Thought and Action from Augustus to Augustine* (Oxford, 1944), pp. 213-215.
89. Cf. J. H. Waszink, ed., *Quinti Septimi Florentis Tertulliani De anima* (Amsterdam, 1947), for a detailed comparison.
90. Cf. WA 10-I-1: 457, where the words of Jesus about 'the blind leading the blind' (Mt 15.14) are cited as a 'proverb.'
91. Cf. WA 44: 483, where a verbatim quotation from the *Gloria in excelsis* of the Mass is left unnoted.
92. A good illustration is the word 'nature,' whose meaning in relation both to dogma and to the development of usage has been investigated in C. S. Lewis, *Studies in Words* (Cambridge, Eng., 1960), pp. 24-74.
93. See pp. 116-117 below.
94. A. N. Whitehead, *Science and the Modern World* (New York, 1952), p. 49; see also A. Nygren, 'The Role of the Self-Evident in History,' *Journal of Religion,* 28 (1948): 235-241.
95. Abiel Holmes (1763-1837), minister of the First Congregational Church in Cambridge, Mass., 1792-1829, was the son-in-law and biographer of Ezra Stiles.
96. O. W. Holmes, Jr., to L. Einstein, Aug. 9, 1921, *The Holmes-Einstein Letters,* ed. J. B. Peabody (New York, 1964), p. 197.
97. See, for one example, the autobiography of E. S. Ames, *Beyond Theology* (Chicago, 1959), pp. 27-35.
98. Mosheim, *Institutiones historiae ecclesiasticae antiquae et recentioris,* quoted in Heussi, *Kirchengeschichtschreibung,* p. 72.
99. E. S. Morgan, *The Gentle Puritan: A Life of Ezra Stiles, 1727-95* (New Haven, 1962), pp. 376-377.
100. Cf. G. W. Glick, *The Reality of Christianity: A Study of*

Adolf von Harnack as Historian and Theologian (New York, 1967), pp. 280–302.
101. Zahn-Harnack, *Harnack*, p. 180.
102. O. Dibelius, *In the Service of the Lord: The Autobiography of Bishop Otto Dibelius*, tr. M. Ilford (New York, 1964), pp. 43–46.
103. D. Bonhoeffer to A. Harnack, Dec. 18, 1929, D. Bonhoeffer, *Gesammelte Schriften* (4v.; Munich, 1958–61), 3:18–19; see M. Bosanquet, *The Life and Death of Dietrich Bonhoeffer* (New York, 1968), pp. 57–60.
104. 'Rede zum Gedächtnis Adolf von Harnacks am 15. Juni 1930 in der Kaiser-Wilhelm-Gesellschaft,' *Gesammelte Schriften*, 3:59–61.
105. Only one of his books is available in English: *The Angels and the Liturgy*, tr. Ronald Walls (London, 1964).
106. E. Peterson, 'Briefwechsel mit Adolf Harnack und ein Epilog,' *Theologische Traktate* (Munich, 1951), pp. 299–321.
107. Glick, *Reality of Christianity*, 258.
108. A. von Harnack, *What Is Christianity?* (new ed.; New York, 1957), p. 300.
109. G. Biemer, *Newman on Tradition*, tr. K. Smyth (New York, 1967), pp. 33–67.
110. J. H. Newman, *Apologia pro vita sua*, ed. M. J. Svaglic (Oxford, 1967), pp. 100–111.
111. G. Krüger, *Was heisst und zu welchem Ende studiert man Dogmengeschichte?* (Freiburg, 1895).
112. See p. 182, n. 145.
113. F. Loofs, 'Dogmengeschichte,' PRE³ 4:752–764 (still the best brief introduction to the subject); 'Doctrine, History of,' *The New Schaff-Herzog Encyclopedia of Religious Knowledge* (13v.; Grand Rapids, Mich., 1953–54), 3:460–463.
114. For a recent summary of the problem, cf. K. Aland, 'Dogmengeschichte,' *Die Religion in Geschichte und Gegenwart* (6v.; 3d ed.; Tübingen, 1957–63), 2:230–234.
115. J. Kunze, 'Loci theologici,' PRE³ 11:570–572.
116. In W. Münscher, *Lehrbuch der christlichen Dogmengeschichte*, ed. D. von Coelln (2v.; 3d ed.; Cassel, 1832–34), 1:76–98, the doctrine of the angels is presented in isolation from the doctrine of God as Creator, 1:141–150, even though, as Münscher himself notes, 1:142, one of the themes of the doctrine of creation was the rejection of the notion of subordinate demiurges.
117. Cf. J. Pelikan, *Obedient Rebels: Catholic Substance and Protestant Principle in Luther's Reformation* (New York and London, 1964), pp. 46–53.

Notes 195

118. A. Harnack, 'Geschichte der Lehre vor der Seligkeit allein durch den Glauben in der alten Kirche,' *Zeitschrift für Theologie und Kirche*, 1 (1891): 82–178.
119. See pp. 10–11 above.
120. R. Schimmelpfennig, *Die Geschichte der Marienverehrung im deutschen Protestantismus* (Paderborn, 1952) is a competent summary.
121. Cf. Münscher, *Lehrbuch*, 1: 284–287.
122. For representative texts and comments, see the convenient collection of C. H. Ratschow, *Lutherische Dogmatik zwischen Reformation und Aufklärung* (2v.; Gütersloh, 1964–66), 1: 21–57, 141–152.
123. See pp. 121–123 below.
124. Cf. T. Tappert et al, eds., *The Book of Concord* (Philadelphia, 1959).
125. P. Schaff, *The Creeds of Christendom* (3v.; New York, 1919), 3: 383–436.
126. Schaff, *Creeds*, 3: 550–597.
127. G. Thomasius, *Die Christliche Dogmengeschichte als Entwicklungs-Geschichte des kirchlichen Lehrbegriffs* (2v.; Erlangen, 1874–76), 2: 237–239, 445–446.
128. See C. Welch, ed., *God and Incarnation in Mid-Nineteenth Century German Theology*, A Library of Protestant Thought (New York, 1965), pp. 25–101.
129. See p. 85 above.
130. See, for example, G. Thomasius, *Christi Person und Werk* (4v.; 2d ed.; Erlangen, 1856–63), 1: 368–447 on both the need and the capacity of redemption according to various theological traditions.
131. R. Seeberg, *Lehrbuch der Dogmengeschichte* (2v.; Leipzig, 1895–98) was the first edition; but unless otherwise indicated, we shall continue to cite the fifth edition (Basel, 1953–54).
132. G. Thomasius, *Die Christliche Dogmengeschichte* (2v.; 2d ed.; Erlangen, 1886–89).
133. Cf. R. Seeberg, *Lehrbuch*, 1: 1–15.
134. Seeberg, *Lehrbuch*, 1: 15, n. 2.
135. Cf. Seeberg, *Lehrbuch*, 1: 19–20, n. 1.
136. Seeberg, *Lehrbuch*: on Augustine, 2: 396–567; on Luther, 4: 1–479.
137. See Glick, *Reality of Christianity*, pp. 29–34.
138. Cf. his comment on Origen, *Lehrbuch der Dogmengeschichte* (3v.; 5th ed.; Tübingen, 1931), 1: 659, n. 3.
139. See pp. 62–63 above.
140. Harnack, *Lehrbuch*, 3: 808–896.
141. Above all see Harnack, *Lehrbuch*, 2: 467–478.
142. Harnack, *Lehrbuch*, 2: 395–400.

143. See p. 60 above.
144. R. M. Grant, ed. *Gnosticism: A Source Book of Heretical Writings from the Early Christian Period* (New York, 1961), pp. 44–46.
145. J. Knox, *Marcion and the New Testament Canon* (Chicago, 1942).
146. See p. 186, n. 230 above.
147. Harnack, *Lehrbuch*, 1:38.
148. See, for example, Harnack, *Lehrbuch*, 3:347–354.
149. This is aimed at the *religionsgeschichtliche Schule*; on Harnack's relation to it, see Glick, *The Reality of Christianity*, pp. 206–215.
150. Harnack, *Lehrbuch* (3d ed.; Leipzig, 1894–97), 1:764–766.
151. Harnack, *Lehrbuch*, 1:806–808.
152. Harnack, *Lehrbuch*, 2:438.
153. Harnack, *Lehrbuch*, 2:440.
154. Harnack, *Lehrbuch*, 2:160–165 and *passim*.
155. J. Ratté, *Three Modernists: Alfred Loisy, George Tyrrell, William L. Sullivan* (New York, 1967), 78–85.
156. 'To Adolf Harnack in long-standing gratitude': O. Ritschl, *Dogmengeschichte des Protestantismus* (4v.; Leipzig and Göttingen, 1908–27), 1:iii.
157. Ritschl, *Dogmengeschichte des Protestantismus*, 1:14–36.
158. Ritschl, *Dogmengeschichte des Protestantismus*, 1:4–5.
159. See p. 62 above.
160. A. C. McGiffert, *A History of Christian Thought* (2v.; reprinted, New York, 1947). The first volume is subtitled 'Early and Eastern from Jesus to John of Damascus'; the second is subtitled 'The West from Tertullian to Erasmus.'
161. Notably *The Apostles' Creed* (New York, 1902) and *The God of the Early Christians* (New York, 1934).
162. NicPNicChFath, 2d series, 1:3–403.
163. A. C. McGiffert, *Protestant Thought Before Kant* (New York, 1961).
164. Cf. Glick, *Reality of Christianity*, pp. 280–302.
165. See the comments, Harnack, *Lehrbuch*, 1:65.
166. But see, for example, the discussion of conditions in the Church in relation to the rise of Montanism, Harnack, *Lehrbuch*, 1:425–444.
167. E. Troeltsch, *The Social Teaching of the Christian Churches*, tr. Olive Wyon, int. H. R. Niebuhr (2v.; New York, 1960).
168. For example, Troeltsch, *Social Teaching*, 1:165–177, where Harnack is cited on almost every page.
169. See Troeltsch's comments of 1921 in Pauck, *Harnack and Troeltsch*, 115; cf. also Zahn-Harnack, *Harnack*, pp. 340–341, on the relation between the two men.

170. Troeltsch, *Social Teaching*, 1:237–245.
171. Cf. H. R. Niebuhr's introduction to the new printing (n. 167 above).
172. Troeltsch, *Social Teaching*, 1:158–161.
173. Troeltsch, *Social Teaching*, 2:569–576.
174. Troeltsch, *Social Teaching*, 2:694–703.
175. As Pauck has put it, 'to some extent, he had outgrown the faculty of theology,' *Harnack and Troeltsch*, p. 81.
176. J. Bach, *Die Dogmengeschichte des Mittelalters* (2v.; Vienna, 1874–75).
177. Cf. Bach, *Dogmengeschichte des Mittelalters*, 1:5–6, on the significance of Chalcedon.
178. Harnack, *Lehrbuch*, 3:380.
179. W. H. Principe, *The Theology of the Hypostatic Union in the Early Thirteenth Century* (4v.; Toronto, 1963–).
180. A. Landgraf, *Dogmengeschichte der Frühscholastik* (4 2-part volumes; Regensburg, 1952–56).
181. 'Die Gnadenlehre' is the subtitle of the first 2-part volume.
182. 'Die Lehre von den Sakramenten' is the subtitle of the third 2-part volume.
183. Cf. Harnack, *Lehrbuch*, 3:740–743, 880–895.
184. Landgraf, *Dogmengeschichte der Frühscholastik*, 3–ii: 207–222.
185. Cf. E. Schillebeeckx, *The Eucharist*, tr. N. D. Smith (New York, 1968), 143.
186. For a good introduction, cf. F. C. Copleston, *Medieval Philosophy* (New York, 1961), pp. 32–41.
187. Cf. J. Reiners, *Der Nominalismus in der Frühscholastik* (Münster, 1910), pp. 25–41.
188. Cf. P. Vignaux, 'Nominalisme,' *Dictionnaire de théologie catholique*, ed. A. Vacant et al (15v.; Paris, 1903–50), 11:717–784.
189. P. Vignaux, 'Sur Luther et Ockham,' *Franziskanische Studien*, 32 (1945):21–30.
190. Cf. C. von Prantl, *Geschichte der Logik im Abendlande* (4v., new ed.; Graz, Austria, 1955), 2:118ff.
191. See É. H. Gilson, *History of Christian Philosophy in the Middle Ages* (New York, 1955), pp. 521–527, with notes.
192. Cf. the passage from Gilson quoted p. 111 below.
193. *Selections from Medieval Philosophers*, ed. R. McKeon (2v.; New York, 1957–58), 1:142–184; *Medieval Philosophy: Selected Readings from Augustine to Buridan*, ed. H. Shapiro (New York, 1964), pp. 104–133.
194. The situation is well summarized by E. R. Fairweather, 'Introduction' to *A Scholastic Miscellany: Anselm to Ockham*, The Library of Christian Classics, 10 (Philadelphia, 1956), pp. 49–53.

195. J. Leclercq, *The Love of Learning and the Desire for God,* tr. C. Misrahi (New York, 1962).
196. Leclercq, *Lore of Learning,* p. 90.
197. Aland, 'Dogmengeschichte,' *Die Religion in Geschichte und Gegenwart*³ 2:234.
198. See pp. 8–10 above.
199. Cf. the introduction to *Augustine: De haeresibus,* ed. L. G. Müller (Washington, 1956).
200. Cf. J. A. Fitzmyer, 'The Qumran Scrolls, the Ebionites and their Literature,' *Theological Studies,* 16 (1955):338.
201. Athanasius *Epistula de synodis,* 36, PG 26:749; cf. the comments in NicPNicChFath, 2d series, 4:467, n. 7.
202. See C. Moeller, 'Le Chalcédonisme et le néo-chalcédonisme,' Grill-Bacht Konz 1:682–683, who calls this title 'un mot barbare.'
203. For the development of such titles almost *ad absurdum,* see H. G. Beck, *Kirche und theologische Literatur im byzantinischen Reich* (Munich, 1959), p. 291, n. 3.
204. So, for example, F. Loofs, 'Gregor von Nazianz,' PRE³ 7:144–146.
205. F. Loofs, *Theophilus von Antiochien Adversus Marcionem und die anderen theologischen Quellen bei Irenaeus,* TU 46–II:403, n. 1.
206. See p. 25 above.
207. See p. 10 above.
208. See C. N. Cochrane, *Christianity and Classical Culture: A Study of Thought and Action from Augustus to Augustine* (New York, 1944), pp. 327–334.
209. H. v. Schubert, *Bekenntnisbildung und Religionspolitik 1529/30* (Gotha, 1910).
210. Cf. W. Bousset, *Kyrios Christos: Geschichte des Christusglaubens von den Anfängen des Christentums bis Irenaeus* (Göttingen, 1913), pp. 123–125.
211. Augustine *De fide et symbolo* 1, PL 40:181.
212. Denz 125.
213. Denz 301.
214. Schroeder Trent 21 (fifth session).
215. Schroeder Trent 73 (thirteenth session, ch. 1).
216. Formula of Concord, Epitome, 'Rule and Norm,' 1, *Book of Concord,* p. 464.
217. Formula of Concord, Epitome, Art. II, par. 2, *Book of Concord,* p. 470.
218. The Scotch Confession of Faith, Art. I, Schaff, *Creeds,* 3:439.
219. This is evident from the liturgical use of the term 'confess'; cf. G. Lampe, *A Patristic Greek Lexicon* (Oxford, 1961–), p. 257.

220. Thomas Mann, *Joseph und seine Brüder* (2v.; Stockholm, 1966), 1:860.
221. See pp. 19-21 above.
222. Kelly, *Early Christian Creeds*, pp. 14-15.
223. H. Reuter, *Augustinische Studien* (Gotha, 1887), p. 34, n. 1.

Notes to Chapter Four

1. Quoted in A. von Zahn-Harnack, *Adolf von Harnack* (2d ed.; Berlin, 1951), 48.
2. Despite Troeltsch's comparison of Harnack with Wilhelm Dilthey (cf. W. Pauck, *Harnack and Troeltsch: Two Historical Theologians* [New York, 1968], pp. 108-109), the difference between them at this very point was decisive, as Zahn-Harnack, *Harnack*, pp. 426-427, points out.
3. Cf. Cochrane, *Christianity and Classical Culture: A Study of Thought and Action from Augustus to Augustine* (Oxford, 1944), pp. 438-441.
4. Above all in R. G. Collingwood, *The Idea of History* (New York, 1956).
5. See the work of V. Harvey, cited p. 167, n. 43 above.
6. Unfortunately, many of Rahner's historical studies are not being collected in his *Schriften zur Theologie*, but remain scattered in journals and *Festschriften*.
7. K. Barth, *Die protestantische Theologie im 19. Jahrhundert* (Zürich, 1952), portions of which are translated as *Protestant Thought from Rousseau to Ritschl* (New York, 1959).
8. P. Tillich, *Perspectives on 19th and 20th Century Protestant Theology*, ed. C. E. Braaten (New York, 1967).
9. K. Rahner, 'Probleme der Christologie von heute,' *Schriften zur Theologie* (6v.; Cologne, 1964-65), 1:169-222.
10. K. Rahner, 'Dogmatische Erwägungen über das Wissen und Selbstbewusstsein Christi,' *Schriften zur Theologie*, 5:222-245.
11. P. Tillich, *Systematic Theology* (3v.; Chicago, 1951-63), 1:38.
12. P. Tillich, *A History of Christian Thought*, ed. C. E. Braaten (New York, 1968), pp. 79-90 on christology and Chalcedon.
13. Tillich, *History of Christian Thought*, pp. 122-131, on the Pelagian controversy.
14. Cf. K. Barth, *Church Dogmatics* (New York, 1936-), I/1: 68-70.
15. Barth, *Protestantische Theologie*, 14.

16. Barth, *Church Dogmatics*, III/1:152–157 on *creatio ex nihilo*.
17. Barth, *Church Dogmatics*, I/1:413–414.
18. See pp. 50–51 above.
19. Cf. J. R. Geiselmann, *Die Eucharistielehre der Vorscholastik* (Paderborn, 1926), pp. 176–218.
20. Paschasius Radbertus, *De partu virginis*, PL 120:1371–72.
21. See J. J. Fahey, *The Eucharistic Teaching of Ratramnus of Corbie* (Mundelein, 1951), for a competent summary.
22. Paschasius Radbertus, *De corpore et sanguine Domini*, i.2, PL 120:1268.
23. Cf. H. de Lubac, *Corpus mysticum* (Paris, 1949), 151, n. 70, on the use of Ambrose.
24. Ratramnus, *De corpore et sanguine Domini*, ch. 51–69. ed. J. N. Bakhuizen van den Brink (Amsterdam, 1954), pp. 47–52.
25. See p. 122 below.
26. Cf. R. W. Southern, 'Lanfranc of Bec and Berengar of Tours,' *Studies in Medieval History Presented to Sir Frederick Maurice Powicke*, ed. R. W. Hunt et al (Oxford, 1948), pp. 27–48.
27. The most complete account is the 'Notice Bibliographique' added by Bakhuizen van den Brink to his edition, pp. 62–128.
28. H. C. G. Moule, ed., *Bishop Ridley on the Lord's Supper* (London, 1895), pp. 197–248.
29. Bakhuizen van den Brink, *De corpore*, ch. 63–64.
30. E. Renan, *Life of Jesus*, int. J. H. Holmes (New York, 1927), p. 65.
31. Cf. M. J. Lagrange, *Christ and Renan: A Commentary on Ernest Renan's 'Life of Jesus'*, tr. M. Ward (New York, 1928).
32. Collingwood, *Idea of History*, pp. 126–133.
33. B. Croce, *History: Its Theory and Practice*, tr. D. Ainslie (New York, 1960), p. 300.
34. Croce, *History*, p. 310.
35. Collingwood, *Idea of History*, p. 131.
36. Collingwood, *Idea of History*, pp. 131–132.
37. L. v. Ranke, *Weltgeschichte*, ed. H. Michael (7v.; Vienna, n.d. [1928]), 3:414.
38. Ranke, *Weltgeschichte*, 4:13–15.
39. A. von Harnack, *Lehrbuch der Dogmengeschichte* (3v.; 5th ed.; Tübingen, 1931), 2:21, 38.
40. Collingwood, *Idea of History*, p. 175.
41. Harnack, *Lehrbuch*, 2:60.
42. See p. 88 above.

43. V. Lindström, 'Motivforschung,' *Die Religion in Geschichte und Gegenwart* (6v.; 3d ed.; Tübingen, 1957-63), 4:1160-63.
44. E. M. Carlson, *The Reinterpretation of Luther* (Philadelphia, 1948), pp. 39-40.
45. A. Nygren, *Agape and Eros*, tr. P. S. Watson (Philadelphia, 1953), p. 35.
46. Nygren, *Agape and Eros*, p. 37.
47. Nygren, *Agape and Eros*, pp. 449-562, 576-593.
48. G. Aulén, *Christus Victor*, tr. A. G. Hebert (New York, 1969).
49. For a critique of this interpretation, see the study of R. Weingart, cited p. 171, n. 63 above.
50. Aulén, *Christus Victor*, pp. 84-92.
51. Aulén, *Christus Victor*, pp. 20-23.
52. Aulén, *Christus Victor*, pp. 101-122.
53. This idea, which appears in Luther's hymn, 'Christ lag in Todesbanden' (WA 35:443-445), comes from the Easter sequence, 'Victimae paschali laudes.'
54. Aulén, *Christus Victor*, pp. 143-159.
55. M. C. D'Arcy, *The Mind and Heart of Love* (London, 1945).
56. See pp. 85-87 above.
57. Nygren, *Agape and Eros*, pp. 681-737.
58. Aulén, *Christus Victor*, pp. 61-80.
59. Nygren, *Agape and Eros*, p. 39.
60. 'Catholicism is a *complexio oppositorum*, a synthesis of opposed fundamental motifs. In Luther, on the other hand, a clear distinction is made.' Nygren, *Agape and Eros*, p. 739.
61. Cf. K. Holl, 'Martin Luther on Luther,' tr. H. C. E. Midelfort, *Interpreters of Luther: Essays in Honor of Wilhelm Pauck*, ed. J. Pelikan (Philadelphia, 1968), pp. 25-26.
62. Carlson, *Reinterpretation of Luther*, pp. 25-26.
63. Nygren, *Agape and Eros*, p. 35.
64. Carlson, *Reinterpretation of Luther*, p. 39.
65. G. Wingren, *Theology in Conflict*, tr. E. H. Wahlstrom (Philadelphia, 1958).
66. Cf. G. Aulén, *Die Dogmengeschichte im Lichte der Lutherforschung* (Gütersloh, 1933).
67. See R. Bultmann, int. to A. von Harnack, *What Is Christianity?* (new ed., New York, 1957), pp. x-xiii.
68. 2 Clem. 1, *The Apostolic Fathers*, ed. J. B. Lightfoot (London, 1893), p. 86.
69. *Martyrdom of Polycarp* 17, Lightfoot, *Apostolic Fathers*, p. 209; but see the comments of W. R. Schoedel, *The Apostolic Fathers: A New Translation and Commentary*,

ed. R. M. Grant (6v.; Camden, N.J., 1964–), 5:74–75.
70. Cf. R. M. Grant, 'Pliny and the Christians,' *After the New Testament* (Philadelphia, 1967), pp. 55–56.
71. Pliny *Epistulae* 10.96.
72. 1 Cor 16.22; cf. C. F. C. Moule, 'A Reconsideration of Maranatha,' *New Testament Studies*, 6 (1960):307–310.
73. Cf. G. L. Prestige, *God in Patristic Thought* (London, 1956), pp. 76–80.
74. G. Kretschmar, *Studien zur frühchristlichen Trinitätstheologie* (Tübingen, 1956), pp. 134–216.
75. Nygren, *Agape and Eros*, p. 35.
76. É. Gilson, 'Historical Research and the Future of Scholasticism,' *A Gilson Reader: Selected Writings of Étienne Gilson*, ed. A. C. Pegis (New York, 1957), p. 156.
77. See pp. 92–93 above.
78. Cf. Pius XI, 'Mortalium animos,' Denz 3683.
79. See the essay of J. H. Newman, cited p. 169, n. 32 above.
80. Cf., for example, W. Windelband, *A History of Philosophy*, tr. J. H. Tufts (2v.; New York, 1958), 1:210–269; it is only in his discussion of St. Augustine that Windelband even refers to the doctrine of the Trinity, and that in one sentence, p. 280.
81. Cochrane, *Christianity and Classical Culture*, p. 432, pp. 436–437.
82. See, however, his trenchant analysis of St. Athanasius, Cochrane, *Christianity and Classical Culture*, pp. 361–372.
83. Harnack, *Lehrbuch*, 1:698.
84. F. Loofs, *Leitfaden zum Studien der Dogmengeschichte*, ed. K. Aland (6th ed.; Tübingen, 1959), p. 141.
85. Loofs, *Leitfaden*, p. 169.
86. Tillich, *Systematic Theology*, 1:229.
87. Harnack, *Lehrbuch*, 1:207, n.
88. H. A. Wolfson, *The Philosophy of the Church Fathers* (Cambridge, Mass., 1956), pp. 177–182.
89. See p. 88 above.
90. Cf. n. 74 above.
91. Kelly, *Early Christian Creeds* (London, 1952), pp. 49–52.
92. He does have occasional comments, as, for example, on the Arian form of the Sanctus, *Trinitätstheologie*, p. 176, n.
93. Cf. Athanasius *Orationes tres adversus Arianos*, 3. 16, PG 25:356.
94. Athanasius *Orationes tres adversus Arianos*, 1.8, PG 25:29.
95. Athanasius *Orationes tres adversus Arianos*, 2.43, PG 25:237.

Notes

96. Athanasius *Orationes tres adversus Arianos*, 1.34, PG 25:81.
97. D. J. Boorstin, *The Americans: The National Experience* (New York, 1957), p. 436.
98. A good introduction to his scholarship are the studies collected in his *Errand into the Wilderness* (New York, 1964), including the autobiographical preface.
99. Boorstin, *The Americans: The National Experience*, p. 436.
100. A magisterial study is W. Haller, *The Rise of Puritanism* (New York, 1957).
101. A. von Harnack, *The Mission and Expansion of Christianity in the First Three Centuries*, tr. J. Moffatt (New York, 1961), pp. 410–414.
102. Cf. *New English Dictionary* (Oxford, 1888–1928), 8:1621–22.
103. P. Miller, *Orthodoxy in Massachusetts 1630–1650* (new ed.; Boston, 1959), p. xviii.
104. P. Miller, *The New England Mind* (2v.; new ed.; Boston, 1961), 1:372.
105. Cf. W. J. Ong, *Ramus, Method, and the Decay of Dialogue* (Cambridge, Mass., 1958).
106. G. Schrenk, *Gottesreich und Bund im ältern Protestantismus vornehmlich bei Johannes Coccejus* (Gütersloh, 1923).
107. Cf. W. Walker, *The Creeds and Platforms of Congregationalism*, int. D. Horton (Boston, 1960), pp. 97–115.
108. Miller, *New England Mind*, 1:374.
109. See p. 167, n. 32 above.
110. Fisher, *History of Christian Doctrine*, 348–349.
111. Miller, *Errand into the Wilderness*, p. 48.
112. Fisher, *History of Christian Doctrine*, p. 394.
113. Cf. Ong, *Ramus, Method*, pp. 3–16.
114. *Encyclopaedia Britannica* (1910–11), 22:881.
115. Ong, *Ramus, Method*, pp. 295–318.
116. Cf. P. Miller and T. H. Johnson, ed., *The Puritans* (2v.; new ed.; New York, 1963), 1:30, n. 2.
117. Miller, *New England Mind*, 1:118.
118. Cf. E. Rietschel, *Das Problem der sichtbar-unsichtbaren Kirche bei Luther* (Leipzig, 1932).
119. Miller, *New England Mind*, 1:147–148.
120. Miller, *New England Mind*, 1:111–153.
121. Miller, *New England Mind*, 1:397.
122. See p. 95.
123. Significantly, E. Fueter, *Geschichte der neueren Historiographie* (Munich and Berlin, 1911), p. 442, still felt able to say in 1911 that the Marxist view of history did not need to be discussed, since it had only been formulated theoret-

ically but had not produced any works of historical scholarship.
124. Cf. E. Troeltsch, *The Social Teaching of the Christian Churches*, tr. Olive Wyon, int. H. R. Niebuhr (2v.; New York, 1960), 2:994–997.
125. See p. 148 below.
126. C. H. Dawson, *The Judgment of the Nations* (New York, 1942), p. 178. See, on the other hand, J. Meyendorff, 'Justinian, the Empire, and the Church,' *Dumbarton Oaks Papers* 22 (1968):43–60.
127. H. R. Niebuhr, *The Social Sources of Denominationalism* (New York, 1929; reprinted, 1957).
128. H. R. Niebuhr, *The Kingdom of God in America* (New York, 1937; reprinted, 1959). On the relation between the two books, cf. R. S. Michaelsen, 'The Kingdom of God in America and the Task of the Church,' *Faith and Ethics: The Theology of H. Richard Niebuhr*, ed. P. Ramsey (New York, 1965), pp. 270–272.
129. W. L. Sperry, *The Non-Theological Factors in the Making and Unmaking of Church Union*, Faith and Order Pamphlet No. 84 (New York, 1937). (I am indebted for this reference to my colleague, Paul S. Minear.)
130. W. H. C. Frend, *The Donatist Church: A Movement of Protest in Roman North Africa* (Oxford, 1952).
131. See the appendix on 'Extant Donatist Texts,' Frend, *Donatist Church*, pp. 337–338.
132. See, for example, Frend, *Donatist Church*, pp. 210–211, 230.
133. Frend, *Donatist Church*, pp. 25–47.
134. Frend, *Donatist Church*, p. 329.
135. The chapter on 'Factors Relating to the Conversion of North Africa to Christianity,' Frend, *Donatist Church*, 94–111, is an instance of this.
136. Thus there is very little attention to the non-theological factors in a book published shortly before Frend's, G. G. Willis, *Saint Augustine and the Donatist Controversy* (London, 1950), although he does take up the question of Church and State, pp. 127–143.
137. J. McIntyre, *St. Anselm and His Critics: A Re-interpretation of the 'Cur Deus Homo'* (Edinburgh, 1954), p. 186.
138. Harnack, *Lehrbuch*, 3:391–392.
139. H. Cremer, 'Die Wurzeln des Anselmschen Satisfaktionsbegriffs,' *Theologische Studien und Kritiken*, 53 (1880):7–24; Cremer 'Der germanische Satisfaktionsbegriff in der Versöhnungslehre,' *Theologische Studien und Kritiken*, 66 (1893):316–345.

140. Cf. *New English Dictionary* (Oxford, 1888–1928), 12:319–320.
141. Cf. J. T. McNeill and H. M. Gamer, ed, *Medieval Handbooks of Penance* (New York, 1938), pp. 35ff.
142. E. R. Fairweather, ed., *A Scholastic Miscellany: Anselm to Ockham*, The Library of Christian Classics, 10 (Philadelphia, 1956), p. 56.
143. Cf. J. Stirnimann, *Die Praescriptio Tertullians im Lichte des römischen Rechtes und der Theologie* (Freiburg, 1949).
144. Cf. B. Poschmann, *Paenitentia secunda* (Bonn, 1940), pp. 270–348.
145. Cf. Tacitus *Germania* 21.
146. See pp. 74–76 above.
147. See pp. 63–64 above.
148. Cf. H. Chadwick, *Early Christian Thought and the Classical Tradition* (New York, 1966), esp. pp. 95–123.
149. J. Quasten, *Patrology* (3v.; Westminster, Md., 1950–), 2: p. 196.
150. Eusebius *Historia ecclesiastica* 5.28, par. 13–14, Sources Chr 41:77–78.
151. Nestorius *Ad Cyrillum II, Nestoriana*, ed. F. Loofs (Halle, 1905), p. 179.
152. Cf. L. Dewart, *The Future of Belief: Theism in a World Come of Age* (New York, 1966), esp. pp. 144–147.
153. J. Pelikan, *The Shape of Death: Life, Death, and Immortality in the Early Fathers* (New York, 1961), esp. pp. 32–52.
154. E. Troeltsch, *Protestantism and Progress*, tr. W. Montgomery (new ed., Boston, 1958); the German title was *Die Bedeutung des Protestantismus für die Entstehung der modernen Welt*.
155. See the comment of K. Holl, 'Was verstand Luther unter Religion?' *Gesammelte Aufsätze zur Kirchengeschichte*, 1, *Luther* (7th ed.; Tübingen, 1948), pp. 109–110, n. 1.
156. M. Creighton, *History of the Papacy* (5v.; London, 1882–94).
157. M. Creighton, 'Introductory Note,' *Cambridge Modern History* (London, New York, 1902–12), 1:1.
158. R. Blake, *Disraeli* (New York, 1967), p. 406.
159. E. Schwartz, *Kaiser Constantin und die christliche Kirche* (2d ed.; Leipzig, 1936).
160. E. Schwartz, *Zur Geschichte des Athanasius* (Berlin, 1959), pp. 156–168 and *passim*.
161. Cochrane, *Christianity and Classical Culture*, pp. 74—113.
162. E. Gibbon, *The History of the Decline and Fall of the Roman Empire*, ed. J. B. Bury (7v.; London, 1896—1900), 7:308.

163. G. Haendler, *Epochen karolingischer Theologie. Eine Untersuchung über die karolingischen Gutachten zum byzantinischen Bilderstreit* (Berlin, 1958).
164. The dates of their deaths are: Rabanus Maurus, 856; Ratramnus, 868; Paschasius Radbertus, c. 860; Gottschalk, c. 868; Johannes Scotus Erigena, c. 877; Hincmar of Reims, 882; Walafrid Strabo, 849; Servatus Lupus, 862; Prudentius of Troyes, 861.
165. Because of the promulgation of transubstantiation at the Fourth Lateran Council in 1215, there is special interest in his doctrine of the Eucharist, which has been studied by G. Barbéro, *La dottrina eucaristica negli scritti di Innocenzo III* (Rome, 1953).
166. See the definitive work of E. Kantorowicz, *Kaiser Friedrich II* (4th ed.; Berlin, 1936).
167. See the wry comment of Gilson, 'Historical Research,' p. 167, n. 1.
168. É. Gilson, *Dante and Philosophy*, tr. D. Moore (New York, 1963), pp. 153–154.
169. Gilson, *Dante and Philosophy*, pp. 317–327.
170. T. G. Bergin, *Dante* (New York, 1965), pp. 63, 104.
171. See pp. 84–85 above.
172. Cf. W. Elert, *Der Ausgang der altkirchlichen Christologie: Eine Untersuchung über Theodor von Pharan und seine Zeit als Einführung in die alte Dogmengeschichte* (Berlin, 1957), pp. 9–11.
173. Cf. I. Ortiz de Urbina, 'Das Symbol von Chalkedon: Sein Text, sein Werden, seine dogmatische Bedeutung,' Grill-Bacht Konz 1 : 389–418, esp. 398–401.
174. Ortiz de Urbina points out, 'Symbol von Chalkedon,' p. 400, that the phrase 'not parted or divided into two persons [*prosōpa*]' probably came from Theodoret of Cyrus, an Antiochene.
175. Ortiz de Urbina, 'Symbol von Chalkedon,' pp. 400–401.
176. Cf. E. J. Martin, *A History of the Iconoclastic Controversy* (London, 1930).
177. See, for example, O. Ritschl, *Dogmengeschichte des Protestantismus* (4v.; Leipzig and Göttingen, 1908–27), 4 : 70–106.
178. A. Schweitzer, *The Quest of the Historical Jesus*, tr. W. Montgomery, int. F. C. Burkitt (New York, 1961), p. 3.
179. Augustine *De Trinitate*, 1.4.7, PL 42 : 824.
180. See p. 16 above.
181. Cf. J. Pelikan, *Development of Christian Doctrine: Some Historical Prolegomena* (New Haven, 1969), pp. 75–79.
182. Denz 267–268.
183. Denz 371–372.

184. 2v.; London, n.d. [1918].
185. Cf. Heussi, 'Centuriae,' *Harnack-Ehrung* (Leipzig, 1921), pp. 328–334.
186. See p. 40 above.
187. *Geschichte der christlichen Kirche* (1840), pp. 30–31, cited in Heussi, 'Centuriae,' p. 328, n. 2.
188. See p. 181, n. 118 above.
189. Heussi, 'Centuriae,' p. 330.
190. F. C. Baur, *The Epochs of Church Historiography*, ed. and tr. P. C. Hodgson, *Ferdinand Christian Baur on the Writing of Church History*, A Library of Protestant Thought (New York, 1968), p. 84.
191. Cf. P. C. Hodgson, *The Formation of Historical Theology, A Study of Ferdinand Christian Baur* (New York, 1966), pp. 246–247.
192. Hodgson, *Formation of Historical Theology*, pp. 247–248.
193. See p. 183, n. 162 above.
194. Hodgson, *Formation of Historical Theology*, pp. 248–250.
195. S. Runciman, *A History of the Crusades* (3v.; New York, 1964–67), 1 : xi.

Notes to Chapter Five

1. A. von Harnack, 'Legenden als Geschichtsquellen,' *Reden und Aufsätze*, 1:23, quoted in G. W. Glick, *The Reality of Christianity: A Study of Adolf von Harnack as Historian and Theologian* (New York, 1967), p. 94.
2. Cf. W. Pauck, *Harnack and Troeltsch: Two Historical Theologians* (New York, 1968), p. 7.
3. E. Schwartz, *Zur Geschichte des Athanasius* (Berlin, 1959), 185–187 (originally published in 1908).
4. A. von Harnack, *History of Dogma*, tr. N. Buchanan (7v.; new ed.; New York, 1961), 1 : vii–viii.
5. See pp. 47–51 above.
6. See pp. 118–119 above.
7. See pp. 114–117 above.
8. Cf. H. R. Niebuhr, D. D. Williams, J. M. Gustafson, *The Advancement of Theological Education* (New York, 1957), pp. 97–99.
9. Cf. the decree *Optatam totius* (On Priestly Formation), 16, *The Documents of Vatican II*, ed. W. M. Abbott (New York, 1966), p. 452; and the comments of J. Neuner, *Lexikon für Theologie und Kirche*², J. Höfer and K. Rahner, eds. (Freiburg, 1957), *Das zweite Vatikanische Konzil*, 2: pp. 343–344.

10. See p. 50 above.
11. W. Elert, *Die Kirche und ihre Dogmengeschichte* (Munich, 1950), p. 5; *Der Ausgang der altkirchlichen Christologie: Eine Untersuchung über Theodor von Pharan und seine Zeit als Einführung in die alte Dogmengeschichte* (Berlin, 1957), p. 315.
12. See the criticisms of W. Pauck, *The Heritage of the Reformation* (rev. ed.; Glencoe, Ill., 1961), p. 358.
13. A. Seeberg, *Der Katechismus der Urchristenheit* (Leipzig, 1903).
14. Cf. J. N. D. Kelly, *A Commentary on the Pastoral Epistles* (New York, 1963), esp. pp. 13–21.
15. C. Spicq, 'S. Paul et la loi des dépôts,' *Revue biblique*, 40 (1931): 481–502.
16. Cf. H. J. Cadbury, *The Book of Acts in History* (New York, 1955).
17. Eusebius, *The Ecclesiastical History; The Martyrs of Palestine*, ed. H. J. Lawlor and J. E. L. Oulton (2v.; London, 1954), 2:28.
18. J. Pelikan, *The Finality of Jesus Christ in an Age of Universal History: A Dilemma of the Third Century* (London, 1965), pp. 48–57.
19. Cf. J. R. Geiselmann, *Die lebendige Überlieferung als Norm des christlichen Glaubens* (Freiburg, 1959), esp. pp. 146–160.
20. E. A. Ryan, *The Historical Scholarship of Saint Bellarmine* (Louvain, 1936), pp. 149–150.
21. See pp. 40–41 above.
22. Cf. A. L. Olsen, *Chemnitz on Scripture and Tradition* (unpublished Ph.D. dissertation, Harvard University, 1966).
23. J. Pelikan, *Obedient Rebels: Catholic Substance and Protestant Principle in Luther's Reformation* (New York and London, 1964), pp. 49–53.
24. M. Chemnitz, *Examen Concilii Tridentini* (1565–73), ed. E. Preuss (Leipzig, 1915), p. 78.
25. M. Chemnitz, *Loci theologici quibus Ph. Melanchthonis communes loci perspicue explicantur*, ed. P. Leyser (Frankfurt, 1604), 1:245–250.
26. M. Chemnitz, *De duabus naturis in Christo*, summarized in Ritschl, *Dogmengeschichte des Protestantismus*, 4:95–104.
27. Ryan, *Historical Scholarship*, pp. 149–150.
28. Cf. K. Aland, 'The Problem of Anonymity and Pseudonymity in the Christian Literature of the First Two Centuries,' *Journal of Theological Studies*, 12 (1910–11), pp. 39–49.

29. Cf. W. Caven, 'The Testimony of Christ to the Old Testament,' *The Fundamentals* (Chicago, n.d.), 4:46–72.
30. Denz 3394.
31. Ironically, it was in Rome and the West that the Pauline authorship was widely questioned, while in the East there was more general agreement on it.
32. Schroeder Trent 18.
33. Denz 3591.
34. Denz 3831.
35. For an introduction to the history of the problem and its present state, cf. E. Riggenbach, *Das Comma Johanneum* (Gütersloh, 1928).
36. The evidence of the manuscripts is collected in C. Tischendorf, *Novum Testamentum Graece* (8th ed.; Leipzig, 1872), 2:337–341.
37. See, in general, W. Schwarz, *Principles and Problems of Biblical Translation: Some Reformation Controversies and Their Background* (Cambridge, Eng., 1955), pp. 92–166.
38. On its background, cf. F. Delitzsch, *Studien zur Entstehungsgeschichte der Polyglottenbibel des Cardinal Ximenes* (Leipzig, 1871).
39. See B. M. Metzger, *The Text of the New Testament: Its Transmission, Corruption, and Restoration* (New York, 1964), pp. 101–102.
40. Cf. J. Wordsworth and H. J. White, *Novum Testamentum Latine* (3v.; Oxford, 1889–1954), 3:373–374, showing that the manuscripts of the Vulgate do not contain this reading.
41. Schroeder Trent 18–19.
42. See, for example, Harnack, *Lehrbuch*, 1:90, n. 1 and *passim*.
43. Cf. F. Pieper, *Christliche Dogmatik* (3v.; St. Louis, 1917–24), 1:410–415.
44. *Acta sanctae sedis* (Rome, 1865–1908), 29:637.
45. D. Smith, 'The Epistles of John,' *The Expositor's Greek Testament* (5v.; Grand Rapids, Mich., n.d.), 5:195.
46. Cf. T. A Marazuela, 'Nuevo estudio sobre el "Comma Ioanneum," ' *Biblica*, 28 (1947):83–112, 216–235; 29 (1948):52–76.
47. Cf. A. Bludau, *Die Schriftfälschungen der Häretiker: Ein Beitrag zur Textkritik der Bibel* (Münster, 1925), for a discussion of other variants that serve as data for the history of doctrine.
48. See O. Ritschl, *Dogmengeschichte des Protestantismus* (4v.; Leipzig and Göttingen, 1908–27), 1:212–267.

49. Cf. G. L. Prestige, *Fathers and Heretics* (London, 1948), p. 21.
50. Cf. J. H. Nichols, 'The Dilemma of the Free Church Liberal,' *The Christian Century*, 70 (1953): 1074–76.
51. The Vulgate of Rom 5.12 reads: 'Propterea sicut per unum hominem in hunc mundum peccatum intravit, et per peccatum mors, et ita in omnes homines mors pertransiit, in quo omnes peccaverunt.'
52. Cf. J. Schildenberger, 'Die Itala des hl. Augustinus,' *Colligere fragmenta: Festschrift A. Dold* (Beuron, 1952), pp. 84–102, on the problem of Augustine's Bible.
53. Augustine *De nuptiis et concupiscentia* 2.2.3, PL 44:438; NicPNicChFath 5:284.
54. Cf. B. Altaner, *Kleine patristische Schriften* (Berlin, 1967), 129–153.
55. Augustine *Contra duas epistulas Pelagianorum ad Bonifatium* 4.4.7, PL 44:614; NicPNicChFath 5:419.
56. Hilary the Deacon, *Commentaria in epistolas beati Pauli*, PL 17:97.
57. Cf. pp. 17–19 above.
58. Cf. J. Pelikan, *Development of Christian Doctrine: Some Historical Prolegomena* (New Haven, 1969), pp. 73–94.
59. Ambrose, *De exessu fratris sui Satyri* 2.6, PL 16:1374.
60. J. Gross, *Geschichte des Erbsündendogmas: Ein Beitrag zur Geschichte des Problems vom Ursprung des Übels* (Munich, 1960–).
61. Cf. H. Haag, *Is Original Sin in Scripture?*, tr. D. Thompson (New York, 1969), esp. pp. 95–100.
62. For a critique of word study, cf. J. Barr, *The Semantics of Biblical Language* (Oxford, 1961), pp. 21–45.
63. For a critique, as applied to the interpretation of Gnosticism, cf. C. Colpe, *Die religionsgeschichtliche Schule* (Göttingen, 1961).
64. J. Pelikan, *The Christian Intellectual* (New York, 1965), pp. 50–59.
65. J. Pelikan, *Luther the Expositor* (St. Louis, 1959), pp. 122–131, 174–190.
66. These have since been reprinted (Grand Rapids, Mich., 1957).
67. See p. 113 above.
68. Cf. G. L. Prestige, *God in Patristic Thought* (London, 1956), pp. 112–128.
69. W. Jaeger, *The Theology of the Early Greek Philosophers* (Oxford, 1947), pp. 112–117.
70. Cf. H. A. Wolfson, *Philo: Foundations of Religious Philosophy in Judaism, Christianity and Islam* (2v.; Cambridge, Mass., 1947), 1:226–240 and *passim*.

71. Cf. R. M. Grant, *After the New Testament* (Philadelphia, 1967), pp. 70–82.
72. F. L. Cross, ed., *The Oxford Dictionary of the Christian Church* (London, 1958), p. 610.
73. J. R. Harris, *The Origin of the Prologue to St. John's Gospel* (Cambridge, Eng., 1917).
74. Cf. P. Heinisch, *Die persönliche Weisheit des Alten Testaments in religionsgeschichtlicher Beleuchtung* (Münster, 1923), esp. pp. 58–62.
75. See J. Daniélou, *The Theology of Jewish Christianity*, tr. J. Baker (London, 1964), pp. 88–107.
76. Daniélou, *Theology of Jewish Christianity*, pp. 166–168.
77. Cf., for example, C. K. Barrett, *The Gospel According to St. John* (London, 1956), pp. 127–129.
78. R. Bultmann, *Theologie des Neuen Testaments* (Tübingen, 1953), p. 411.
79. One exception is A. von Harnack, *Lehrbuch der Dogmengeschichte* (3v.; 5th ed.; Tübingen, 1931), 1:587, n. 1.
80. Harnack, *Lehrbuch*, 1:559, 568.
81. A. von Harnack, 'über das gnostische Buch "Pistis Sophia," ' TU 7–2:1–114.
82. See, for example, *Lehrbuch*, 1:124, n. 1.
83. Harnack, *Lehrbuch*, 2:203.
84. Athanasius *Orationes tres adversus Arianos* 2.16.18–2.22.82, PG 26:184–321.
85. J. Pelikan, *The Light of the World: A Basic Image in Early Christian Thought* (New York, 1962), pp. 55ff.
86. G. Kretschmar, *Studien zur frühchristlichen Trinitätstheologie* (Tübingen, 1956), p. 60.
87. Justin *Dialogus cum Tryphone Judaeo* 61, PG 6:616.
88. Cf., for example, the questionable *Expositio in Proverbia*, 8.80–90, PG 17:184–185.
89. Pelikan, *Luther the Expositor*, pp. 5–31.
90. See the monumental work of H. de Lubac, *Exégèse médiévale: Les quatre sens de l'Écriture* (3v.; Paris, 1959–61).
91. Cf., for example, T. C. Bergin, *Dante* (New York, 1965), pp. 102–103, 250–254.
92. 'Patristic theology is purely and simply the study of the sacred writings: the Fathers are essentially *tractatores, expositores sacrae Scripturae*.' Y. M.-J. Congar, *Tradition and Traditions: An Historical and a Theological Essay*, tr. M. Naseby and T. Rainborough (New York, 1967), p. 382.
93. H. Küng, *The Council in Action*, tr. C. Hastings (New York, 1963), pp. 159–195.
94. Küng, *Council in Action*, pp. 183–189.

95. See p. 70 above.
96. Cf. G. P. Gooch, *History and Historians in the Nineteenth Century* (2d ed.; Boston, 1959), pp. 459–469.
97. See Harnack's memorial address for Mommsen (Nov. 5, 1903), *Aus Wissenschaft und Leben* (2v.; Giessen, 1911), 2:323–332.
98. A. von Zahn-Harnack, *Adolf von Harnack* (2d ed.; Berlin, 1951), p. 196.
99. For example, R. Seeberg, *Lehrbuch der Dogmengeschichte* (4v.; 5th ed.; Basel, 1953–54), 1:4–15.
100. Cf. Schwartz, *Zur Geschichte des Athanasius*, pp. 117–168.
101. See pp. xii–xiii above.
102. Cf. J. L. Neve, *A History of Christian Thought* (2v.; Philadelphia, 1943–46), 2:180.
103. Cf. pp. 49–50 above.
104. W. Nigg, *Das Buch der Ketzer* (Zürich, 1949), pp. 9–21.
105. Cf. H. Butterfield, 'The Reconstruction of an Historical Episode,' *Man on His Past* (Cambridge, Eng., 1955), pp. 143–167.
106. The problem is summarized in H. Chadwick, *Early Christian Thought and the Classical Tradition* (New York, 1966), pp. 67–94.
107. W. Völker, *Das Vollkommenheitsideal des Origenes* (Tübingen, 1931).
108. Cf. F. v. Hügel, *The Mystical Element of Religion as Studied in Saint Catherine of Genoa and Her Friends* (2v.; London, 1961), 2:259–275.
109. J. Daniélou, *Origen*, tr. W. Mitchell (New York, 1955), p. 293.
110. See pp. 21–24 above.
111. H. de Lubac, *Histoire et esprit: L'intelligence de l'Écriture d'après Origène* (Paris, 1950), pp. 47–91.
112. The problem is complicated by the Latin translation of Rufinus, which, especially in the preface, may have made Origen more orthodox than the Greek text warranted.
113. See the work of R. F. Evans, *Pelagius: Inquiries and Reappraisals* (New York, 1968).
114. Cf. Seeberg, *Lehrbuch*, 3:703–728.
115. See Seeberg, *Lehrbuch*, 4:464–469 for a summary.
116. See p. 38 above.
117. G. Thomasius, *Die Christliche Dogmengeschichte als Entwicklungs-Geschichte des kirchlichen Lehrbegriffs* (2v.; Erlangen, 1874–76), 1:322.
118. Thomasius, *Dogmengeschichte*, 1:330.
119. See pp. 68–70 above.
120. Elert, *Ausgang der altkirchlichen Christologie*, pp. 54–55.

121. Cf. A. Grillmeier, *Christ in Christian Tradition: From the Apostolic Age to Chalcedon (451)*, tr. J. S. Bowden (New York, 1965), pp. 344–347 and *passim*.
122. For example, the citation of Ps 68.19 in Eph 4.8 was an allusion, not a 'messianic' proof, Theodore of Mopsuestia *Commentarii*, 1:166.
123. Cf. R. A. Greer, *Theodore of Mopsuestia: Exegete and Theologian* (Westminster, Eng., 1961), pp. 100–101.
124. Harnack, *Lehrbuch*, 2:340.
125. R. Seeberg, *Text Book of the History of Doctrines*, tr. C. E. Hay (2v.; Grand Rapids, Mich., 1952), 1:247–248.
126. Seeberg, *Lehrbuch*, 2:196, n. 1.
127. Seeberg, *Lehrbuch*, 2:187.
128. M. Jugie, *Nestorius et la controverse nestorienne* (Paris, 1912).
129. C. Pesch, *Nestorius als Irrlehrer: Zur Erläuterung einer wichtigen theologischen Prinzipienfrage* (Paderborn, 1921).
130. H. B. Swete, ed., *Theodori episcopi Mopsuesteni in epistolas B. Pauli Commentarii* (2v.; Cambridge, Eng., 1880–82).
131. J. M. Vosté, ed., *Theodori Mopsuesteni Commentarius in Evangelium Iohannis Apostoli* (2v.; Paris, 1940); R. Devreesse, ed., *Le commentaire de Théodore de Mopsueste sur les Psaumes* (Rome, 1939).
132. A. Mingana, ed., *Commentary of Theodore of Mopsuestia on the Nicene Creed* (Cambridge, Eng., 1932); A. Mingana, ed., *Commentary of Theodore of Mopsuestia on the Lord's Prayer and on the Sacraments of Baptism and the Eucharist* (Cambridge, Eng., 1933); R. Tonneau, ed., *Les homélies catéchétiques de Théodore de Mopsueste*, Studi e testi: 145.
133. Cf. R. A. Norris, *Manhood and Christ: A Study in the Christology of Theodore of Mopsuestia* (Oxford, 1963), pp. 246–262.
134. F. Loofs, ed., *Nestoriana: Die Fragmente des Nestorius* (Halle, 1905).
135. Loofs, *Nestoriana*, 4.
136. F. Nau, ed., *Nestorius: Le livre d'Héraclide de Damas* (Paris, 1910).
137. Grillmeier, *Christ in Christian Tradition*, pp. 496–505.
138. E. Benz, *Die Ostkirche im Lichte der protestantischen Geschichtsschreibung von der Reformation bis zur Gegenwart* (Freiburg, 1952).
139. F. Loofs, *Leitfaden zum Studium der Dogmengeschichte*, ed. K. Aland (6th ed.; Tübingen, 1959), p. 261, who devotes six lines to the question.
140. Cf. S. Runciman, *The Eastern Schism: A Study of the*

Papacy and the Eastern Churches during the XIth and XIIth Centuries (Oxford, 1956), pp. 29–32.
141. Pelikan, *Development of Doctrine*, pp. 131–136.
142. P. Sherrard, *The Greek East and the Latin West: A Study in the Christian Tradition* (London, 1959), pp. 61–72.
143. 'It is clear that the differences in the uses quoted by Photius were not the real cause of the schism,' L. Bréhier, 'The Greek Church: Its Relations with the West up to 1054,' *Cambridge Medieval History* (8v.; London-New York, 1911–36), 4:250.
144. See the monograph cited earlier, p. 206, n. 163.
145. Cf. M. Rackl, 'Die griechische Übersetzung der Summa theologiae des hl. Thomas von Aquin,' *Byzantinische Zeitschrift*, 24 (1915):48–60.
146. K. Holl, *Enthusiasmus und Bussgewalt beim griechischen Mönchtum* (Leipzig, 1898).
147. I. Hausherr, 'La méthode d'oraison des hésychastes,' *Orientalia christiana analecta*, 9 (1933):97–209.
148. W. Nölle, 'Hesychasmus und Yoga,' *Byzantinische Zeitschrift*, 47 (1938):95–103.
149. J. Meyendorff, *Introduction à l'étude de Grégoire Palamas* (Louvain, 1959).
150. See p. 77 above.
151. Cf. J. M. Reu, *Luther and the Scriptures* (Columbus, 1949).
152. E. Bizer, *Fides ex auditu* (Neukirchen, 1958) precipitated a fresh discussion of the question; cf. B. Lohse, ed., *Der Durchbruch der reformatorischen Erkenntnis bei Luther* (Darmstadt, 1968).
153. R. Hermann, *Luthers These 'Gerecht und Sünder zugleich'* (2d ed.; Gütersloh, 1960) is the standard monograph.
154. *In epistolam S. Pauli ad Galatas Commentarius*, WA, 40–I: pp. 39–668; tr. J. Pelikan, *Luther's Works*, ed. J. Pelikan and H. Lehmann (St. Louis and Philadelphia, 1955–), 26:1–27:149.
155. R. H. Bainton, *Here I Stand: A Life of Martin Luther* (New York, 1950).
156. H. Bornkamm, 'Probleme der Lutherbiographie,' *Lutherforschung heute*, ed. V. Vajta (Berlin, 1958), p. 15.
157. J. Köstlin, *Martin Luther: Sein Leben und seine Schriften*, ed. G. Kawerau (2v.; Berlin, 1903).
158. Erik H. Erikson, *Young Man Luther: A Study in Psychoanalysis and History* (New York, 1958).
159. On the problem, cf. Bornkamm, 'Probleme der Lutherbiographie,' pp. 20–21.
160. L. Edel, *Literary Biography* (New York, 1959), pp. 91–122.
161. W. L. Langer, 'The Next Assignment,' *American Historical*

Review, 63 (1958): 283–304, reprinted in B. Mazlish, ed., *Psychoanalysis and History* (New York, 1963), pp. 87–107.
162. E. Jones, *The Life and Work of Sigmund Freud* (3v.; New York, 1953–55).
163. L. Edel, *Henry James* (New York, 1953–).
164. P. Althaus, *Luthers Haltung im Bauernkrieg* (Basel, 1953).
165. Cf. G. Franz, 'Bauernkrieg,' *Die Religion in Geschichte und Gegenwart* (6v.; 3d ed.; Tübingen, 1957–63), 1:927–930.
166. see p. 62 above.
167. P. Hefner, *Faith and the Vitalities of History: A Theological Study Based on the Work of Albrecht Ritschl* (New York, 1966), pp. 88–111.
168. See pp. 4–7 above.
169. Zahn-Harnack, *Harnack*, pp. 130–131.
170. Lord Acton, *Lectures on Modern History* (New York, 1966), p. 44.
171. See pp. 56–57 above.
172. H. Stephan, *Geschichte der deutschen evangelischen Theologie seit dem deutschen Idealismus*, ed. M. Schmidt (2d ed.; Berlin, 1960), p. 179.
173. K. Barth, *Die protestantische Theologie im 19. Jahrhundert* (Zürich, 1952), p. 379.
174. F. Schleiermacher, *Der christliche Glaube nach den Grundsätzen der evangelischen Kirche im Zusammenhange dargestellt*, ed. M. Redeker (7th ed.; Berlin, 1960), 1:137.
175. Schleiermacher, *Christlicher Glaube*, 1:148–154.
176. H. Fagerberg, *Bekenntnis, Kirche und Amt in der deutschen konfessionellen Theologie des 19. Jahrhunderts* (Uppsala, 1952).
177. Cf. S. Hebart, *Wilhelm Löhes Lehre von der Kirche, ihrem Amt und Regiment* (Neuendettelsau, 1939), pp. 221–222.
178. A. Ritschl, *Schleiermachers Reden über die Religion und ihre Nachwirkungen auf die evangelische Kirche Deutschlands* (Bonn, 1890).
179. Hefner, *Faith and the Vitalities of History*, pp. 26–70.
180. Cf. F. Kattenbusch, *Die deutsche evangelische Theologie seit Schleiermacher: Ihre Leistungen und ihre Schäden* (5th ed.; Giessen, 1926), pp. 63–64.
181. See pp. 70–72 above.
182. J. Knox, *The Church and the Reality of Christ* (New York, 1962), pp. 13–36 and *passim*.
183. Both at the first and at the third International Congress for Luther Research, Luther's doctrine of the Church was a principal theme; cf. W. Maurer and J. Pelikan, 'Luthers Lehre von der Kirche,' *Lutherforschung heute*, ed. V. Vajta

(Berlin, 1958), 85–110; W. Maurer, R. H. Esnault, and J. Pelikan, 'Die Frage nach der Kontinuität der Kirche,' *Kirche, Mystik, Heiligung und das Natürliche bei Luther*, ed. I. Asheim (Göttingen, 1967), pp. 95–155.
184. J. T. McNeill, *The History and Character of Calvinism* (New York, 1957), pp. 214–215.
185. Cf. M. Bévenot, 'Introduction' to Cyprian, *The Lapsed. The Unity of the Catholic Church*, AncChrWr 25:6–8, summarizing his earlier research.
186. G. H. Tavard, *Holy Writ or Holy Church: The Crisis of the Protestant Reformation* (New York, 1959), pp. 195–209.
187. J. Hergenröther, *Photius* (3v.; Regensburg, 1867–69); this has now been largely superseded by F. Dvornik, *The Photian Schism: History and Legend* (Cambridge, 1948).
188. See p. 77 above.
189. Cf. M. Grabmann, *Geschichte der scholastischen Methode* (2v.; Graz, 1957), 1:22, n. 2.
190. Cf. C. N. Cochrane, *Christianity and Classical Culture: A Study of Thought and Action From Augustus to Augustine* (Oxford, 1944), pp. 456–516.
191. See p. 37 above.
192. This tendency has been criticized and corrected by R. Prenter, *Spiritus Creator*, tr. J. M. Jensen (Philadelphia, 1953), pp. 173–184.
193. Pauck, *Heritage of the Reformation*, p. 334.
194. Denz 3878.
195. Pauck, *Harnack and Troeltsch*, pp. 89–90.

Notes to Conclusion

1. Cf. pp. 8–9 on continuity.
2. See the essays of K. Rahner cited p. 199, n. 9–10 above.
3. H. Küng, *The Church*, tr. R. and R. Ockenden (New York, 1968), pp. 203–260; 388–393.
4. Denz 3812.
5. Denz 3830.
6. Cf. P. S. Minear, *Images of the Church in the New Testament* (Philadelphia, 1960), pp. 173–220.
7. A. N. Whitehead, *Process and Reality* (New York, 1960), pp. 122–123.
8. Cf. J. Knox, *Jesus: Lord and Christ* (New York, 1958), pp. 51–57 and *passim*.
9. Cf. A. Grillmeier, *Christ in Christian Tradition: From the Apostolic Age to Chalcedon (451)*, tr. J. S. Bowden (New York, 1965), pp. 159–163.

10. J. Maritain, *Existence and the Existent*, tr. L. Galantière and G. B. Phelan (New York, 1948), p. 45.
11. Maritain, *Existence and the Existent*, p. 45.
12. H. R. Niebuhr, *The Meaning of Revelation* (New York, 1960), pp. 38–42.
13. G. S. Haight, *George Eliot: A Biography* (New York, 1968), p. 120.
14. W. S. Churchill, *The Second World War* (6v.; New York, 1961), 1:560.
15. Churchill, *Second World War*, 1:565.
16. Denz 301.
17. See especially pp. 149–155 above.
18. F. L. Cross, ed., *The Oxford Dictionary of the Christian Church* (London, 1958), p. 1375.
19. On the reasons for the change, cf. C. Welch, *In This Name: The Doctrine of the Trinity in Contemporary Theology* (New York, 1952), pp. 3–76.
20. F. Schleiermacher, *Der christliche Glaube nach den Grundsätzen der evangelischen Kirche im Zusammenhange dargestellt*, ed. M. Redeker (7th ed.; Berlin, 1960), 2:147, on the states of humiliation and exaltation.
21. Cf. W. Pauck, *Harnack and Troeltsch: Two Historical Theologians* (New York, 1968), pp. 84–86.
22. A. C. Outler, *The Christian Tradition and the Unity We Seek* (New York, 1957), pp. 65–101.
23. Cf. É. Gilson, *The Philosophy of St. Bonaventure*, tr. I. Trethowan and F. J. Sheed (Paterson, N.J., 1965), pp. 447–449.
24. T. Tappert et al, eds., *The Book of Concord* (Philadelphia, 1959), p. 25 (translation my own).

Bibliography

Adam, A. *Lehrbuch der Dogmengeschichte*. Gütersloh: Mohr, 1965–.
Augusti, J. C. W. *Lehrbuch der christlichen Dogmengeschichte*. Leipzig: Dyk, 1805.
Aulén, G. *Dogmhistoria*. Stockholm: Norstedt, 1917.
Bach, J. *Die Dogmengeschichte des Mittelalters vom christologischen Standpunkte*. 2 vols. Vienna: Braumüller, 1873–75.
Baiks, J. S. *The Development of Doctrine in the Early Church*. 2 vols. London: C. H. Kelly, 1900–01.
Barth, K. *Die protestantische Theologie im 19. Jahrhundert*. Zürich: Evangelischer Verlag, 1947.
———. *Protestant Thought: From Rousseau to Ritschl*. New York: Harper, 1959.
Baumgarten-Crusius, L. F. O. *Kompendium der christlichen Dogmengeschichte*. 2 vols. Leipzig: Breitkopf and Härtel, 1840–46.
———. *Lehrbuch der christlichen Dogmengeschichte*. 2 vols. Jena: Cröker, 1832.
Baur, F. C. *Lehrbuch der Dogmengeschichte*. Tübingen: Fues, 1847.
———. *Vorlesungen über die christliche Dogmengeschichte*. 3 vols. Leipzig: Fues, 1865–67.
Beck, H. G. *Kirche und theologische Literatur im byzantinischen Reich*. Munich: Beck, 1959.
Beck, K. *Christliche Dogmengeschichte bis auf die neueste Gegenwart in gedrängter Uebersicht*. Tübingen: Osiander, 1864.

Berthold, L. *Handbuch der Dogmengeschichte.* 2 vols. Erlangen, 1822–23.
Bethune-Baker, J. F. *An Introduction to the Early History of Christian Doctrine.* London: Methuen, 1903.
Bonwetsch, N. *Grundriss der Dogmengeschichte.* Gütersloh, 1908.
Daniélou, J. *The Development of Christian Doctrine Before the Council of Nicaea.* Translated and edited by John A. Baker. London: Darton Longman and Todd, 1964–.
Dorner, A. J. *Die Entstehung der christlichen Glaubenslehren.* Munich: J. F. Lehmann, 1906.
———. *Grundriss der Dogmengeschichte. Entwickelungsgeschichte der christlichen Lehrbildungen.* Berlin: Reimer, 1899.
Ebrard, J. H. A. *Handbuch der christlichen Kirchen- und Dogmengeschichte.* 4 vols. Erlangen: 1865–66.
Elert, W. *Der Ausgang der altkirchlichen Christologie.* Berlin: Lutherisches Verlagshaus, 1957.
Engelhardt, J. G. V. *Dogmengeschichte.* 2 vols. Neustadt: J. C. Engelhardt, 1839.
Fisher, G. P. *History of Christian Doctrine.* New York: C. Scribner's Sons, 1896.
Gasz, W. *Geschichte der protestantischen Dogmatik in ihrem Zusammengange mit der Theologie überhaupt.* 4 vols. Berlin, 1854–67.
Gieseler, J. C. L. *Dogmengeschichte.* Bonn: 1855.
Ginoulhiac, J. M. A. *Histoire du dogme catholique pendant les trois premiers siècles.* 2d ed. 3 vols. Paris: A. Durand, 1866.
Grabmann, M. *Die Geschichte der scholastischen Methode.* 2 vols. Freiburg and St. Louis: Herder, 1909–11.
Hagenbach, K. R. *Lehrbuch der Dogmengeschichte.* 3 vols. in 2. Leipzig: Weidman, 1840–41.
———. *A History of Christian Doctrines.* 3 vols. Translated from the 5th (last) German Edition, with additions from other sources. Introduction by E. H. Plumptre. Edinburgh: T. and T. Clark, 1880–85.
———. *Tabellarische Uebersicht der Dogmengeschichte bis auf die Reformation.* Basel, 1828.
Hägglund, B. *Teologins historia: en dogmhistorisk översikt.* Lund: 1963.
———. *History of Theology.* Translated by G. Lund. St. Louis: Concordia, 1969.
Harnack, A. von. *Grundriss der Dogmengeschichte.* 2 vols. Freiburg: J. C. B. Mohr, 1889–91.
———. *Outlines of the History of Dogma.* Translated by E. K. Mitchell. Boston: Beacon Press, 1957. Introduction by P. Rieff.

———. *Lehrbuch der Dogmengeschichte*. 3 vols. Freiburg: J. C. B. Mohr, 1886–94.

———. *History of Dogma*. Edited by B. Bruce. Translated by N. Buchanan et al. 7 vols. London: Williams and Norgate, 1897–1910.

Heick, O. W. *A History of Christian Thought*. 2 vols. Philadelphia: Fortress Press, 1965–66.

Hirsch, E. *Geschichte der neuern evangelischen Theologie im Zusammenhang mit den allgemeinen Bewegungen des europäischen Denkens*. 5 vols. Gütersloh: C. Bertelsmann, 1949.

Kahnis, K. F. A. *Der Kirchenglaube historisch-genetisch dargestellt*. Leipzig: Dörffling und Franke, 1864.

Kelly, J. N. D. *Early Christian Doctrines*. New York: Harper, 1958.

Klee, H. *Lehrbuch der Dogmengschichte*. 2 vols. Mainz: 1837–38.

Köhler, W. *Dogmengeschichte als Geschichte des christlichen Selbstbewusstseins*. 2 vols. Zürich: M. Niehan, 1943–51.

Landerer, M. A. *Neueste Dogmengeschichte*. Heilbronn: Altenburg, 1881.

Landgraf, A. M. *Dogmengeschichte de Frühscholastik*. 4 vols. in 8. Regensburg: Pustet, 1952–55.

Lange, S. G. *Ausführliche Geschichte der Dogmen oder der Glaubenslehren der christlichen Kirche*. Leipzig: Gerhard Fleischer dem Jüngern, 1796.

Lentz, C. G. H. *Geschichte der christlichen Dogmen in pragmatischer Entwicklung*. 2 vols. Helmstedt, 1834–35.

Lohse, B. *Epochen der Dogmengeschichte*. Stuttgart: Kreuz, 1963.

———. *A Short History of Christian Doctrine*. Translated by F. E. Stoeffler. Philadelphia: Fortress, 1966.

Loofs, F. *Leitfaden für seine Vorlesungen über Dogmengeschichte*. Halle: M. Niemeyer, 1889.

McGiffert, A. C. *A History of Christian Thought*. 2 vols. New York: C. Scribner's, 1932–33.

Marheineke, P. *Christliche Dogmengeschichte*. Berlin: Duncker und Humboldt, 1849.

Meier, F. K. *Lehrbuch der Dogmengeschichte für akademische Vorlesungen*. Giessen, 1840.

Münscher, W. *Handbuch der christlichen Dogmengeschichte*. 4 vols. Marburg, 1797–1809.

———. *Lehrbuch der christlichen Dogmengeschichte*. Marburg, 1811.

Münter, F. *Handbuch der ältesten christlichen Dogmengeschichte*. 2 vols. Göttingen, 1804–06.

Neander, A. *Christliche Dogmengeschichte*. Berlin, 1857.

Neve, J. L. *A History of Christian Thought.* 2 vols. Philadelphia: United Lutheran Publication House, 1943–46.

Nitzsch, F. *Grundriss der christlichen Dogmengeschichte.* Berlin: Teil, 1870.

Noack, L. *Die christliche Dogmengeschichte nach ihrem organischen Entwicklungsgange.* Erlangen: Enke, 1853.

Nygren, A. *Agape and Eros.* Translated by Philip S. Watson. Philadelphia: Westminster, 1953.

Oberman, H. A. *The Harvest of Medieval Theology.* Cambridge, Mass.: Harvard University Press, 1963.

Ritschl, O. *Dogmengeschichte des Protestantismus.* 4 vols. Leipzig: J. C. Hinrichs, 1908–27.

Ruperti, F. A. *Geschichte der Dogmen oder Darstellung der Glaubenslehren des Christentums.* Berlin, 1851.

Schickedanz, J. H. *Versuch einer Geschichte der christlichen Glaubenslehre und der merkwürdigen Systeme, Kompendien, Normalschriften und Katechismen.* Braunschweig, 1827.

Schmid, H. *Lehrbuch der Dogmengeschichte.* Nördlingen: C. H. Beck, 1860.

Schnappinger, B. M. *Entwurf einer katholisch-christlichen Religions- und Dogmengeschichte.* Karlsruhe: Macklots, 1808.

Schwane, J. *Dogmengeschichte.* 4 vols. Münster: Theissing, 1862–90.

Seeberg, R. *Lehrbuch der Dogmengeschichte.* 2 vols. Erlangen: A. Deichert, 1895–98.

———. *Textbook of the History of Doctrines.* Translated by C. E. Hay. 2 vols in 1. Grand Rapids: Baker Book House, 1958.

Thomasius, G. *Die christliche Dogmengeschichte als Entwicklungsgeschichte des kirchlichen Lehrbegriffs.* 2 vols. Erlangen: A. Deichert, 1874–76.

Tillich, P. *A History of Christian Thought.* Revised and edited by Carl E. Braaten. 2d ed. New York: Harper and Row, 1968.

———. *Perspectives on 19th and 20th Century Protestant Theology.* New York: Harper and Row, 1967.

Tixeront, J. *Histoire des dogmes dans l'antiquité chrétienne.* 3 vols. Paris: V. Lecoffre, 1906–12.

———. *History of Dogmas.* Translated by H. L. Brianceau from the 5th French Edition. 3 vols. St. Louis: B. Herder, 1910–16.

Vorländer, C. *Tabellarisch-übersichtliche Darstellung der Dogmengeschichte, nach Neanders dogmengeschichtlichen Vorlesungen.* 2 vols. Hamburg and Gotha, 1835–55.

Werner, J. *Dogmengeschichtliche Tabellen zum monarchianischen, trinitarischen und christologischen Streite.* Gotha: Prethes, 1893.

Werner, M. *Die Entstehung des christlichen Dogmas problemgeschichtlich dargestellt.* Bern: P. Haupt, 1941.

———. *The Formation of Christian Dogma: An Historical Study of Its Problem.* Translated by S. G. F. Brandon. London: A. and C. Black, 1957. Rewritten in shortened form by the author from his *Die Entstehung des christlichen Dogmas*, with an introduction by the translator.

Wiegand, F. L. L. *Dogmengeschichte.* Berlin: W. de Gruyter, 1928.

Wundemann, J. C. *Geschichte der christlichen Glaubenslehre vom Zeitalter des Athanasius bis Gregor dem Grossen.* 2 vols. Leipzig, 1798.

Zeller, P. *Christliche Dogmengeschichte.* Handbuch der theologischen Wissenschaften. 2 vols. Nördlingen: C. H. Beck, 1884.

Zobl, J. *Dogmengeschichte der katholischen Kirche.* Innsbruck, 1865.

Index of Names

Abelard, Peter, xviii, 12–15, 27–9, 31, 107
Abgar, of Edessa, 35
Aepinus, Johannes, 39
Aland, Kurt, 93
Ambrose, of Milan, 19, 103, 123, 136
Ames, William, 116
Anastasius I, Pope, 23
Anslem of Canterbury, 92–3, 107, 119
Aristotle, 3, 26–7, 81, 92, 119, 122–3, 144
Arminius, Jacobus, 78
Arnold, Gottfried, 48–50, 58, 142
Athanasius of Alexandria, 22, 56–7, 75, 78–9, 121, 139–40
Augustine of Hippo, 4, 7, 12, 16–19, 31, 37, 51, 75, 78, 86, 96, 100, 113, 124, 136–7
Aulén, Gustaf, 107–8

Bach, Joseph, 90–2
Bainton, Roland H., 36, 148
Bardy, Gustave, 41
Barlaam of Calabria, 147
Barnes, H. E., 34

Baronius, Caesar, 41–2, 54
Barth, Karl, 52, 65–6, 100–2, 141
Basil of Caesarea, 79
Baur, Ferdinand Christian, 7–8, 40–1, 52–6, 58, 68, 125–6
Bellarmine, Robert, 132–3
Bernard of Clairvaux, 143
Blake, Robert, 121
Blondus, Flavius, 34
Boethius, 29–30
Bonaventure, 143, 161
Bonhoeffer, Dietrich, 82
Bonwetsch, Nathanael, xvii
Boorstin, Daniel J., 114–15
Bornkamm, Heinrich, 148
Bossuet, Jacques Bénigne, 45
Bucer, Martin, 11
Bultmann, Rudolf, 109, 139, 152
Burckhardt, Jacob, 34

Calvin, John, 33, 61, 153
Carlson, Edgar M., 106
Chadwick, Owen, 45
Charlemagne, 122
Chemnitz, Martin, 133
Christlieb, Max, 59
Chrysostom, John, 75

226   *Index*

Churchill, Winston, 2, 159
Clement of Alexandria, 46, 158
Cochrane, Charles Norris, 112–13, 122
Collingwood, R. G., xvii, 104–6, 109
Constantine I, Emperor, 35
Creighton, Mandell, 121
Cremer, Hermann, 119
Croce, Benedetto, 104
Cyprian of Carthage, 17–19, 136, 153
Cyril of Alexandria, 8, 75, 143
Cyril of Jerusalem, xvi

Damasus I, Pope, 30
Daniélou, Jean, 143
Dante Alighieri, 123
D'Arcy, Martin C., 108
Dawson, Christopher, 118
De Maistre, Joseph, 56
Dibelius, Martin, 152
Dibelius, Otto, 82
Dillman, Christian, 65
Dilthey, Wilhelm, 105
Dionysius the Areopagite, Pseudo–, 29, 107

Eck, Johann, 36–7
Edel, Leon, 148
Elert, Werner, xi–xii, 131
Epiphanius of Salamis, 22
Erasmus of Rotterdam, 134–5
Erigena, Johannes Scotus, 103, 122
Erikson, Erik, 148
Euclid, 119
Eudemus of Rhodes, 3
Eusebius of Caesarea, 8–10, 22, 35, 41, 49, 94, 131–2

Fairweather, Eugene R., 119
Fisher, George Park, xvi, 116
Fisher, John, 103

Flacius Illyricus, Matthias, 37, 40–1
Flückiger, Felix, 66
Franks, Robert S., 124
Frederick II, Emperor, 122
Frend, W. H. C., 118
Freud, Sigmund, 148
Fueter, Eduard, xvii

Gay, Peter, 43, 47–8
Gibbon, Edward, xviv, 43–8
Gilson, Étienne, 123
Glick, G. Wayne, 64–5
Goethe, Johann Wolfgang von, 3
Gooch, G. P., 33–4
Gottschalk of Orbais, 122
Grabmann, Martin, 13, 27
Gregory of Nazianzus, 79
Gregory of Nyssa, xvi, 79
Gregory the Wonder-Worker, 21–2
Grundtvig, Nikolai F. S., 57
Guicciardini, Francesco, 34

Hagenbach, Karl Rudolf, xiii
Haight, Gordon S., 159
Harnack, Adolf von, 58–67, and *passim*
Harris, J. Rendel, 138–9
Hegel, Georg Wilhelm Friedrich, 52–3, 81, 126
Heraclitus, 138
Hergenröther, Joseph, 153–4
Hesiod, 3
Heussi, Karl, 41, 125
Hincmar of Reims, 122
Hippolytus of Rome, 71, 119
Hirsch, Emanuel, 48
Holl, Karl, 62, 70
Holmes, Oliver Wendell, Jr., 81
Honorius I, Pope, 42
Hus, Jan, 36

Ignatius of Antioch, xiv, 59
Innocent III, Pope, 122

Index

Jaeger, Werner, 3
James, Henry, 148
Jerome, 23, 30–1
John of the Cross, 143
John of Damascus, 26, 123, 146
Jones, Ernest, 148
Jugie, Martin, 144
Justin Martyr, 75, 140
Justinian I, Emperor, 23, 25, 105

Kant, Immanuel, 125
Khomyakov, Alexei, 57
Kliefoth, 152
Knowles, David, 51
Knox, John, 152
Köstlin, Julius, 148
Kretschmar, Georg, 114, 140
Krüger, Gustav, 83, 93
Kuhn, Johann Evangelist, 4

Landgraf, Artur, 91–3
Langer, William L., 148
Lawlor, Hugh Jackson, 131–2
Leclercq, Jean, 93
Leo I, Pope, 123
Lietzmann, Hans, 70
Lightfoot, Joseph, 138
Loehe, Wilhelm, 152
Lohmeyer, Ernst, 72
Loofs, Friedrich, 61, 62, 83–4, 87, 94, 113, 145
Lovejoy, Arthur O., 14–15
Lucian of Antioch, 22
Luther, Martin, 11, 24, 33, 36–41, 61, 77–8, 85–7, 90, 107–8, 138, 147–8, 153–4

McGiffert, Arthur Cushman, 89
Machiavelli, Niccolò, 34
McIntyre, John, 119
McNeill, John T., 153
Mann, Thomas, 97
Manning, Henry Edward, 150
Mansi, Giovanni, 51

Marcion of Pontus, 60, 66, 87
Marheinecke, Philipp Konrad, 142
Maritain, Jacques, 158
Melanchthon, Philipp, 24, 39, 133
Mennas of Constantinople, 23
Middleton, Conyers, 45
Miller, Perry, 115–17
Möhler, Johann Adam, xi, 4, 55–7
Mommsen, Theodor, 141
Monrad, D. G., 36
Morgan, Edmund S., 82
Mosheim, Johann Lorenz von, 48–50, 81–2
Münscher, Wilhelm, 50–1

Neander, Johann August, 65
Nestorius of Constantinople, 38, 119–20, 143–5
Nevin, John, 57
Newman, John Henry, 19–20, 45, 56–8, 83
Niebuhr, H. Richard, 118, 159
Nigg, Walter, 142
Nygren, Anders, 106–8, 110

Ockham, William of, 143
Oecolampadius, Johannes, 38–9
Origen of Alexandria, xiv, 6, 16, 21–5, 140, 142–3
Outler, Albert C., 160
Owen, John, 116

Palamas, Gregory, 147
Parmenian, 16
Paschasius Radbertus, 10, 102–3, 122
Pauck, Wilhelm, 60–1
Pelagius, 143
Pesch, Christian, 144
Peterson, Erik, 67, 82
Philo of Alexandria, 74, 138
Photius of Constantinople, 153–4

Pius X, Pope, 24
Pius XII, Pope, 155, 157
Polman, Pontien, 41
Preger, Johann Wilhelm, 41
Prudentius of Troyes, 122

Rabanus Maurus, 122
Rahner, Karl, 100–1
Ramus, Peter, 115–6
Ranke, Leopold von, 104–5, 109
Ratramnus of Corbie, 10, 102–3, 122
Renan, Ernest, 104
Reuter, Hermann, 98
Ridley, Nicholas, 103
Ritschl, Albrecht, 65, 102, 149, 152
Ritschl, Otto, 88–9
Roscellinus, 92
Rufinus of Aquileia, 23, 35–6
Runciman, Steven, 37, 127–8
Ryan, E. A., 132–3

Sandys, J. E., xv
Savigny, Friedrich Karl von, 52
Schaff, Philip, 57
Schleiermacher, Friedrich Daniel Ernst, 25, 53, 65, 125, 151–2, 160
Schwartz, Eduard, 121–2
Schweitzer, Albert, 72–3, 123
Seeberg, Alfred, 131
Seeberg, Erich, 50
Seeberg, Reinhold, xvi–xvii, 86–7, 144
Semler, Johann Salomo, 50, 130
Sergius of Constantinople, 42
Servatus Lupus, 122
Smend, Friedrich, 59
Socrates Scholasticus, 9
Soranus of Ephesus, 79
Sozomen, 9
Spencer, Herbert, 159
Stiles, Ezra, 82
Strigel, Victorinus, 78

Tauler, Johann, 143
Taylor, Henry Osborn, 27
Tertullian of Carthage, 6, 15, 18, 46, 60, 71, 74, 79, 119
Theodore of Mopsuestia, xvi, 8, 144–5
Theodore of Studios, 123
Theodosius II, Emperor, 95
Theophilus of Alexandria, 23
Thomas Aquinas, xviii, 28–32, 77, 92–3, 123, 154, 160–1
Thomasius, Gottfried, 85–8, 143–4
Thompson, James Westfall, xvii
Tillich, Paul, 100–1, 113
Troeltsch, Ernst, 54, 89–90, 120, 155, 160

Uhlhorn, Gerhard, 59

Valla, Lorenzo, 35–6, 71
Venerius of Milan, 23
Vilmar, August, 152
Vincent of Lérins, xviii, 4–7, 19, 21
Völker, Walter, 142

Walafrid Strabo, 122
Weiss, Johannes, 72–3
Werner, Martin, 73–4
Whitehead, Alfred North, 1, 10, 80, 95
Willis, Geoffrey Grimshaw, 17
Windelband, Wilhelm, 52
Wingren, Gustaf, 109
Wulf, Maurice de, 29

Zahn-Harnack, Agnes von, 82, 141
Zwingli, Ulrich, 33

www.ingramcontent.com/pod-product-compliance
Lightning Source LLC
Chambersburg PA
CBHW062013220426
43662CB00010B/1310